SUPER COOKERY

Chocolate & Baking

p

This is a Parragon Book
This edition published in 2003

Parragon
Queen Street House
4 Queen Street
Bath BA1 1HE, UK

ISBN: 1-40540-114-1

A copy of the CIP data for this book is available from the British Library, upon request

Printed in China

Note

Cup measurements used in this book are for American cups. Tablespoons are assumed to be 15 ml. Unless otherwise stated, milk is assumed to be full fat, eggs are medium and pepper is freshly ground black pepper.

Contents

Introduction

Chocolate is one of life's luxuries and one of the few that we can all afford. This book contains all of the recipes you need to enjoy this luxury at any time of the day. For example, you could wake up to Pain au Chocolat, or have a tasty chocolate biscuit with morning coffee. You could indulge in a hot chocolate pudding at lunch time, have a sumptuous slice of chocolate cake with afternoon tea, luxuriate with a rich chocolate dessert as part of an evening meal and round off the end of the day with a hot chocolate toddy. Whilst this might seem to be taking things too far, even for the most hardened chocoholic, why not tempt yourself with a perfect chocolate treat now and then. Go on, spoil yourself!

Chocolate is produced from the beans of the cacao tree, which originated in South America, and now grows in Africa, the West Indies, the tropical parts of America and the Far East. Cacao beans are large pods – once harvested, both the pulp from the pods and the bean are allowed to ferment in the sun. The pulp evaporates and the bean develops its chocolatey flavour. The outer skin is then removed and the beans are left in the sun for a little longer or roasted. Finally, they are shelled and the kernels are used for making cocoa and chocolate.

The kernels have to be ground and processed to produce a thick mixture or paste called "cocoa solids", and it is this that we refer to when gauging the quality of chocolate. The cocoa solids are then pressed to remove some of the fat – 'cocoa butter'. They are then further processed to produce the product that we know and love as chocolate.

STORING CHOCOLATE

Store chocolate in a cool, dry place away from direct heat or sunlight. Most chocolate can be stored for about one year. It can be stored in the refrigerator, but make sure it is well wrapped as it will pick up flavours from other foods. Chocolate decorations can be stored in airtight containers and interleaved with non-stick baking parchment. Dark chocolate will keep for four weeks and milk and white chocolate for two weeks.

MELTING CHOCOLATE

Chocolate should not be melted over direct heat, except when melted with other ingredients and even then the heat should be very low.

Break the chocolate into small, equal-sized pieces and place them in a heatproof bowl. Place over a pan of hot water, making sure the base is not in contact with the water. Once the chocolate starts to melt, stir gently and if necessary leave over the water a little longer. No drops of water or steam should come into contact with the melted chocolate as it will solidify.

To melt chocolate in the microwave, break it into small pieces and place in microwave-proof bowl. Timing will vary according to the type and quantity of chocolate. As a guide, melt 125 g/4½ oz dark chocolate on High for two minutes and white or milk chocolate for two-three minutes on Medium. Stir the chocolate and leave to stand for a few minutes, then stir again. Return to the microwave for a further 30 seconds if necessary.

SETTING CHOCOLATE

Chocolate sets best at 65° F/18° C although it will set (more slowly) in a slightly hotter room. If possible, set chocolate for decorations in a cool room. If set in the refrigerator, it may develop a white bloom.

TYPES OF CHOCOLATE

Dark Chocolate *can contain anything from 30% to 75% cocoa solids. It has a slightly sweet flavour and a dark colour. It is the chocolate most used in cooking. For everyday cooking and the majority of the recipes for dark chocolate, choose one with around 50% cocoa solids. However, dark chocolate with a higher cocoa solid content will give a richer, more intense, flavour. This chocolate is often called luxury or continental chocolate and has a cocoa solid content of between 70-75%. Occasionally it is essential to use a better chocolate and I have indicated in the individual recipes where this is the case.*

Milk Chocolate, *as its name suggests, contains milk and has a lovely creamy, mild and sweet flavour. It is mostly used as an eating chocolate, rather than in cooking. However, it does have its place in chocolate cooking, especially for decorations and when a milder, creamy flavour is required. It is more sensitive to heat than dark chocolate so care must be taken when melting it.*

White Chocolate *contains a lower cocoa butter content and cocoa solids. It can be quite temperamental when used in cooking. Always choose a luxury cooking white chocolate to avoid problems and take great care not to overheat when melting. White chocolate is useful for colour contrast especially when decorating cakes.*

Couverture *is the preferred chocolate for professionals (it retains a high gloss after melting and cooling) but it requires tempering and is only available from specialist suppliers and has therefore not been used in this book.*

Chocolate-Flavoured Cake Covering *is an inferior product not generally used by true chocolate lovers. However, it has a high fat content, making it easier to handle when making some decorations such as curls or caraque. If you do not want to compromise the flavour too much, but have difficulty making the decorations with pure chocolate, try adding a few squares of chocolate-flavoured cake covering to a good quality chocolate.*

Chocolate Chips *are available in dark, milk and white chocolate varieties, and are used for baking and decoration.*

Coco Powder *is the powder left after the cocoa butter has been pressed from the roasted and ground beans. It is unsweetened and bitter in flavour. It gives a good, strong chocolate flavour when used in cooking.*

In addition to the chocolate recipes, this book brings you all the skills you need to recreate some of the best-loved traditional baking dishes. It also shows you how to experiment with some of the exciting contemporary ingredients now readily available in leading supermarkets.

Clear step-by-step instructions guide you through the techniques needed to mastermind all the baking favourites that have been savoured and enjoyed from generation to generation.

FAMILY FAVOURITES

Experience the sweet pleasure of a wonderful selection of everyday and special occasion desserts as you learn how to make rich, gooey and irresistible puddings such Pavlova, Fruit Crumble, Queen of Puddings and tasty sticky chocolate puddings. Everyone's favourite is sure to be included. This book also helps you to perfect your baking skills so you are guaranteed to have success each time you prepare a dish, whether it is an elaborate cheesecake or a fruity crumble. The only problem will be deciding which recipe to try next

BREADS & SAVOURIES

Making bread at home is great fun and allows you to experiment with all sorts of ingredients, such as sun-dried tomatoes, garlic, mangoes and olive oil, to create versatile and delicious variations of modern breads. Easy-blend yeast also makes the task of making bread-making less labourious these days. Chapter 4 also shows you how to spice-up all sorts of savouries with exciting adaptations of traditional flans, pies and scones.

VEGETARIAN COOKING

Vegetarian recipes full of delicious wholesome ingredients, which are every bit as good as traditional baking favourites, have been created for those following a vegetarian diet.

CAKES & BISCUITS

Transform traditional cakes and biscuits into a real tea-time extravaganza with some new adaptations of old favourites.

Irresistible cake recipes are included, as are delicious biscuit (cookie) recipes. These recipes are quick and easy to make and are sure to be winners with all of the family.

PUDDINGS

Puddings are always a great treat at the end of a meal, but they must be balanced with the rest of the food. Rich puddings after a heavy main course will not be popular. This book provides a myriad of ideas, both light and more substantial, to round off a meal in a perfect manner. Ice cream may be the perfect choice after a heavy roast main dish, while a tasty fruit tart will complement a fish main course perfectly.

MAKING CAKES

With all baking recipes, there are some basic principles that apply, and this is especially true of cake making:

- Start by reading the recipe all the way through.
- Weigh all the ingredients accurately and do basic preparation, such as grating and chopping, before you start cooking.
- Basic cake-making ingredients should be kept at room temperature.
- Mixtures that are creamed together, a process which involves mixing butter and sugar together, should be almost white and have a 'soft dropping' consistency. This can be done by hand, but using a hand-held electric mixer will save you time and effort.
- 'Folding in' is achieved by using a metal spoon or spatula and working as gently as possible to fold through the flour or dry ingredients in a figure-of-eight movement.
- Do not remove a cake from the oven until it is fully cooked. To test if a cake is cooked, press the surface lightly with your fingertips – it should feel springy to the touch. Alternatively, insert a fine metal skewer into the centre of the cake – it will come out clean if the cake is cooked through.
- Leave cakes in their tins (pans) to cool before carefully turning out on to a wire rack to cool completely.

MAKING PIES & TARTS

When making the pies or tarts in the book, follow these basic principles:

- Sieve (strain) the dry ingredients into a large mixing bowl, add the diced fat and toss it through the flour.
- Gently rub the fat between your fingertips a little at a time until the mixture looks like fine breadcrumbs and, as you rub in the mixture, lift your hands up to aerate the mixture as it falls back into the bowl.
- Bind the mixture with iced water or other liquid, using just enough to make a soft dough. Wrap the dough and leave to chill for at least 30 minutes.

Cakes & Gateaux

It is hard to resist the pleasure of a sumptuous piece of chocolate cake and no baking book would be complete without a selection of family cakes and gateaux – there are plenty to choose from in this chapter. You can spend several indulgent hours in the kitchen making that perfect extravagant gateau or to knock up a quick cake for afternoon tea, the choice is yours. The more experimental among you can vary the fillings or decorations used according to what takes your fancy.

Alternatively, follow our easy step-by-step instructions and look at our pictures to guide you to perfect results. The gateaux in this book will be perfectly at home on the dessert table – they are a feast for the eyes and will keep all hardened cake addicts in ecstasy. The recipes are ideal for those who find a slice of cake comforting at any time of day, as many of them are made with surprising ease.

Chocolate Almond Cake

Serves 8–10

INGREDIENTS

175 g/6 oz dark chocolate
175 g/6 oz/¾ cup butter
125 g/4½ oz caster (superfine) sugar
4 eggs, separated
1/4 tsp cream of tartar
50 g/1¾ oz/⅓ cup self-raising flour
125 g/4½ oz/1¼ cups ground almonds
1 tsp almond flavouring (extract)

TOPPING:
125 g/4½ oz milk chocolate
25 g/1 oz/2 tbsp butter
4 tbsp double (heavy) cream

TO DECORATE:
25 g/1 oz/2 tbsp toasted flaked almonds
25 g/1 oz dark chocolate, melted

1 Lightly grease and line the base of a 23 cm/9 inch round springform tin (pan). Break the chocolate into small pieces and place in a small pan with the butter. Heat gently, stirring until melted and well combined.

2 Place 100 g/3½ oz/ 7 tbsp of the caster (superfine) sugar in a bowl with the egg yolks and whisk until pale and creamy. Add the melted chocolate mixture, beating until well combined.

3 Sieve (strain) the cream of tartar and flour together and fold into the chocolate mixture with the ground almonds and almond flavouring (extract).

4 Whisk the egg whites in a bowl until standing in soft peaks. Add the remaining caster (superfine) sugar and whisk for about 2 minutes by hand, or 45–60 seconds, if using an electric whisk, until thick and glossy. Fold the egg whites into the chocolate mixture and spoon into the tin (pan). Bake in a preheated oven, 190°C/ 375°F/ Gas Mark 5, for 40 minutes until just springy to the touch. Let cool.

5 Heat the topping ingredients in a bowl over a pan of hot water. Remove from the heat and beat for 2 minutes. Let chill for 30 minutes. Transfer the cake to a plate and spread with the topping. Scatter with the almonds and drizzle with melted chocolate. Leave to set for 2 hours before serving.

2

4

4

Chocolate Tray Bake

Serves 15

INGREDIENTS

350 g/12 oz/3 cups self-raising flour, sieved (strained)
3 tbsp cocoa powder, sieved (strained)
225 g/8 oz/1 cup caster (superfine) sugar
225 g/8 oz/1 cup soft margarine
4 eggs, beaten
4 tbsp milk
50 g/1¾ oz/⅓ cup milk chocolate chips
50 g/1¾ oz/⅓ cup dark chocolate chips
50 g/1¾ oz/⅓ cup white chocolate chips
icing (confectioners') sugar, to dust

1 Grease a 33 x 24 x 5 cm/ 13 x 9 x 2 inch cake tin (pan) with a little butter or margarine.

2 Place all of the ingredients except for the chocolate chips and icing (confectioners') sugar in a large mixing bowl and beat together until smooth.

3 Beat in the milk, dark and white chocolate chips.

4 Spoon the mixture into the prepared cake tin (pan) and level the top. Bake in a preheated oven, 180°C/350°F/Gas Mark 4, for 30-40 minutes until risen and springy to the touch. Leave to cool in the tin (pan).

5 Once cool, dust with icing (confectioners') sugar. Cut into squares to serve.

COOK'S TIP

If liked, serve warm with whipped cream for a delicious dessert.

COOK'S TIP

The cake can be frozen, wrapped well in the tin (pan), for 2 months. Defrost at room temperature.

VARIATION

For an attractive finish, cut thin strips of paper and lay in a criss-cross pattern on top of the cake. Dust with icing (confectioners') sugar, then remove the paper strips.

Low-Fat Chocolate & Pineapple Cake

Serves 9

INGREDIENTS

150 g/5½ oz/⅔ cup low-fat spread
125 g/4½ oz caster (superfine) sugar
100 g/3½ oz/¾ cup self-raising flour, sieved (strained)
3 tbsp cocoa powder, sieved (strained)
1½ tsp baking powder
2 eggs
225g/8 oz can pineapple pieces in natural juice
125 ml/4 fl oz/½ cup low-fat thick natural yogurt
about 1 tbsp icing (confectioners') sugar
grated chocolate, to decorate

1 Lightly grease a 20 cm/8 inch square cake tin (pan).

2 Place the low-fat spread, caster (superfine) sugar, flour, cocoa powder, baking powder and eggs in a large mixing bowl. Beat with a wooden spoon or electric hand whisk until smooth.

3 Pour the cake mixture into the prepared tin (pan) and level the surface. Bake in a preheated oven, 190°C/325°F/Gas Mark 5, for 20-25 minutes or until springy to the touch. Leave to cool slightly in the tin (pan) before transferring to a wire rack to cool completely.

4 Drain the pineapple, chop the pineapple pieces and drain again. Reserve a little pineapple for decoration, then stir the rest into the yogurt and sweeten to taste with icing (confectioners') sugar.

5 Spread the pineapple and yogurt mixture over the cake and decorate with the reserved pineapple pieces. Sprinkle with the grated chocolate.

COOK'S TIP

Store the cake, undecorated, in an airtight container for up to 3 days. Once decorated, refrigerate and use within 2 days.

Chocolate & Orange Cake

Serves 8–10

INGREDIENTS

175 g/6 oz/¾ cup caster (superfine) sugar
175 g/6 oz/¾ cup butter or block margarine
3 eggs, beaten
175 g/6 oz/1½ cups self-raising flour, sieved (strained)
2 tbsp cocoa powder, sieved (strained)
2 tbsp milk
3 tbsp orange juice
grated rind of ½ orange

ICING:
175 g/6 oz/1 cup icing (confectioners') sugar
2 tbsp orange juice

1 Lightly grease a 20 cm/ 8 inch deep round cake tin (pan).

2 Beat together the sugar and butter or margarine in a bowl until light and fluffy. Gradually add the eggs, beating well after each addition. Carefully fold in the flour.

3 Divide the mixture in half. Add the cocoa powder and milk to one half, stirring until well combined. Flavour the other half with the orange juice and rind.

4 Place spoonfuls of each mixture into the prepared tin (pan) and swirl together with a skewer, to create a marbled effect. Bake in a preheated oven, 190°C/375°F/Gas Mark 5, for 25 minutes or until springy to the touch.

5 Leave the cake to cool in the tin (pan) for a few minutes before transferring to a wire rack to cool completely.

6 To make the icing, sift the icing (confectioners') sugar into a mixing bowl and mix in enough of the orange juice to form a smooth icing. Spread the icing over the top of the cake and leave to set before serving.

VARIATION

Add 2 tablespoons of rum or brandy to the chocolate mixture instead of the milk. The cake also works well when flavoured with grated lemon rind and juice instead of the orange.

2

3

4

Family Chocolate Cake

Serves 8–10

INGREDIENTS

125 g/4½ oz/½ cup soft margarine
125 g/4½ oz/½ cup caster (superfine) sugar
2 eggs
1 tbsp golden (light corn) syrup
125 g/4½ oz/1 cup self-raising flour, sieved (strained)
2 tbsp cocoa powder, sieved (strained)

FILLING AND TOPPING:
50 g/1¾ oz/¼ cup icing (confectioners') sugar, sieved (strained)
25 g/1 oz/2 tbsp butter
100 g/3½ oz white or milk cooking chocolate
a little milk or white chocolate, melted (optional)

1 Lightly grease two 18 cm/7 inch shallow cake tins (pans).

2 Place all of the ingredients for the cake in a large mixing bowl and beat with a wooden spoon or electric hand whisk to form a smooth mixture.

3 Divide the mixture between the prepared tins (pans) and level the tops. Bake in a preheated oven, 190°C/325F/Gas Mark 5, for 20 minutes or until springy to the touch. Cool for a few minutes in the tins (pans) before transferring to a wire rack to cool completely.

4 To make the filling, beat the icing (confectioners') sugar and butter together in a bowl until light and fluffy. Melt the cooking chocolate and beat half into the icing mixture. Use the filling to sandwich the 2 cakes together.

5 Spread the remaining melted cooking chocolate over the top of the cake. Pipe circles of contrasting melted milk or white chocolate and feather into the cooking chocolate with a cocktail stick (toothpick), if liked. Leave to set before serving.

COOK'S TIP

Ensure that you eat this cake on the day of baking, as it does not keep well.

2

3

4

Chocolate & Vanilla Loaf Cake

Serves 10

INGREDIENTS

175 g/6 oz/¾ cup caster (superfine) sugar
175 g/6 oz/¾ cup soft margarine
½ tsp vanilla flavouring (extract)
3 eggs
225 g/8 oz/2 cups self-raising flour, sieved (strained)
50 g/1¾ oz dark chocolate
icing (confectioners') sugar, to dust

1 Lightly grease a 450 g/ 1 lb loaf tin (pan).

2 Beat together the sugar and soft margarine in a bowl until light and fluffy.

3 Beat in the vanilla flavouring (extract). Gradually add the eggs, beating well after each addition. Carefully fold in the self-raising flour.

4 Divide the mixture in half. Melt the dark chocolate and stir into one half of the mixture until well combined.

5 Place the vanilla mixture in the tin (pan) and level the top. Spread the chocolate layer over the vanilla layer.

6 Bake in a preheated oven, 190°C/375°F/Gas Mark 5, for 30 minutes or until springy to the touch.

7 Leave to cool in the tin (pan) for a few minutes before transferring to a wire rack to cool completely.

8 Serve the cake dusted with icing (confectioners') sugar.

COOK'S TIP

Freeze the cake undecorated for up to 2 months. Defrost at room temperature.

VARIATION

If liked, the mixtures can be marbled together with a cocktail stick (toothpick).

Chocolate Tea Bread

Serves 10

INGREDIENTS

175 g/6 oz/¾ cup butter, softened
100 g/3½ oz light muscovado sugar
4 eggs, lightly beaten
225 g/8 oz dark chocolate chips
100 g/3½ oz/½ cup raisins
50 g/1¾ oz/½ cup chopped walnuts
finely grated rind of 1 orange
225 g/8 oz/2 cups self-raising flour

1 Lightly grease a 900 g/2 lb loaf tin (pan) and line the base with baking parchment.

2 Cream together the butter and sugar in a bowl until light and fluffy.

3 Gradually add the eggs, beating well after each addition. If the mixture begins to curdle, beat in 1–2 tablespoons of the flour.

4 Stir in the chocolate chips, raisins, walnuts and orange rind. Sieve (strain) the flour and carefully fold it into the mixture.

5 Spoon the mixture into the prepared loaf tin (pan) and make a slight dip in the centre of the top with the back of a spoon.

6 Bake in a preheated oven, 170°C/325°F/Gas Mark 3, for 1 hour or until a fine skewer inserted into the centre of the loaf comes out clean.

7 Leave to cool in the tin (pan) for 5 minutes, before carefully turning out and leaving on a wire rack to cool completely.

8 Serve the tea bread cut into thin slices.

VARIATION

Use white or milk chocolate chips instead of dark chocolate chips, or a mixture of all three, if desired. Dried cranberries instead of the raisins also work well in this recipe.

COOK'S TIP

This tea bread can be frozen, well wrapped, for up to 3 months. Defrost at room temperature.

2

5

6

Apricot & Chocolate Ring

Serves 12

INGREDIENTS

75 g/2¾ oz/⅓ cup butter, diced
450 g/1 lb/4 cups self-raising flour, sieved (strained)
50 g/1¾ oz/4 tbsp caster (superfine) sugar
2 eggs, beaten
150 ml/1/4 pint/⅔ cup milk

FILLING AND DECORATION:
25 g/1 oz/2 tbsp butter, melted
150 g/5½ oz ready-to-eat dried apricots, chopped
100 g/3½ oz dark chocolate chips
1–2 tbsp milk, to glaze
25 g/1 oz dark chocolate, melted

1 Grease a 25 cm/10 inch round cake tin (pan) and line the base with baking parchment.

2 Rub the butter into the flour until the mixture resembles fine breadcrumbs. Stir in the caster (superfine) sugar, eggs and milk to form a soft dough.

3 Roll out the dough on a lightly floured surface to form a 35 cm/14 inch square.

4 Brush the melted butter over the surface of the dough. Mix together the apricots and chocolate chips and spread them over the dough to within 2.5 cm/1 inch of the top and bottom.

5 Roll up the dough tightly, like a Swiss roll, and cut it into 2.5 cm/1 inch slices. Stand the slices in a ring around the edge of the prepared tin (pan) at a slight tilt. Brush with a little milk.

6 Bake in a preheated oven, 180°C/350°F/Gas Mark 4, for 30 minutes or until cooked and golden. Leave to cool in the tin (pan) for about 15 minutes, then transfer to a wire rack to cool.

7 Drizzle the melted chocolate over the ring, to decorate.

COOK'S TIP

This cake is best served very fresh, ideally on the day it is made. It is fabulous served slightly warm.

Chocolate Fruit Loaf

Serves 10

INGREDIENTS

- 350 g/12 oz/3 cups strong white flour
- 25 g/1 oz/¼ cup cocoa powder
- 25 g/1 oz/5 tsp caster (superfine) sugar
- 6 g sachet easy blend yeast
- 1/4 tsp salt
- 225 ml/8 fl oz/1 cup tepid water
- 25 g/1 oz/2 tbsp butter, melted
- 75 g/2¾ oz/5 tbsp glacé (candied) cherries, chopped roughly
- 75 g/2¾ oz/½ cup dark chocolate chips
- 50 g/1¾ oz/⅓ cup sultanas (golden raisins)
- 75 g/2¾ oz no-soak dried apricots, roughly chopped

GLAZE:

- 1 tbsp caster (superfine) sugar
- 1 tbsp water

1 Lightly grease a 900 g/2 lb loaf tin (pan). Sieve (strain) the flour and cocoa into a large mixing bowl. Stir in the sugar, yeast and salt.

2 Mix together the tepid water and butter. Make a well in the centre of the dry ingredients and add the liquid. Mix well with a wooden spoon, then use your hands to bring the dough together. Turn out on to a lightly floured surface and knead for 5 minutes, until a smooth elastic dough forms. Return to a clean bowl, cover with a damp tea towel and leave to rise in a warm place for about 1 hour or until doubled in size.

3 Turn the dough out on to a floured surface and knead for 5 minutes. Roll out to a rectangle about 1 cm/½ inch thick and the same width as the length of the tin (pan). Scatter the cherries, chocolate chips, sultanas (golden raisins) and chopped apricots over the dough. Carefully roll up the dough, like a Swiss roll, enclosing the filling. Transfer to the loaf tin (pan), cover with a damp tea towel and leave to rise for 20 minutes or until the top of the dough is level with the top of the tin (pan).

4 To make the glaze, mix together the sugar and water, then brush it over the top of the loaf. Bake in a preheated oven, 200°C/400°F/Gas Mark 6, for 30 minutes or until well risen. Serve.

Mocha Layer Cake

Serves 8–10

INGREDIENTS

200 g/7¾ oz/1 cup self-raising flour
1/4 tsp baking powder
4 tbsp cocoa powder
100 g/3½ oz/7 tbsp caster (superfine) sugar
2 eggs
2 tbsp golden (light corn) syrup
150 ml/¼ pint/⅔ cup sunflower oil
150 ml/¼ pint/⅔ cup milk

FILLING:
1 tsp instant coffee
1 tbsp boiling water
300 ml/½ pint/1¼ cups double (heavy) cream
25 g/1 oz/2 tbsp icing (confectioners') sugar

TO DECORATE:
50 g/1¾ oz flock chocolate
chocolate caraque icing (confectioners') sugar, to dust

1 Lightly grease three 18 cm/7 inch cake tins (pans).

2 Sieve (strain) the flour, baking powder and cocoa powder into a large mixing bowl. Stir in the sugar. Make a well in the centre and stir in the eggs, syrup, oil and milk. Beat with a wooden spoon, gradually mixing in the dry ingredients to make a smooth batter. Divide the mixture between the prepared tins (pans).

3 Bake in a preheated oven, 180°C/350°F/Gas Mark 4, for 35–45 minutes or until springy to the touch. Leave in the tins (pans) for 5 minutes, then turn out on to a wire rack to cool completely.

4 Dissolve the instant coffee in the boiling water and place in a bowl with the cream and icing (confectioners') sugar. Whip until the cream is just holding it's shape. Use half of the cream to sandwich the 3 cakes together. Spread the remaining cream over the top and sides of the cake. Lightly press the flock chocolate into the cream around the edge of the cake.

5 Transfer to a serving plate. Lay the caraque over the top of the cake. Cut a few thin strips of baking parchment and place on top of the caraque. Dust lightly with icing (confectioners') sugar, then carefully remove the paper. Serve.

Chocolate Lamington Bar Cake

Serves 8–10

INGREDIENTS

175 g/6 oz/¾ cup butter or block margarine
175 g/6 oz/¾ cup caster (superfine) sugar
3 eggs, lightly beaten
150 g/5½ oz/1¼ cups self-raising flour
2 tbsp cocoa powder
125 g/4½ oz/¾ cup icing (confectioners') sugar
50 g/1¾ oz dark chocolate, broken into pieces
5 tbsp milk
1 tsp butter
about 8 tbsp desiccated (shredded) coconut
150 ml/¼ pint double (heavy cream), whipped

1 Lightly grease a 450 g/1 lb loaf tin (pan) – preferably a long, thin tin (pan) about 7.5 x 25 cm/3 x 10 inches.

2 Cream together the butter and sugar in a bowl until light and fluffy. Gradually add the eggs, beating well after each addition. Sieve (strain) together the flour and cocoa. Fold into the mixture.

3 Pour the mixture into the prepared tin (pan) and level the top. Bake in a preheated oven, 180°C/350°F/Gas Mark 4, for 40 minutes or until springy to the touch. Leave to cool for 5 minutes in the tin (pan), then turn out on to a wire rack to cool completely.

4 Place the chocolate, milk and butter in a heatproof bowl set over a pan of hot water. Stir until the chocolate has melted. Add the icing (confectioners') sugar and beat until smooth. Leave to cool until the icing is thick enough to spread, then spread it all over the cake. Sprinkle with the desiccated (shredded) coconut and allow the icing to set.

5 Cut a V-shape wedge from the top of the cake. Put the cream in a piping bag fitted with a plain or star nozzle (tip). Pipe the cream down the centre of the wedge and replace the wedge of cake on top of the cream. Pipe another line of cream down either side of the wedge of cake. Serve.

Rich Chocolate Layer Cake

Serves 10–12

INGREDIENTS

7 eggs
200 g/7 oz/1¾ cups caster (superfine) sugar
150 g/5½ oz/1¼ cups plain (all-purpose) flour
50 g/1¾ oz/½ cup cocoa powder
50 g/1¾ oz/4 tbsp butter, melted

FILLING:
200 g/7 oz dark chocolate
125 g/4½ oz/½ cup butter
50 g/1¾ oz/4 tbsp icing (confectioners') sugar

TO DECORATE:
75 g/2¾ oz/10 tbsp toasted flaked almonds, crushed lightly
small chocolate curls or grated chocolate

1 Grease a deep 23 cm/ 9 inch square cake tin (pan) and line the base with baking parchment.

2 Whisk the eggs and caster (superfine) sugar in a mixing bowl with an electric whisk for about 10 minutes, or until the mixture is very light and foamy and the whisk leaves a trail that lasts a few seconds when lifted.

3 Sieve (strain) the flour and cocoa together and fold half into the mixture. Drizzle over the melted butter and fold in the rest of the flour and cocoa. Pour into the prepared tin (pan) and bake in a preheated oven, 180°C/350°F/ Gas Mark 4, for 30–35 minutes or until springy to the touch. Leave to cool slightly, then remove from the tin (pan) and cool completely on a wire rack. Wash and dry the tin (pan) and return the cake to it.

4 To make the filling, melt the chocolate and butter together, then remove from the heat. Stir in the icing (confectioners') sugar, leave to cool, then beat until thick enough to spread.

5 Halve the cake lengthways and cut each half into 3 layers. Sandwich the layers together with three-quarters of the chocolate filling. Spread the remainder over the cake and mark a wavy pattern on the top. Press the almonds on to the sides. Decorate with chocolate curls or grated chocolate.

3

5

5

Chocolate & Mango Layer Cake

Serves 12

INGREDIENTS

50 g/1¾ oz/½ cup cocoa powder
150 ml/¼ pint/⅔ cup boiling water
6 large eggs
350 g/12 oz/1½ cups caster (superfine) sugar
300 g/10½ oz/2½ cups self-raising flour
2 x 400 g/14 oz cans mango
1 tsp cornflour (cornstarch)
425 ml/¾ pint/generous 1¾ cups double (heavy) cream
75 g/2¾ oz dark flock chocolate or grated chocolate

1 Grease a deep 23 cm/9 inch round cake tin (pan) and line the base with baking parchment.

2 Place the cocoa powder in a small bowl and gradually add the boiling water; blend to form a smooth paste.

3 Place the eggs and caster (superfine) sugar in a mixing bowl and whisk until the mixture is very light and foamy and the whisk leaves a trail that lasts a few seconds when lifted. Fold in the cocoa mixture. Sieve (strain) the flour and fold into the mixture.

4 Pour the mixture into the tin (pan) and level the top. Bake in a preheated oven, 170°C/325°F/Gas Mark 3, for about 1 hour or until springy to the touch.

5 Leave to cool in the tin (pan) for a few minutes then turn out and cool completely on a wire rack. Peel off the lining paper and cut the cake into 3 layers.

6 Drain the mangoes and place a quarter of them in a food processor and purée until smooth. Mix the cornflour (cornstarch) with about 3 tbsp of the mango juice to form a smooth paste. Add to the mango purée. Transfer to a small pan and heat gently, stirring until the purée thickens. Leave to cool.

7 Chop the remaining mango. Whip the cream and reserve about one quarter. Fold the mango into the remaining cream and use to sandwich the layers of cake together. Place on a serving plate. Spread some of the remaining cream around the side of the cake. Press the flock or grated chocolate lightly into the cream. Pipe cream rosettes around the top. Spread the mango purée over the centre.

2

3

6

Devil's Food Cake

Serves 8

INGREDIENTS

100 g/3½ oz dark chocolate
250 g/9 oz/2¼ cups self-raising flour
1 tsp bicarbonate of soda (baking soda)
225 g/8 oz/1 cup butter
400 g/14 oz/2⅔ cups dark muscovado sugar
1 tsp vanilla flavouring (extract)
3 eggs
125 ml/4 fl oz/½ cup buttermilk
225 ml/8 fl oz/2 cups boiling water

FROSTING:
300 g/10½ oz/1⅓ cups caster (superfine) sugar
2 egg whites
1 tbsp lemon juice
3 tbsp orange juice
candied orange peel, to decorate

1 Lightly grease two 20 cm/8 inch shallow round cake tins (pans) and line the bases. Melt the chocolate in a pan. Sieve (strain) the flour and bicarbonate of soda (baking soda) together.

2 Beat the butter and sugar in a bowl until pale and fluffy. Beat in the vanilla flavouring (extract) and the eggs, one at a time and beating well after each addition. Add a little flour if the mixture begins to curdle.

3 Fold the melted chocolate into the mixture until well blended. Gradually fold in the remaining flour, then stir in the buttermilk and boiling water.

4 Divide the mixture between the tins (pans) and level the tops. Bake in a preheated oven, 190°C/375°F/Gas Mark 5, for 30 minutes until springy to the touch. Leave to cool in the tin (pan) for 5 minutes, then transfer to a wire rack to cool completely.

5 Place the frosting ingredients in a large bowl set over a pan of gently simmering water. Whisk, preferably with an electric beater, until thickened and forming soft peaks. Remove from the heat and whisk until the mixture is cool.

6 Sandwich the 2 cakes together with a little of the frosting, then spread the remainder over the sides and top of the cake, swirling it as you do so. Decorate with the candied orange peel.

Chocolate Carrot Cake

Serves 10–12

INGREDIENTS

5 eggs
150 g/5$\frac{1}{2}$ oz/$\frac{2}{3}$ cup caster (superfine) sugar
150 g/5$\frac{1}{2}$ oz/1$\frac{1}{4}$ cups plain (all-purpose) flour
40 g/1$\frac{1}{2}$ oz/$\frac{1}{3}$ cup cocoa powder
175 g/6 oz carrots, peeled and finely grated
50 g/1$\frac{3}{4}$ oz/$\frac{1}{2}$ cup chopped walnuts
2 tbsp sunflower oil
350 g/12 oz medium fat soft cheese
175 g/6 oz/1 cup icing (confectioners') sugar
175 g/6 oz milk or dark chocolate, melted

1 Lightly grease and line the base of a 20 cm/8 inch deep round cake tin (pan).

2 Place the eggs and sugar in a large mixing bowl set over a pan of gently simmering water and whisk until very thick. Lift the whisk up and let the mixture drizzle back – it will leave a trail for a few seconds when thick enough.

3 Remove the bowl from the heat. Sieve (strain) the flour and cocoa powder into the bowl and carefully fold in. Fold in the carrots, walnuts and oil until just combined.

4 Pour into the prepared tin (pan) and bake in a preheated oven, 190°C/ 375°F/Gas Mark 5, for 45 minutes or until well risen and springy to the touch. Leave to cool slightly then turn out on to a wire rack to cool completely.

5 Beat together the soft cheese and icing (confectioners') sugar until combined. Beat in the melted chocolate. Split the cake in half and sandwich together again with half of the chocolate mixture. Cover the top of the cake with the remainder of the chocolate mixture, swirling it with a knife. Leave to chill or serve at once.

COOK'S TIP

The undecorated cake can be frozen for up to 2 months. Defrost at room temperature for 3 hours or overnight in the refrigerator.

2

3

5

Chocolate Yogurt Cake

Serves 8–10

INGREDIENTS

150 ml/¼ pint/⅔ cup vegetable oil
150 ml/¼ pint/⅔ cup whole milk natural yogurt
175 g/6 oz/1¼ cups light muscovado sugar
3 eggs, beaten
100 g/3½ oz/¾ cup wholemeal (whole wheat) self-raising flour
125 g/4½ oz/1 cup self-raising flour, sieved (strained)
2 tbsp cocoa powder
1 tsp bicarbonate of soda (baking soda)
50 g/1¾ oz dark chocolate, melted

FILLING AND TOPPING:
150 ml/¼ pint/⅔ cup whole milk natural yogurt
150 ml/¼ pint/⅔ cup double (heavy) cream
225 g/8 oz fresh soft fruit, such as strawberries or raspberries

1 Grease a deep 23 cm/9 inch round cake tin (pan) and line the base with baking parchment.

2 Place the oil, yogurt, sugar and beaten eggs in a large mixing bowl and beat together until well combined. Sieve (strain) the flours, cocoa powder and bicarbonate of soda (baking soda) together and beat into the bowl until well combined. Beat in the melted chocolate.

3 Pour into the prepared tin (pan) and bake in a preheated oven, 180°C/350°F/Gas Mark 4, for 45-50 minutes or until a fine skewer inserted into the centre comes out clean. Leave to cool in the tin (pan) for 5 minutes, then turn out on to a wire rack to cool completely. When cold, split the cake into 3 layers.

4 To make the filling, place the yogurt and cream in a large mixing bowl and whisk well until the mixture stands in soft peaks.

5 Place one layer of cake on to a serving plate and spread with some of the cream. Top with a little of the fruit (slicing larger fruit such as strawberries). Repeat with the next layer. Top with the final layer of cake and spread with the rest of the cream. Arrange more fruit on top and cut the cake into wedges to serve.

2

3

5

Chocolate Layer Log

Serves 8–10

INGREDIENTS

125 g/4½ oz/½ cup soft margarine
125 g/4½ oz/½ cup caster (superfine) sugar
2 eggs
100 g/3½ oz/¾ cup self-raising flour
25 g/1 oz/¼ cup cocoa powder
2 tbsp milk

WHITE CHOCOLATE BUTTER CREAM:
75 g/2¾ oz white chocolate
2 tbsp milk
150 g/5½ oz/⅔ cup butter
125 g/4½ oz/¾ cup icing (confectioners') sugar
2 tbsp orange-flavoured liqueur
large dark chocolate curls, to decorate

1 Grease and line the sides of two 400 g/14 oz food cans.

2 Beat together the margarine and sugar in a bowl until light and fluffy. Gradually add the eggs, beating well after each addition. Sieve (strain) together the flour and cocoa powder and fold into the cake mixture. Fold in the milk.

3 Divide the mixture between the two prepared cans. Stand the cans on a baking tray (cookie sheet) and bake in a preheated oven, 180°C/ 350°F/Gas Mark 4, for 40 minutes or until springy to the touch. Leave to cool for about 5 minutes in the cans, then turn out and leave to cool completely on a wire rack.

4 To make the butter cream, put the chocolate and milk in a pan and heat gently until the chocolate has melted, stirring until well combined. Leave to cool slightly. Beat together the butter and icing (confectioners') sugar until light and fluffy. Beat in the orange liqueur. Gradually beat in the chocolate mixture.

5 To assemble, cut both cakes into 1 cm/½ inch thick slices, then reassemble them by sandwiching the slices together with some of the butter cream.

6 Place the cake on a serving plate and spread the remaining butter cream over the top and sides. Decorate with the chocolate curls, then serve the cake cut diagonally into slices.

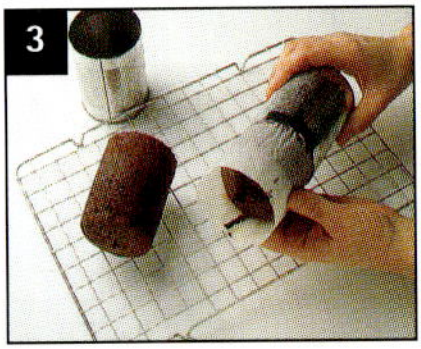

Chocolate & Orange Mousse Cake

Serves 12

INGREDIENTS

175 g/6 oz/¾ cup butter
175 g/6 oz/¾ cup caster (superfine) sugar
4 eggs, lightly beaten
200 g/7 oz/1¾ cups self-raising flour
1 tbsp cocoa powder
50 g/1¾ oz dark orange-flavoured chocolate, melted

ORANGE MOUSSE:
2 eggs, separated
50 g/1¾ oz/4 tbsp caster (superfine) sugar
200 ml/7fl oz/¾ cup freshly squeezed orange juice
2 tsp gelatine
3 tbsp water
300 ml/½ pint/1¼ cups double (heavy) cream
peeled orange slices, to decorate

1 Grease a 20 cm/8 inch springform cake tin (pan) and and line the base. Beat the butter and sugar in a bowl until light and fluffy. Gradually add the eggs, beating well after each addition. Sieve (strain) together the cocoa and flour and fold into the cake mixture. Fold in the chocolate.

2 Pour into the prepared tin (pan) and level the top. Bake in a preheated oven, 180°C/350°F/Gas Mark 4, for 40 minutes or until springy to the touch. Leave to cool for 5 minutes in the tin (pan), then turn out and leave to cool completely on a wire rack. Cut the cold cake into 2 layers.

3 To make the orange mousse, beat the egg yolks and sugar until light, then whisk in the orange juice. Sprinkle the gelatine over the water in a small bowl and allow to go spongy, then place over a pan of hot water and stir until dissolved. Stir into the mousse.

4 Whip the cream until holding its shape, reserve a little for decoration and fold the rest into the mousse. Whisk the egg whites until standing in soft peaks, then fold in. Leave in a cool place until starting to set, stirring occasionally.

5 Place half of the cake in the tin (pan). Pour in the mousse and press the second cake layer on top. Chill until set. Transfer to a dish, pipe cream rosettes on the top and arrange orange slices in the centre.

2

3

5

Chocolate Roulade

Serves 6–8

INGREDIENTS

150 g/5½ oz dark chocolate
6 eggs
175 g/6 oz/¾ cup caster (superfine) sugar
25 g/1 oz/¼ cup plain (all-purpose) flour
1 tbsp cocoa powder
2 tbsp water

FILLING:
300 ml/½ pint/1¼ cups double (heavy) cream
75 g/2¾ oz sliced strawberries

TO DECORATE:
icing (confectioners') sugar
chocolate leaves (see below)

1 Line a 37.5 x 25 cm/15 x 10 inch Swiss roll tin (pan). Melt the chocolate in the water, stirring. Leave to cool slightly.

2 Place the eggs and sugar in a bowl and whisk for 10 minutes, or until the mixture is pale and foamy and the whisk leaves a trail when lifted. Whisk in the chocolate in a thin stream. Sieve (strain) the flour and cocoa together and fold into the mixture. Pour into the tin; level the top.

3 Bake in a preheated oven, 200°C/400°F/ Gas Mark 6, for 12 minutes. Dust a sheet of baking parchment with a little icing (confectioners') sugar. Turn out the roulade and remove the lining paper. Roll up the roulade with the fresh parchment inside. Place on a wire rack, cover with a damp tea towel and leave to cool.

4 Whisk the cream until just holding its shape. Unroll the roulade and scatter over the fruit. Spread three-quarters of the cream over the roulade and re-roll. Dust with icing (confectioners') sugar. Place the roulade on a plate. Pipe the rest of the cream down the centre and decorate with chocolate leaves.

5 To make chocolate leaves, wash some rose or holly leaves and pat dry. Melt some chocolate and brush over the leaves. Set aside to harden. Repeat with 2–3 layers of chocolate. Carefully peel the leaves away from the chocolate.

4

5

5

Chocolate & Coconut Roulade

Serves 8–10

INGREDIENTS

3 eggs
75 g/2¾ oz/⅓ cup caster (superfine) sugar
50 g/1¾ oz/⅓ cup self-raising flour
1 tbsp block creamed coconut, softened with 1 tbsp boiling water
25 g/1 oz desiccated (shredded) coconut
6 tbsp good raspberry conserve

CHOCOLATE COATING:
200 g/7 oz dark chocolate
60 g/2 oz/¼ cup butter
2 tbsp golden (light corn) syrup

RASPBERRY COULIS:
225 g/8 oz fresh or frozen raspberries, thawed if frozen
2 tbsp water
4 tbsp icing (confectioners') sugar

1 Grease and line a 23 x 30 cm/ 9 x 12 inch Swiss roll tin (pan). Whisk the eggs and caster (superfine) sugar in a large mixing bowl with electric beaters for about 10 minutes or until the mixture is very light and foamy and the whisk leaves a trail that lasts a few seconds when lifted.

2 Sieve (strain) the flour and fold in with a metal spoon or a spatula. Fold in the creamed coconut and desiccated (shredded) coconut. Pour into the prepared tin (pan) and bake in a preheated oven, 200°C/400°F/Gas Mark 6, for 10–12 minutes, or until springy to the touch.

3 Sprinkle a sheet of baking parchment with a little caster (superfine) sugar and place on top of a damp tea towel. Turn the cake out on to the paper and carefully peel away the lining paper. Spread the jam over the sponge and roll up from the short end, using the tea towel to help you. Place seam-side down on a wire rack and leave to cool completely.

4 To make the coating, melt the chocolate and butter, stirring. Stir in the golden (light corn) syrup; leave to cool for 5 minutes. Spread it over the roulade and leave to set. To make the coulis, purée the fruit in a food processor with the water and sugar; sieve to remove the seeds. Cut the roulade into slices and serve with the coulis.

2

3

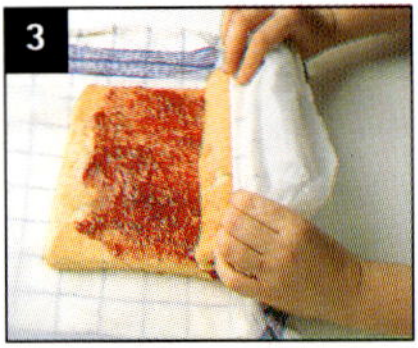
3

Almond & Hazelnut Gateau

Serves 8–10

INGREDIENTS

4 eggs
100 g/3½ oz/7 tbsp caster (superfine) sugar
50 g/1¾ oz/½ cup ground almonds
50 g/1¾ oz/½ cup ground hazelnuts
50 g/1¾ oz/⅓ cup plain (all-purpose) flour
50 g/1¾ oz/½ cup flaked almonds

FILLING:
100 g/3½ oz dark chocolate
15 g/½ oz/1 tbsp butter
300 ml/½ pint/1¼ cups double (heavy) cream
icing (confectioners') sugar, to dust

1 Grease two 18 cm/7 inch round sandwich tins (pans) and line the bases with baking parchment.

2 Whisk the eggs and caster (superfine) sugar in a large mixing bowl with electric beaters for about 10 minutes, or until the mixture is very light and foamy and the whisk leaves a trail that lasts a few seconds when lifted.

3 Fold in the ground nuts, sieve (strain) the flour and fold in with a metal spoon or spatula. Pour into the prepared tins (pans).

4 Scatter the flaked almonds over the top of one of the cakes. Bake both of the cakes in a preheated oven, 190°C/375°F/Gas Mark 5, for 15–20 minutes or until springy to the touch.

5 Leave the cakes to cool slightly in the tins (pans). Carefully remove the cakes from the tins (pans) and transfer them to a wire rack to cool completely.

6 To make the filling, melt the chocolate, remove from the heat and stir in the butter. Leave to cool slightly. Whip the cream until just holding its shape, then fold in the melted chocolate until mixed.

7 Place the cake without the extra almonds on a serving plate and spread the filling over it. Leave to set slightly, then place the almond-topped cake on top of the filling and leave to chill for about 1 hour. Dust with icing (confectioners') sugar and serve.

3

4

7

Chocolate & Walnut Cake

Serves 8–12

INGREDIENTS

4 eggs
125 g/4½ oz/½ cup caster (superfine) sugar
125 g/4½ oz/1 cup plain (all-purpose) flour
1 tbsp cocoa powder
25 g/1 oz/2 tbsp butter, melted
75 g/2¾ oz dark chocolate, melted
150 g/5½ oz/1¼ cups finely chopped walnuts

ICING:
75 g/2¾ oz dark chocolate
125 g/4½ oz/½ cup butter
200 g/7 oz/1¼ cups icing (confectioners') sugar
2 tbsp milk
walnut halves, to decorate

1 Grease a 18 cm/7 inch deep round cake tin (pan) and line the base. Place the eggs and caster (superfine) sugar in a mixing bowl and whisk with electric beaters for 10 minutes, or until the mixture is light and foamy and the whisk leaves a trail that lasts a few seconds when lifted.

2 Sieve (strain) together the flour and cocoa powder and fold in with a metal spoon or spatula. Fold in the melted butter and chocolate, and the chopped walnuts. Pour into the prepared tin (pan) and bake in a preheated oven, 160°C/325°F/Gas Mark 3, and bake for 30–35 minutes or until springy to the touch.

3 Leave to cool in the tin (pan) for 5 minutes, then transfer to a wire rack to cool completely. Cut the cold cake into 2 layers.

4 To make the icing, melt the dark chocolate and leave to cool slightly. Beat together the butter, icing (confectioners') sugar and milk in a bowl until the mixture is pale and fluffy. Whisk in the melted chocolate.

5 Sandwich the 2 cake layers with some of the icing and place on a serving plate. Spread the remaining icing over the top of the cake with a palette knife (spatula), swirling it slightly as you do so. Decorate the cake with the walnut halves and serve.

Dobos Torte

Serves 8

INGREDIENTS

3 eggs
100 g/3½ oz/7 tbsp caster (superfine) sugar
1 tsp vanilla flavouring (extract)
100 g/3½ oz/½ cup plain (all-purpose) flour

FILLING:
175 g/6 oz dark chocolate
175 g/6 oz/¾ cup butter
2 tbsp milk
350 g/12 oz/2 cups icing (confectioners') sugar

CARAMEL:
100 g/3½ oz/7 tbsp granulated sugar
4 tbsp water

1 Draw four 18 cm/7 inch circles on sheets of baking parchment. Place 2 of them upside down on 2 baking trays (cookie sheets). Whisk the eggs and caster (superfine) sugar in a large mixing bowl with electric beaters for 10 minutes, or until the mixture is light and foamy and the whisk leaves a trail. Fold in the vanilla flavouring (extract). Sieve (strain) the flour and fold in with a metal spoon or a spatula. Spoon a quarter of the mixture on to one of the trays (sheets) and spread out to the size of the circle. Repeat with the other circle. Bake in a preheated oven, 200°C/400°F/Gas Mark 6, for 5–8 minutes or until golden brown. Cool on wire racks. Repeat with the remaining mixture.

2 To make the filling, melt the chocolate and cool slightly. Beat the butter, milk and icing (confectioners') sugar until pale and fluffy. Whisk in the chocolate.
Place the sugar and water for the caramel in a heavy-based pan and heat gently, stirring until the sugar dissolves. Boil gently until the syrup is pale golden. Remove from the heat. Pour over one layer of the cake to cover the top. Leave to harden slightly, then mark into 8 portions with an oiled knife.
Remove the cakes from the paper and trim the edges. Sandwich the layers together with some of the filling, finishing with the caramel-topped cake. Place on a serving plate and spread the sides with the filling mixture, using a comb scraper if you have one. Pipe rosettes around the top of the cake.

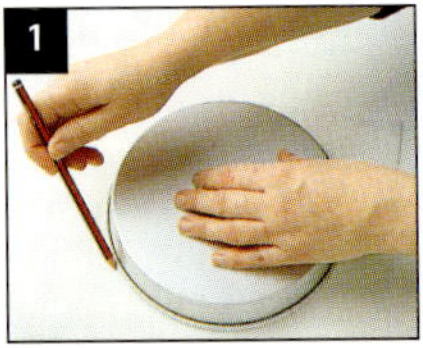
1

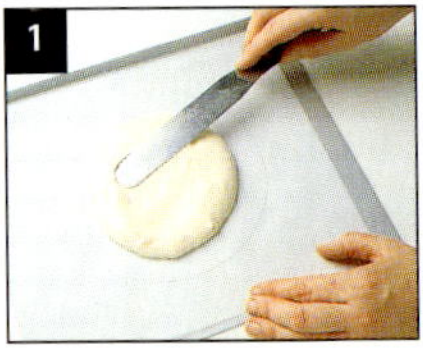
1

2

Bistvitny Torte

Serves 10

INGREDIENTS

CHOCOLATE TRIANGLES:
- 25 g/1 oz dark chocolate, melted
- 25 g/1 oz white chocolate, melted

CAKE:
- 175 g/6 oz/¾ cup soft margarine
- 175 g/6 oz/¾ cup caster (superfine) sugar
- ½ tsp vanilla flavouring (extract)
- 3 eggs, lightly beaten
- 225 g/8 oz/2 cups self-raising flour
- 50 g/1¾ oz dark chocolate

SYRUP:
- 125 g/4½ oz/½ cup sugar
- 6 tbsp water
- 3 tbsp brandy or sherry
- 150 ml/¼ pint/⅔ cup double (heavy) cream

1 Grease a 23 cm/9 inch ring tin (pan). To make the triangles, place a sheet of baking parchment on to a baking tray (cookie sheet) and place alternate spoonfuls of the dark and white chocolate on to the paper. Spread together to form a thick marbled layer; leave to set. Cut into squares, then into triangles.

2 To make the cake, beat the margarine and sugar until light and fluffy. Beat in the vanilla flavouring (extract). Gradually add the eggs, beating well after each addition. Fold in the flour. Divide the mixture in half. Melt the dark chocolate and stir into one half.

3 Place spoonfuls of each mixture into the prepared tin (pan) and swirl together with a skewer to create a marbled effect.

4 Bake in a preheated oven, 190°C/375°F/Gas Mark 5, for 30 minutes, or until the cake is springy to the touch. Leave to cool in the tin (pan) for a few minutes, then transfer to a wire rack to cool completely.

5 To make the syrup, place the sugar in a small pan with the water and heat until the sugar has dissolved. Boil for 1–2 minutes. Remove from the heat and stir in the brandy or sherry. Leave the syrup to cool slightly then spoon it slowly over the cake, allowing it to soak into the sponge. Whip the cream and pipe swirls of it on top of the cake. Decorate with the chocolate triangles.

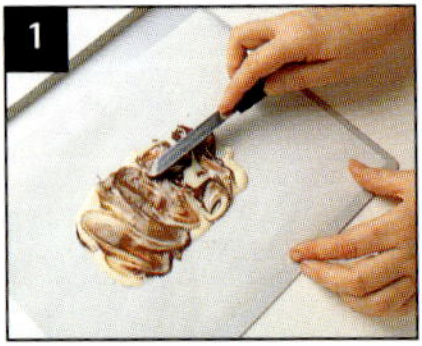

Sachertorte

Serves 10–12

INGREDIENTS

175 g/6 oz dark chocolate
150 g/5½ oz/⅔ cup unsalted butter
150 g/5½ oz/⅔ cup caster (superfine) sugar
6 eggs, separated
150 g/5½ oz/1¼ cups plain (all-purpose) flour

ICING AND FILLING:
175 g/6 oz dark chocolate
5 tbsp strong black coffee
175 g/6 oz/1 cup icing (confectioners') sugar
6 tbsp good apricot preserve
50 g/1¾ oz dark chocolate, melted

1 Grease a 23 cm/9 inch springform cake tin (pan) and line the base. Melt the chocolate. Beat the butter and 75 g/2¾ oz/⅓ cup of the sugar until pale and fluffy. Add the egg yolks and beat well. Add the chocolate in a thin stream, beating well. Sieve (strain) the flour; fold it into the mixture. Whisk the egg whites until they stand in soft peaks. Add the remaining sugar and whisk for 2 minutes by hand, or 45–60 seconds if using an electric whisk, until glossy. Fold half into the chocolate mixture, then fold in the remainder.

2 Spoon into the prepared tin (pan) and level the top. Bake in a preheated oven, 150°C/300°F/ Gas Mark 2, for 1–1¼ hours until a skewer inserted into the centre comes out clean. Cool in the tin (pan) for 5 minutes, then transfer to a wire rack to cool completely.

3 To make the icing, melt the chocolate and beat in the coffee until smooth. Sieve (strain) the icing (confectioners') sugar into a bowl. Whisk in the melted chocolate mixture to give a thick icing. Halve the cake. Warm the jam, spread over one half of the cake and sandwich together. Invert the cake on a wire rack. Spoon the icing over the cake and spread to coat the top and sides. Leave to set for 5 minutes, allowing any excess icing to drop through the rack. Transfer to a serving plate and leave to set for at least 2 hours.

4 To decorate, spoon the melted chocolate into a small piping bag and pipe the word 'Sacher' or 'Sachertorte' on the top of the cake. Leave it to harden before serving the cake.

Sachertorte

Dark & White Chocolate Torte

Serves 10

INGREDIENTS

4 eggs
100 g/3½ oz/7 tbsp cup caster (superfine) sugar
100 g/3½ oz/¾ cup plain (all-purpose) flour

DARK CHOCOLATE CREAM:
300 ml/½ pint/⅔ cup double (heavy) cream
150 g/5½ oz dark chocolate, broken into small pieces

WHITE CHOCOLATE ICING:
75 g/2¾ oz white chocolate
15 g/½ oz/1 tbsp butter
1 tbsp milk
50 g/1¾ oz/4 tbsp icing (confectioners') sugar
chocolate caraque

1 Grease a 20 cm/8 inch round springform tin (pan) and line the base. Whisk the eggs and caster (superfine) sugar in a large mixing bowl with electric beaters for about 10 minutes, or until the mixture is very light and foamy and the whisk leaves a trail that lasts a few seconds when lifted.

2 Sieve (strain) the flour and fold in with a metal spoon or spatula. Pour into the prepared tin (pan) and bake in a preheated oven, 180°C/350°F/Gas Mark 4, for 35–40 minutes, or until springy to the touch. Leave to cool slightly, then transfer to a wire rack to cool completely. Cut the cold cake into 2 layers.

3 To make the chocolate cream, place the cream in a saucepan and bring to the boil, stirring. Add the chocolate and stir until melted and well combined. Remove from the heat and leave to cool. Beat with a wooden spoon until thick.

4 Sandwich the 2 cake layers back together with the chocolate cream and place on a wire rack.

5 To make the icing, melt the chocolate and butter together and stir until blended. Whisk in the milk and icing (confectioners') sugar. Whisk for a few minutes until the icing is cool. Pour it over the cake and spread with a palette knife (spatula) to coat the top and sides. Decorate with chocolate caraque and leave to set.

Chocolate Ganache Cake

Serves 10–12

INGREDIENTS

175 g/6 oz/$^{3}/_{4}$ cup butter
175 g/6 oz/$^{3}/_{4}$ cup caster (superfine) sugar
4 eggs, lightly beaten
200 g/7 oz/1$^{3}/_{4}$ cups self-raising flour
1 tbsp cocoa powder
50 g/1$^{3}/_{4}$ oz dark chocolate, melted

GANACHE:
450ml/16 fl oz/2 cups double (heavy) cream
375 g/13 oz dark chocolate, broken into pieces

TO FINISH:
200 g/7 oz chocolate-flavoured cake covering

1 Lightly grease a 20 cm/8 inch springform cake tin (pan) and line the base. Beat the butter and sugar until light and fluffy. Gradually add the eggs, beating well after each addition. Sieve (strain) together the flour and cocoa. Fold into the cake mixture. Fold in the melted chocolate.

2 Pour into the prepared tin (pan) and level the top. Bake in a preheated oven, 180°C/350°F/ Gas Mark 4, for 40 minutes or until springy to the touch. Leave to cool for 5 minutes in the tin (pan), then turn out on to a wire rack and leave to cool completely . Cut the cold cake into 2 layers.

3 To make the ganache, place the cream in a pan and bring to the boil, stirring. Add the chocolate and stir until melted and combined. Pour into a bowl and whisk for about 5 minutes or until the ganache is fluffy and cool.

4 Reserve one-third of the ganache. Use the remaining ganache to sandwich the cake together and spread over the top and sides of the cake.

5 Melt the cake covering and spread it over a large sheet of baking parchment. Cool until just set. Cut into strips a little wider than the height of the cake. Place the strips around the edge of the cake, overlapping them slightly.

6 Pipe the reserved ganache in tear drop or shells to cover the top of the cake. Chill for 1 hour.

1

4

5

Bûche de Noël

Serves 8–10

INGREDIENTS

CAKE:
4 eggs
100 g/3½ oz/7 tbsp caster (superfine) sugar
75 g/2¾ oz/⅔ cup self-raising flour
2 tbsp cocoa powder

ICING:
150 g/5½ oz dark chocolate
2 egg yolks
150 ml/¼ pint/⅔ cup milk
125 g/4½ oz/½ cup butter
50 g/1¾ oz/4 tbsp icing (confectioners') sugar
2 tbsp rum (optional)

TO DECORATE:
a little white glacé or royal icing
icing (confectioners') sugar, to dust
holly or Christmas cake decorations

1 Grease and line a 30 x 23 cm/12 x 9 inch Swiss roll tin (pan). Whisk the eggs and caster (superfine) sugar in a bowl with electric beaters for 10 minutes, or until the mixture is very light and foamy and the whisk leaves a trail. Sieve (strain) the flour and cocoa powder and fold in. Pour into the prepared tin (pan) and bake in a preheated oven, 200°C/400°F/Gas Mark 6, for 12 minutes or until springy to the touch. Turn out on to a piece of baking parchment which has been sprinkled with a little caster (superfine) sugar. Peel off the lining paper and trim the edges. Cut a small slit halfway into the cake about 1 cm/½ inch from one short end. Starting at that end, roll up tightly, enclosing the paper. Place on a wire rack to cool.

2 To make the icing, break the chocolate into pieces and melt it over a pan of hot water. Beat in the egg yolks, whisk in the milk and cook until the mixture thickens enough to coat the back of a wooden spoon, stirring. Cover with dampened greaseproof paper and cool. Beat the butter and sugar until pale and fluffy. Beat in the custard and rum, if using. Unroll the sponge, spread with one-third of the icing and roll up again. Place on a serving plate. Spread the remaining icing over the cake and mark with a fork to give the effect of bark. Leave to set. Pipe white icing to form the rings of the log. Sprinkle with sugar and decorate.

Chocolate Truffle Cake

Serves 12

INGREDIENTS

75 g/2¾ oz/⅓ cup butter
75 g/2¾ oz/⅓ cup caster (superfine) sugar
2 eggs, lightly beaten
75 g/2¾ oz/⅔ cup self-raising flour
½ tsp baking powder
25 g/1 oz/¼ cup cocoa powder
50 g/1¾ oz ground almonds

TRUFFLE TOPPING:
350 g/12 oz dark chocolate
100 g/3½ oz butter
300 ml/½ pint/1¼ cups double (heavy) cream
75 g/2¾ oz/1¼ cups plain cake crumbs
3 tbsp dark rum

TO DECORATE:
Cape gooseberries
50 g/1¾ oz dark chocolate, melted

1 Lightly grease a 20 cm/ 8 inch round springform tin (pan) and line the base. Beat together the butter and sugar until light and fluffy. Gradually add the eggs, beating well after each addition.

2 Sieve (strain) the flour, baking powder and cocoa powder together and fold into the mixture along with the ground almonds. Pour into the prepared tin (pan) and bake in a preheated oven, 180°C/ 350°F/Gas Mark 4, for 20–25 minutes or until springy to the touch. Leave to cool slightly in the tin (pan), then transfer to a wire rack to cool completely. Wash and dry the tin (pan) and return the cooled cake to the tin (pan).

3 To make the topping, heat the chocolate, butter and cream in a heavy-based pan over a low heat and stir until smooth. Cool, then chill for 30 minutes. Beat well with a wooden spoon and chill for a further 30 minutes. Beat the mixture again, then add the cake crumbs and rum, beating until well combined. Spoon over the sponge base and chill for 3 hours.

4 Meanwhile, dip the Cape gooseberries in the melted chocolate until partially covered. Leave to set on baking parchment. Transfer the cake to a serving plate; decorate with Cape gooseberries.

White Chocolate Truffle Cake

Serves 12

INGREDIENTS

2 eggs
50 g/1¾ oz/4 tbsp caster (superfine) sugar
50 g/1¾ oz/⅓ cup plain (all-purpose) flour
50 g/1¾ oz white chocolate, melted

TRUFFLE TOPPIING:
300 ml/½ pint/1¼ cups double (heavy) cream
350 g/12 oz white chocolate, broken into pieces
250 g/9 oz Quark or fromage frais

TO DECORATE:
dark, milk or white chocolate, melted
cocoa powder, to dust

1 Grease a 20 cm/8 inch round springform tin (pan) and line the base. Whisk the eggs and caster (superfine) sugar in a mixing bowl for 10 minutes, or until the mixture is very light and foamy and the whisk leaves a trail that lasts a few seconds when lifted. Sieve (strain) the flour and fold in with a metal spoon. Fold in the melted white chocolate. Pour into the tin (pan) and bake in a preheated oven, 180°C/350°F/Gas Mark 4, for 25 minutes or until springy to the touch. Leave to cool slightly, then transfer to a wire rack until completely cold. Return the cold cake to the tin (pan).

2 To make the topping, place the cream in a pan and bring to the boil, stirring to prevent it sticking to the bottom of the pan. Cool slightly, then add the white chocolate pieces and stir until melted and combined. Remove from the heat and leave until almost cool, stirring, then stir in the Quark or fromage frais. Pour the mixture on top of the cake and chill for 2 hours. Remove the cake from the tin (pan) and transfer to a serving plate.

3 To make large chocolate curls, pour melted chocolate on to a marble or acrylic board and spread it thinly with a palette knife (spatula). Leave to set at room temperature. Using a scraper, push through the chocolate at a 25° angle until a large curl forms. Remove each curl as you make it and leave to chill until set. Decorate the cake with chocolate curls and sprinkle with a little cocoa powder.

2

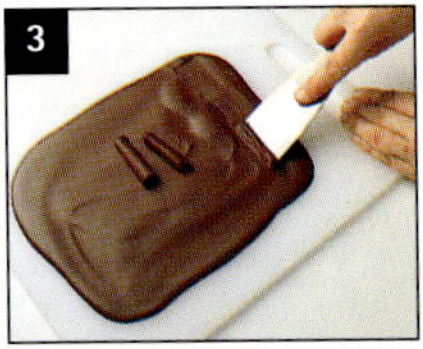
3

3

Chocolate & Raspberry Vacherin

Serves 10–12

INGREDIENTS

3 egg whites
175 g/6 oz/¾ cup caster (superfine) sugar
1 tsp cornflour (cornstarch)25 g/1 oz dark chocolate, grated

FILLING:
175 g/6 oz dark chocolate
450 ml/16 fl oz/2 cups double (heavy) cream, whipped
350 g/12 oz fresh raspberries
a little melted chocolate, to decorate

1 Draw 3 rectangles, 10 x 25 cm/4 x 10 inches, on sheets of baking parchment and place on 2 baking trays (cookie sheets).

2 Whisk the egg whites in a mixing bowl until standing in soft peaks, then gradually whisk in half of the sugar and continue whisking until the mixture is very stiff and glossy.

3 Carefully fold in the rest of the sugar, the cornflour (cornstarch) and grated chocolate with a metal spoon or a spatula.

4 Spoon the meringue mixture into a piping bag fitted with a 1 cm/½ inch plain nozzle (tip) and pipe lines across the rectangles.

5 Bake in a preheated oven, 140°C/275°F/Gas Mark 1, for 1½ hours, changing the positions of the baking trays (cookie sheets) halfway through. Without opening the oven door, turn off the oven and leave the meringues to cool in the oven, then peel away the paper.

6 To make the filling, melt the chocolate and spread it over 2 of the meringue layers. Leave the filling to harden.

7 Place 1 chocolate-coated meringue on a plate and top with about one-third of the cream and raspberries. Gently place the second chocolate-coated meringue on top and spread with half of the remaining cream and raspberries.

8 Place the last meringue on the top and decorate it with the remaining cream and raspberries. Drizzle a little melted chocolate over the top and serve.

Tropical Fruit Vacherin

Serves 10–12

INGREDIENTS

6 egg whites
275 g/9½ oz/generous 1 cup caster (superfine) sugar
75 g/2¾ oz/¾ cup desiccated (shredded) coconut

FILLING AND TOPPING:
90 g/3 oz dark chocolate, broken into pieces
3 egg yolks
3 tbsp water
1 tbsp rum (optional)
50 g/1¾ oz/4 tbsp caster (superfine) sugar
450 ml/16 fl oz/2 cups double (heavy) cream
selection of tropical fruits, sliced or cut into bite size pieces

1. Draw 3 circles, 20 cm/8 inch each, on sheets of baking parchment and place on baking trays (cookie sheets).

2. Whisk the egg whites until standing in soft peaks, then gradually whisk in half of the sugar and continue whisking until the mixture is very stiff and glossy. Carefully fold in the remaining sugar and the coconut.

3. Spoon the mixture into a piping bag fitted with a star nozzle (tip) and cover the circles with piped swirls. Bake in a preheated oven, 140°C/275°F/Gas Mark 1, for 1½ hours, changing the position of the trays (sheets) halfway through. Without opening the oven door, turn off the oven and leave the meringues to cool in the oven, then peel away the paper.

4. To make the filling, place the chocolate pieces, egg yolks, water, rum, if using, and sugar in a small bowl and place it over a pan of gently simmering water. Cook over a low heat, stirring, until the chocolate has melted and the mixture has thickened. Cover with a disc of baking parchment and leave until cold.

5. Whip the cream and fold two-thirds of it into the chocolate mixture. Sandwich the meringue layers together with the chocolate mixture. Place the remaining cream in a piping bag fitted with a star nozzle (tip) and pipe around the edge of the meringue. Arrange the tropical fruits in the centre.

1

2

3

Olive Oil, Fruit & Nut Cake

Serves 8

INGREDIENTS

225 g/8 oz/2 cups self-raising flour
50 g/1¾ oz/9 tsp caster (superfine) sugar
125 ml/4 fl oz/½ cup milk
4 tbsp orange juice
150 ml/¼ pint/⅔ cup olive oil
100 g/3½ oz mixed dried fruit
25 g/1 oz pine kernels (nuts)

1 Grease an 18 cm/7 inch cake tin (pan) and line with baking parchment.

2 Sieve (strain) the flour into a bowl and stir in the caster (superfine) sugar.

3 Make a well in the centre of the dry ingredients and pour in the milk and orange juice. Stir the mixture with a wooden spoon, beating in the flour and sugar.

4 Pour in the olive oil, stirring well so that all of the ingredients are evenly mixed.

5 Stir the mixed dried fruit and pine kernels (nuts) into the mixture and spoon into the prepared tin (pan).

6 Bake in a preheated oven, 180°C/350°F/ Gas Mark 4, for about 45 minutes until the cake is golden and firm to the touch.

7 Leave the cake to cool in the tin (pan) for a few minutes, then transfer to a wire rack to cool.

8 Serve the cake warm or cold and cut into slices.

COOK'S TIP

Pine kernels (nuts) are best known as the flavouring ingredient in the classic Italian pesto, but here they give a delicate, slightly resinous flavour to this cake.

Chocolate & Pear Sponge Cake

Serves 6

INGREDIENTS

175 g/6 oz/¾ cup butter, softened
175 g/6 oz/1 cup soft brown sugar
3 eggs, beaten
150 g/5½ oz/1¼ cups self-raising flour
15 g/½ oz/2 tbsp cocoa powder
2 tbsp milk
2 small pears, peeled, cored and sliced

1 Grease a 23 cm/8 inch loose-bottomed cake tin (pan) and line the base with baking parchment.

2 In a bowl, cream together the butter and soft brown sugar until pale and fluffy.

3 Gradually add the beaten eggs to the creamed mixture, beating well after each addition.

4 Sieve (strain) the self-raising flour and cocoa powder into the creamed mixture and fold in gently until all of the ingredients are combined.

5 Stir in the milk, then spoon the mixture into the prepared tin (pan). Level the surface with the back of a spoon or a knife.

6 Arrange the pear slices on top of the cake mixture, arranging them in a radiating pattern.

7 Bake in a preheated oven, 180°C/350°F/Gas Mark 4, for about 1 hour until the cake is just firm to the touch.

8 Leave the cake to cool in the tin (pan), then transfer to a wire rack until completely cold before serving.

COOK'S TIP

Serve the cake with melted chocolate drizzled over the top for a delicious dessert.

Caraway Madeira Cake

Serves 8

INGREDIENTS

225 g/8 oz/1 cup butter, softened
175 g/6 oz/1 cup soft brown sugar
3 eggs, beaten
350 g/12 oz/3 cups self-raising flour
1 tbsp caraway seeds
grated rind of 1 lemon
6 tbsp milk
1 or 2 strips of citron peel

1 Grease and line a 900 g/2 lb loaf tin (pan).

2 In a bowl, cream together the butter and soft brown sugar until pale and fluffy.

3 Gradually add the beaten eggs, beating well after each addition.

4 Sieve (strain) the flour into the bowl and gently fold into the creamed mixture.

5 Add the caraway seeds, lemon rind and the milk and fold in until thoroughly blended.

6 Spoon the mixture into the prepared tin (pan) and level the surface with a palette knife (spatula).

7 Bake in a preheated oven, 160°C/325°F/Gas Mark 3, for 20 minutes.

8 Remove the cake from the oven, place the pieces of citron peel on top of the cake and return it to the oven for a further 40 minutes or until the cake is well risen and a fine skewer inserted into the centre comes out clean.

9 Leave the cake to cool in the tin (pan) before turning out and transferring to a wire rack until completely cold.

COOK'S TIP

Citron peel is available in the baking section of supermarkets. If it is unavailable, you can substitute it with chopped mixed peel.

Clementine Cake

Serves 8

INGREDIENTS

2 clementines
175 g/6 oz/¾ cup butter, softened
175 g/6 oz/¾ cup caster (superfine) sugar
3 eggs, beaten
175 g/6 oz/1½ cups self-raising flour
3 tbsp ground almonds
3 tbsp single (light) cream

GLAZE AND TOPPING:
6 tbsp clementine juice
2 tbsp caster (superfine) sugar
3 white sugar cubes, crushed

1 Grease an 18 cm/7 inch round tin (pan) and line the base with baking parchment.

2 Pare the rind from the clementines and chop the rind finely. In a bowl, cream together the butter, sugar and clementine rind until pale and fluffy.

3 Gradually add the beaten eggs to the mixture, beating well after each addition.

4 Gently fold in the self-raising flour followed by the ground almonds and the single (light) cream. Spoon the mixture into the prepared tin (pan).

5 Bake in a preheated oven, 180°C/350°F/ Gas Mark 4, for about 55-60 minutes or until a fine skewer inserted into the centre comes out clean. Leave to cool slightly.

6 To make the glaze, put the clementine juice into a small saucepan with the caster (superfine) sugar. Bring to the boil and simmer for 5 minutes.

7 Drizzle the glaze over the cake until it has been absorbed and sprinkle with the crushed sugar cubes.

COOK'S TIP

If you prefer, chop the rind from the clementines in a food processor or blender together with the sugar in step 2. Tip the mixture into a bowl with the butter and begin to cream the mixture.

Glacé Fruit Cake

Serves 8

INGREDIENTS

175 g/6 oz/3/4 cup butter, softened
175 g/6 oz/3/4 cup caster (superfine) sugar
3 eggs, beaten
175 g/6 oz self-raising flour, sieved (strained)
25 g/1 oz ground rice
finely grated rind of 1 lemon
4 tbsp lemon juice
125 g/4 1/2 oz/2/3 cup glacé (candied) fruits, chopped
icing (confectioners') sugar, for dusting (optional)

1 Lightly grease an 18 cm/7 inch cake tin (pan) and line with baking parchment.

2 In a bowl, whisk together the butter and caster (superfine) sugar until light and fluffy.

3 Add the beaten eggs a little at a time. Fold in the flour and ground rice.

4 Add the grated lemon rind and juice, followed by the chopped glacé fruits. Lightly mix all the ingredients together.

5 Spoon the mixture into the prepared tin (pan) and level the surface with the back of a spoon or a knife.

6 Bake in a preheated oven, 180°C/350°F/Gas Mark 4, for 1 hour - 1 hour 10 minutes until well risen or until a fine skewer inserted into the centre of the cake comes out clean.

7 Leave the cake to cool in the tin (pan) for 5 minutes, then turn out on to a wire rack to cool completely.

8 Dust well with icing (confectioners') sugar, if using, before serving.

COOK'S TIP

Wash and dry the glacé (candied) fruits before chopping them. This will prevent the fruits sinking to the bottom of the cake during cooking.

2

3

4

White Chocolate & Apricot Squares

Makes 12 bars

INGREDIENTS

125 g/4½ oz/½ cup butter
175 g/6 oz white chocolate, chopped
4 eggs
125 g/4½ oz/½ cup caster (superfine) sugar
200 g/7 oz/1 ¾ cups plain (all-purpose) flour, sieved (strained)
1 tsp baking powder
pinch of salt
100 g/3½ oz ready-to-eat dried apricots, chopped

1 Lightly grease a 20 cm/9 inch square cake tin (pan) and line the base with a sheet of baking parchment.

2 Melt the butter and chocolate in a heatproof bowl set over a saucepan of simmering water. Stir frequently with a wooden spoon until the mixture is smooth and glossy. Leave the mixture to cool slightly.

3 Beat the eggs and caster (superfine) sugar into the butter and chocolate mixture until well combined.

4 Fold in the flour, baking powder, salt and chopped dried apricots and mix well.

5 Pour the mixture into the tin (pan) and bake in a preheated oven, 180°C/350°F/Gas Mark 4, for 25-30 minutes.

6 The centre of the cake may not be completely firm, but it will set as it cools. Leave in the tin (pan) to cool.

7 When the cake is completely cold turn it out and slice into bars or squares.

VARIATION

Replace the white chocolate with milk or dark chocolate, if you prefer.

2

3

4

Crunchy Fruit Cake

Serves 8–10

INGREDIENTS

- 100 g/3$\frac{1}{2}$ oz/$\frac{1}{3}$ cup butter, softened
- 100g/3$\frac{1}{2}$ oz/$\frac{1}{2}$ cup caster (superfine) sugar
- 2 eggs, beaten
- 50 g/1$\frac{3}{4}$ oz/$\frac{1}{3}$ cup self-raising flour, sieved (strained)
- 100 g/3$\frac{1}{2}$ oz/$\frac{2}{3}$ cup polenta (cornmeal)
- 1 tsp baking powder
- 225 g/8 oz mixed dried fruit
- 25 g/ 1oz pine kernels (nuts)
- grated rind of 1 lemon
- 4 tbsp lemon juice
- 2 tbsp milk

1 Grease an 18 cm/7 inch cake tin (pan) and line the base with baking parchment.

2 In a bowl, whisk together the butter and sugar until light and fluffy.

3 Whisk in the beaten eggs a little at a time, whisking well after each addition.

4 Fold the flour, baking powder and polenta (cornmeal) into the mixture until well blended.

5 Stir in the mixed dried fruit, pine kernels (nuts), grated lemon rind, lemon juice and milk.

6 Spoon the mixture into the prepared tin (pan) and level the surface.

7 Bake in a preheated oven, 180°C/350°F/Gas Mark 4, for about 1 hour or until a fine skewer inserted into the centre of the cake comes out clean.

8 Leave the cake to cool in the tin (pan) before turning out.

VARIATION

To give a more crumbly light fruit cake, omit the polenta (cornmeal) and use 150 g/5$\frac{1}{2}$ oz/1$\frac{1}{4}$ cups self-raising flour instead.

Chocolate Slab Cake with Frosting

Serves 10–12

INGREDIENTS

225 g/8 oz/1 cup butter
100 g/3½ oz dark chocolate, chopped
150 ml/¼ pint/⅔ cup water
300 g/10½ oz/2½ cups plain (all-purpose) flour
2 tsp baking powder
275 g/9½ oz/1⅔ cups soft brown sugar
150 ml/¼ pint/⅔ cup soured cream
2 eggs, beaten

FROSTING:
200 g/7 oz dark chocolate
6 tbsp water
3 tbsp single (light) cream
1 tbsp butter, chilled

1 Grease a 33 x 20 cm/ 13 x 8 inch square cake tin (pan) and line the base with baking parchment. In a saucepan, melt the butter and chocolate with the water over a low heat, stirring frequently.

2 Sieve (strain) the flour and baking powder into a mixing bowl and stir in the sugar.

3 Pour the hot chocolate liquid into the bowl and then beat well until evenly mixed. Stir in the soured cream, followed by the eggs.

4 Pour the mixture into the prepared tin (pan) and bake in a preheated oven, 190°C/ 375°F/ Gas Mark 5, for 40-45 minutes.

5 Leave the cake to cool in the tin (pan), then turn it out on to a wire rack. Leave to cool completely.

6 To make the frosting, melt the chocolate with the water in a saucepan over a very low heat, stir in the cream and remove from the heat. Stir in the chilled butter, then pour the frosting over the cooled cake, using a spatula to spread it evenly over the top of the cake.

Chocolate & Almond Torte

Serves 10

INGREDIENTS

225 g/8 oz dark chocolate, broken into pieces
3 tbsp water
150 g/5½ oz/1 cup soft brown sugar
175 g/6 oz/¾ cup butter, softened
25 g/1 oz/¼ cup ground almonds
3 tbsp self-raising flour
5 eggs, separated
100 g 3½ oz/¼ cup blanched almonds, chopped finely
icing (confectioners') sugar, for dusting
double (heavy) cream, to serve (optional)

1 Grease a 23 cm/9 inch loose-bottomed cake tin (pan) and base line with baking parchment.

2 In a saucepan set over a very low heat, melt the chocolate with the water, stirring until smooth. Add the sugar and stir until dissolved, taking the pan off the heat to prevent it overheating.

3 Add the butter in small amounts until it has melted into the chocolate. Remove from the heat and lightly stir in the ground almonds and flour. Add the egg yolks one at a time, beating well after each addition.

4 In a large mixing bowl, whisk the egg whites until they stand in soft peaks, then fold them into the chocolate mixture with a metal spoon. Stir in the chopped almonds. Pour the mixture into the tin (pan) and level the surface with a palette knife (spatula).

5 Bake in a preheated oven, 180°C/350°F/ Gas Mark 4, for about 40-45 minutes until well risen and firm (the cake will crack on the surface during cooking).

6 Leave the cake to cool in the tin (pan) for 30-40 minutes, then turn it out on to a wire rack to cool completely. Dust with icing (confectioners') sugar and serve in slices with double (heavy) cream, if using.

2

3

3

Carrot Cake

Makes 12 bars

INGREDIENTS

125 g/4½ oz/1 cup self-raising flour
pinch of salt
1 tsp ground cinnamon
125 g/4½ oz/¾ cup soft brown sugar
2 eggs
100 ml/3½ fl oz/scant ½ cup sunflower oil
125 g/4½ oz carrot, peeled and grated finely
25 g/1 oz/⅓ cup desiccated (shredded) coconut
25 g/1 oz/⅓ cup walnuts, chopped
walnut pieces, for decoration

FROSTING:
50 g/1¾ oz/10 tsp butter, softened
50 g/1¾ oz full fat soft cheese
225 g/8 oz/1½ cups icing (confectioners') sugar, sieved (strained)
1 tsp lemon juice

1 Lightly grease a 20 cm/8 inch square cake tin (pan) and line with baking parchment.

2 Sieve (strain) the flour, salt and ground cinnamon into a large bowl and stir in the brown sugar. Add the eggs and oil to the dry ingredients and mix well.

3 Stir in the grated carrot, desiccated (shredded) coconut and chopped walnuts.

4 Pour the mixture into the prepared tin (pan) and bake in a preheated oven, 180°C/350°F/Gas Mark 4, for 20-25 minutes or until just firm to the touch. Leave to cool in the tin (pan).

5 Meanwhile, make the cheese frosting. In a bowl, beat together the butter, full fat soft cheese, icing (confectioners') sugar and lemon juice until the mixture is fluffy and creamy.

6 Turn the cake out of the tin (pan) and cut into 12 bars or slices. Spread with the frosting and then decorate with walnut pieces.

2

3

5

Lemon Syrup Cake

Serves 8

INGREDIENTS

200 g/7 oz/1¾ cups plain (all-purpose) flour
2 tsp baking powder
200 g/7 oz/1 cup caster (superfine) sugar
4 eggs
150 ml/¼ pint/⅔ cup soured cream
grated rind 1 large lemon
4 tbsp lemon juice
150 ml/¼ pint/⅔ cup sunflower oil

SYRUP:
4 tbsp icing (confectioners') sugar
3 tbsp lemon juice

1 Lightly grease a 20 cm/8 inch loose-bottomed round cake tin (pan) and line the base with baking parchment.

2 Sieve (strain) the flour and baking powder into a mixing bowl and stir in the sugar.

3 In a separate bowl, whisk the eggs, soured cream, lemon rind, lemon juice and oil together.

4 Pour the egg mixture into the dry ingredients and mix well until evenly combined.

5 Pour the mixture into the prepared tin (pan) and bake in a preheated oven, 180°C 350°F/Gas Mark 4, for 45-60 minutes until risen and golden brown.

6 To make the syrup, mix together the icing (confectioners') sugar and lemon juice in a small saucepan. Stir over a low heat until just beginning to bubble and turn syrupy.

7 As soon as the cake comes out of the oven prick the surface with a fine skewer, then brush the syrup over the top. Leave the cake to cool completely in the tin (pan) before turning out and serving.

COOK'S TIP

Pricking the surface of the hot cake with a skewer ensures that the syrup seeps right into the cake.

3

4

7

Orange Kugelhopf Cake

Serves 6–8

INGREDIENTS

225 g/8 oz/1 cup butter, softened
225 g/8 oz/1 cup caster (superfine) sugar
4 eggs, separated
425 g/15 oz/3¾ cups plain (all-purpose) flour
3 tsp baking powder
pinch of salt
300 ml/½ pint/1¼ cups fresh orange juice
1 tbsp orange flower water
1 tsp grated orange rind

SYRUP:
200 ml/7 fl oz/¾ cup orange juice
200 g/7 oz/1 cup granulated sugar

1 Grease and flour a 25 cm/10 inch kugelhopf tin (pan) or deep ring mould (mold).

2 Cream together the butter and caster (superfine) sugar until light. Add the egg yolks one at a time, whisking well after each addition.

3 Sieve (strain) together the flour, salt and baking powder in a bowl. Fold the flour mixture and the orange juice alternately into the creamed mixture. Stir in the orange flower water and orange rind.

4 Whisk the egg whites until they reach the soft peak stage and fold them into the mixture.

5 Pour into the prepared mould (mold) and bake in a preheated oven, 180°C/350°F/Gas Mark 4, for 50-55 minutes or until a metal skewer inserted into the centre of the cake comes out clean.

6 In a saucepan, bring the orange juice and sugar to the boil, then simmer for 5 minutes until the sugar has dissolved.

7 Remove the cake from the oven and leave in the tin (pan) to cool for 10 minutes. Prick the top of the cake with a skewer and brush over half of the syrup. Cool for 10 minutes, then invert on to a wire rack over a deep plate and brush the remaining syrup over the entire cake. Serve.

3

4

7

Coconut Cake

Serves 6-8

INGREDIENTS

225 g/8 oz/ self-raising flour (self-rising) flour
pinch of salt
100 g/3½ oz/½ cup butter, cut into small pieces
100 g/3½ oz/½ cup demerara (brown crystal) sugar
100 g/3½ oz/1 cup desiccated (shredded) coconut, plus extra for sprinkling
2 eggs, beaten
4 tbsp milk

1 Grease a 900 g/2 lb loaf tin and line the base with baking parchment.

2 Sieve (strain) the flour and salt into a mixing bowl and rub in the butter with your fingers until the mixture resembles fine breadcrumbs.

3 Stir in the sugar, coconut, eggs and milk and mix to a soft dropping consistency.

4 Spoon the mixture into the prepared tin (pan) and level the surface. Bake in a preheated oven, 160°C/325°F/Gas Mark 3, for 30 minutes.

5 Remove the cake from the oven and sprinkle with the reserved coconut. Return the cake to the oven and cook for a further 30 minutes until well risen and golden and a fine skewer inserted into the centre comes out clean.

6 Leave the cake to cool in the tin (pan) before turning out and transferring to a wire rack to cool completely before serving.

COOK'S TIP

The flavour of this cake is enhanced by storing it in a cool dry place for a few days before eating.

2

3

3

Apple Cake with Cider

Serves 6–8

INGREDIENTS

225 g/8 oz/2 cups self-raising flour
1 tsp baking powder
75 g/$2^3/_4$ oz/$^1/_3$ cup butter, cut into small pieces
75 g/$2^3/_4$ oz/$^1/_3$ cup caster (superfine) sugar
50 g/$1^3/_4$ oz dried apple, chopped
75 g/$2^3/_4$ oz/5 tbsp raisins
150 ml/$^1/_4$ pint/$^2/_3$ cup sweet cider
1 egg, beaten
175 g/6 oz raspberries

1 Grease a 20 cm/8 inch cake tin (pan) and line with baking parchment.

2 Sieve (strain) the flour and baking powder into a mixing bowl and rub in the butter with your fingers until the mixture resembles fine breadcrumbs.

3 Stir in the caster (superfine) sugar, chopped dried apple and raisins, and mix well.

4 Pour in the sweet cider and egg and mix together until thoroughly blended. Stir in the raspberries vey gently so they do not break up.

5 Pour the mixture into the prepared cake tin (pan).

6 Bake in a preheated oven, 190°C/375°F/ Gas Mark 5, for about 40 minutes until risen and lightly golden. Leave the cake to cool in the tin (pan), then turn out on to a wire rack. Leave until completely cold before serving.

VARIATION

If you don't want to use cider, replace it with clear apple juice, if you prefer.

3

4

4

Spiced Apple Ring

Serves 8

INGREDIENTS

175 g/6 oz/¾ cup butter, softened
175 g/6 oz/¾ cup caster (superfine) sugar
3 eggs, beaten
175 g/6 oz/1½ cups self-raising flour
1 tsp ground cinnamon
1 tsp ground mixed spice (allspice)
2 dessert apples, cored and grated
2 tbsp apple juice or milk
25 g/1 oz/¼ cup flaked (slivered) almonds

1 Lightly grease a 25 cm/10 inch ovenproof ring mould (mold).

2 In a mixing bowl, cream together the butter and sugar until light and fluffy. Gradually add the beaten eggs, beating well after each addition, until fully incorporated.

3 Sieve (strain) the flour and spices, then carefully fold them into the creamed mixture.

4 Stir in the grated apples and the apple juice or milk and mix to a soft dropping consistency.

5 Sprinkle the almonds around the base of the mould (mold) and spoon the cake mixture on top. Level the surface with the back of the spoon.

6 Bake in a preheated oven, 180°C/350°F/Gas Mark 4, for 30 minutes until well risen and a fine skewer inserted into the centre comes out clean.

7 Leave the cake to cool in the tin (pan) before turning out and transferring to a wire rack to cool completely. Serve the apple ring cut into slices.

COOK'S TIP

This cake can also be made in an 18 cm/7 inch round cake tin (pan) if you do not have an ovenproof ring mould (mold).

4

5

5

Marbled Chocolate Cake

Serves 8

INGREDIENTS

175 g/6 oz/¾ cup butter, softened
175 g/6 oz/¾ cup caster (superfine) sugar
3 eggs, beaten
150 g/5½ oz/1¼ cups self-raising (self-rising) flour, sieved (strained)
25 g/1 oz/¼ cup cocoa powder, sieved (strained)
5-6 tbsp orange juice
grated rind of 1 orange

1 Lightly grease a 25 cm/10 inch ovenproof ring mould (mold).

2 In a mixing bowl, cream together the butter and sugar with an electric whisk for about 5 minutes.

3 Add the beaten egg a little at a time, whisking well after each addition.

4 Fold the flour into the creamed mixture carefully, then spoon half of the mixture into a separate mixing bowl.

5 Fold the cocoa powder and half of the orange juice into one bowl and mix gently.

6 Fold the orange rind and remaining orange juice into the other bowl and mix gently.

7 Place spoonfuls of each of the mixtures alternately into the mould (mold), then drag a skewer through the mixture to create a marbled effect.

8 Bake in a preheated oven, 180°C/350°F/Gas Mark 4, for about 30-35 minutes until well risen and a skewer inserted into the centre comes out clean.

9 Leave the cake to cool in the mould (mold) before turning out on to a wire rack.

VARIATION

For a richer chocolate flavour, add 40 g/1¾ oz chocolate drops to the cocoa mixture.

5

6

7

Coffee & Almond Streusel Cake

Serves 8

INGREDIENTS

275 g/9½ oz/1¼ cups plain (all-purpose) flour
1 tbsp baking powder
75 g/2¾ oz/⅓ cup caster (superfine) sugar
150 ml/¼ pint/⅔ cup milk
2 eggs
100 g/3½ oz/½ cup butter, melted and cooled
2 tbsp instant coffee mixed with 1 tbsp boiling water
50 g/1¾ oz/⅓ cup almonds, chopped
icing (confectioners' sugar), for dusting

TOPPING:
75 g/2¾ oz/½ cup self-raising flour
75 g/2¾ oz/⅓ cup demerara (brown crystal) sugar
25 g/1 oz/6 tsp butter, cut into small pieces
1 tsp ground mixed spice (allspice)
1 tbsp water

1 Grease a 23 cm/9 inch loose-bottomed round cake tin (pan) and line with baking parchment. Sieve (strain) together the flour and baking powder into a mixing bowl, then stir in the caster (superfine) sugar.

2 Whisk the milk, eggs, butter and coffee mixture together and pour on to the dry ingredients. Add the chopped almonds and mix lightly together. Spoon the mixture into the tin (pan).

3 To make the topping, mix the flour and demerara (brown crystal) sugar together. Rub in the butter until the mixture is crumbly. Sprinkle in the ground mixed spice (allspice) and the water and bring the mixture together in loose crumbs. Sprinkle the topping over the cake mixture.

4 Bake in a preheated oven, 190°C/375°F/Gas Mark 5, for 50 minutes-1 hour. Cover loosely with foil if the topping starts to brown too quickly. Leave to cool in the tin (pan), then turn out. Dust with icing (confectioners') sugar just before serving.

2

2

3

Sugar-Free Fruit Cake

Serves 8–10

INGREDIENTS

350 g/12 oz/3 cups plain (all-purpose) flour
2 tsp baking powder
1 tsp ground mixed spice (allspice)
125 g/4½ oz/½ cup butter, cut into small pieces
75 g/2¾ oz ready-to-eat dried apricots, chopped
75 g/2¾ oz dates, chopped
75 g/2¾ oz/⅓ cup glacé (candied) cherries, chopped
100 g/3½ oz/⅔ cup raisins
125 ml/4 fl oz/½ cup milk
2 eggs, beaten
grated rind of 1 orange
5-6 tbsp orange juice
3 tbsp runny honey

1 Grease a 20 cm/8 inch round cake tin (pan) and line the base with baking parchment.

2 Sieve (strain) the flour, baking powder and ground mixed spice (allspice) into a large mixing bowl.

3 Rub in the butter until the mixture resembles fine breadcrumbs.

4 Carefully stir in the apricots, dates, glacé (candied) cherries and raisins with the milk, beaten eggs, grated orange rind and orange juice.

5 Stir in the honey and mix everything together to form a soft dropping consistency. Spoon into the prepared cake tin (pan) and level the surface.

6 Bake in a preheated oven, 180°C/350°F/Gas Mark 4, for 1 hour until a fine skewer inserted into the centre of the cake comes out clean.

7 Leave the cake to cool in the tin (pan) before turning out.

VARIATION

For a fruity alternative, replace the honey with 1 mashed ripe banana, if you prefer.

3

4

5

Almond Cake

Serves 8

INGREDIENTS

100 g/3½ oz/⅓ cup soft tub margarine
50 g/1¾ oz/3 tbsp soft brown sugar
2 eggs
175 g/6 oz/1½ cups self-raising flour
1 tsp baking powder
4 tbsp milk
2 tbsp runny honey
50 g/1¾ oz/½ cup flaked almonds

SYRUP:
150 ml/¼ pint/⅔ cup runny honey
2 tbsp lemon juice

1 Grease an 18 cm/7 inch round cake tin (pan) and line with baking parchment.

2 Place the margarine, brown sugar, eggs, flour, baking powder, milk and honey in a large mixing bowl and beat well for about 1 minute until all of the ingredients are thoroughly mixed together.

3 Spoon into the prepared tin (pan), level the surface with the back of a spoon or a knife and sprinkle with the almonds.

4 Bake in a preheated oven, 180°C/350°F/ Gas Mark 4, for about 50 minutes or until the cake is well risen.

5 Meanwhile, make the syrup. Combine the honey and lemon juice in a small saucepan and simmer for about 5 minutes or until the syrup starts to coat the back of a spoon.

6 As soon as the cake comes out of the oven, pour over the syrup, allowing it to seep into the middle of the cake.

7 Leave the cake to cool for at least 2 hours before slicing.

2

3

6

Gingerbread

Makes 12 bars

INGREDIENTS

150 g/5½ oz/⅔ cup butter
175 g/6 oz/1 cup soft brown sugar
2 tbsp black treacle (molasses)
225 g/8 oz/2 cups plain (all-purpose) flour
1 tsp baking powder
2 tsp bicarbonate of soda (baking soda)
2 tsp ground ginger
150 ml/¼ pint/⅔ cup milk
1 egg, beaten
2 dessert apples, peeled, chopped and coated with 1 tbsp lemon juice

1 Grease a 23 cm/9 inch square cake tin (pan) and line with baking parchment.

2 Melt the butter, sugar and treacle (molasses) in a pan over a low heat. Leave the mixture to cool.

3 Sieve (strain) the flour, baking powder, bicarbonate of soda (baking soda) and ginger into a mixing bowl.

4 Stir in the milk, beaten egg and cooled buttery liquid, followed by the chopped apples coated with the lemon juice.

5 Mix everything together gently, then pour the mixture into the prepared tin (pan).

6 Bake in a preheated oven, 170°C/325°F/Gas Mark 3, for 30-35 minutes until the cake has risen and a fine skewer inserted into the centre comes out clean.

7 Leave the cake to cool in the tin (pan) before turning out and cutting into 12 bars.

VARIATION

If you enjoy the flavour of ginger, try adding 25 g (1 oz) stem (candied) ginger, chopped finely, to the mixture in step 3.

2

4

5

Pear & Ginger Cake

Serves 4–6

INGREDIENTS

200 g/7 oz/14 tbsp unsalted butter, softened
175 g/6 oz caster (superfine) sugar
175 g/6 oz self-raising flour, sifted
3 tsp ginger
3 eggs, beaten
450 g/1 lb dessert (eating) pears, peeled, cored and thinly sliced
1 tbsp soft brown sugar

1 Lightly grease and line the base of a deep 20.5 cm/8 inch cake tin (pan).

2 Using a whisk, combine 175 g/6 oz of the butter with the sugar, flour, ginger and eggs and mix to form a smooth consistency.

3 Spoon the cake mixture into the prepared tin (pan), levelling the surface.

4 Arrange the pear slices over the cake mixture. Sprinkle with the brown sugar and dot with the remaining butter.

5 Bake in a preheated oven, at 180°C/350°F/ Gas Mark 4, for 35–40 minutes or until the cake is golden and feels springy to the touch.

6 Serve the pear and ginger cake warm, with ice cream or cream, if you wish.

COOK'S TIP

Soft, brown sugar is often known as Barbados sugar. It is a darker form of light brown soft sugar.

COOK'S TIP

To test whether the cake is cooked through, insert a fine metal skewer into the centre of the cake. If the skewer comes out clean the cake is cooked through.

Eggless Sponge Cake

Serves 8

INGREDIENTS

225 g/8 oz/1¾ cups self-raising wholemeal (self-rising whole wheat) flour
2 tsp baking powder
175 g/6 oz/¾ cup caster (superfine) sugar
6 tbsp sunflower oil
250 ml/9 fl oz/1 cup water
1 tsp vanilla flavouring (extract)
4 tbsp strawberry or raspberry reduced-sugar spread
caster (superfine) sugar, for dusting

1 Grease two 20 cm/8 inch sandwich cake tins (layer pans) and line them with baking parchment.

2 Sieve (strain) the flour and baking powder into a large mixing bowl, stirring in any bran remaining in the sieve. Stir in the caster (superfine) sugar.

3 Pour in the sunflower oil, water and vanilla flavouring (extract) and mix well for about 1 minute until the mixture is a smooth consistency.

4 Divide the mixture between the prepared tins (pans).

5 Bake in a preheated oven, 180°C/350°F/Gas 4, for 25-30 minutes until the centre springs back when lightly touched. Leave to cool in the tins (pans), then turn out and transfer to a wire rack.

6 To serve, remove the baking parchment and place one of the sponges on to a serving plate. Spread with the jam and place the other sponge on top. Dust with a little caster (superfine) sugar.

VARIATION

Use melted vegan butter or margarine instead of the sunflower oil if you prefer, but allow it to cool before adding it to the dry ingredients in step 3.

Small Cakes & Biscuits

This chapter contains everyday delights for baking fans. You are sure to be tempted by our wonderful array of cookies and small cakes. Make any day special with a home-made chocolate biscuit (cookie) to be served with coffee, as a snack or to accompany a special dessert. Although some take a little longer to make, most are quick and easy to prepare and decoration is often simple although you can get carried away if you like!

You'll find recipes for old favourites and some new biscuits (cookies) and small cakes to tickle your taste-buds. Finally, we have given the chocolate treatment to some traditional recipes, turning them into chocoholic delights.

Chocolate Boxes

Makes 4

INGREDIENTS

225 g/8 oz dark chocolate
about 225 g/8 oz bought or ready-made plain or chocolate cake
2 tbsp apricot jam
150 ml/$\frac{1}{4}$ pint/$\frac{2}{3}$ cup double (heavy) cream
1 tbsp maple syrup
100 g/3$\frac{1}{2}$ oz prepared fresh fruit, such as small strawberries, raspberries, kiwi fruit or redcurrants

1 Melt the dark chocolate and spread it evenly over a large sheet of baking parchment. Leave to harden in a cool room.

2 When just set, cut the chocolate into 5 cm/2 inch squares and remove from the paper. Make sure that your hands are as cool as possible and handle the chocolate as little as possible.

3 Cut the cake into two 5 cm/2 inch cubes, then each cube in half. Warm the apricot jam and brush it over the sides of the cake cubes. Carefully press a chocolate square on to each side of the cake cubes to give 4 chocolate boxes with cake at the bottom. Leave to chill for 20 minutes.

4 Whip the double (heavy) cream with the maple syrup until just holding its shape. Spoon or pipe a little of the mixture into each chocolate box.

5 Decorate the top of each box with the prepared fruit. If liked, the fruit can be partially dipped into melted chocolate and allowed to harden before putting into the boxes.

COOK'S TIP

For the best results, keep the boxes well chilled and fill and decorate them just before you want to serve them.

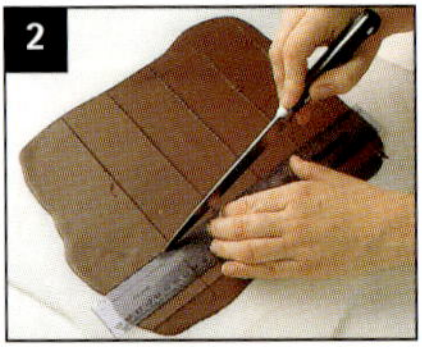

Chocolate Dairy Wraps

Makes 6–8

INGREDIENTS

2 eggs
50 g/1 3/4 oz/4 tbsp caster (superfine) sugar
50 g/1 3/4 oz/1/3 cup plain (all-purpose) flour
1 1/2 tbsp cocoa powder
4 tbsp apricot jam
150 ml/1/4 pint/2/3 cup double (heavy) cream, whipped
icing (confectioners') sugar, to dust

1 Line 2 baking trays (cookie sheets) with pieces of baking parchment. Whisk the eggs and sugar together until the mixture is very light and fluffy and the whisk leaves a trail when lifted.

2 Sift together the flour and cocoa powder. Using a metal spoon or a spatula, gently fold it into the eggs and sugar in a figure of eight movement.

3 Drop rounded tablespoons of the mixture on to the lined baking trays (cookie sheets) and spread them into oval shapes. Make sure they are well spaced as they will spread during cooking.

4 Bake in a preheated oven, 220°C/425°F/Gas Mark 7, for about 6–8 minutes or until springy to the touch. Leave to cool on the baking trays (cookie sheets).

5 When cold, slide the cakes on to a damp tea towel and allow to stand until cold. Carefully remove them from the dampened paper. Spread the flat side of the cakes with jam, then spoon or pipe the whipped cream down the centre of each one.

6 Fold the cakes in half and place them on a serving plate. Sprinkle them with a little icing (confectioners') sugar and serve.

VARIATION

Fold 4 tsp of crème de menthe or 50 g/2 oz melted chocolate into the cream for fabulous alternatives to plain dairy cream.

3

5

5

Chocolate Cup Cakes with White Chocolate Icing

Makes 18

INGREDIENTS

100 g/$3\frac{1}{2}$ oz/ generous $\frac{1}{3}$ cup butter, softened

100 g/$3\frac{1}{2}$ oz/7 tbsp caster (superfine) sugar

2 eggs, lightly beaten

50 g/$1\frac{3}{4}$ oz/$\frac{1}{3}$ cup dark chocolate chips

2 tbsp milk

150 g/$5\frac{1}{2}$ oz/$1\frac{1}{4}$ cups self-raising flour

25 g/1 oz/$\frac{1}{4}$ cup cocoa powder

ICING:

225 g/8 oz white chocolate

150 g/$5\frac{1}{2}$ oz low-fat soft cheese

1 Line an 18 hole bun tray with individual paper cup cases.

2 Beat together the butter and sugar until pale and fluffy. Gradually add the eggs, beating well after each addition. Add a little of the flour if the mixture begins to curdle. Add the milk, then fold in the chocolate chips.

3 Sift together the flour and cocoa powder and fold into the mixture with a metal spoon or spatula. Divide the mixture equally between the paper cases and level the tops.

4 Bake in a preheated oven, 180°C/350°F/Gas Mark 4, for 20 minutes, or until well risen and springy to the touch. Leave to cool on a wire rack.

5 To make the icing, melt the chocolate, then leave to cool slightly. Beat the cream cheese until softened slightly, then beat in the melted chocolate. Spread a little of the icing over each cake and chill for 1 hour before serving.

VARIATION

Add white chocolate chips or chopped pecan nuts to the mixture instead of the dark chocolate chips, if you prefer. You can also add the finely grated rind of 1 orange for a chocolate and orange flavour.

Chocolate Rum Babas

Makes 4

INGREDIENTS

100 g/3½ oz/¾ cup strong plain (all-purpose) flour
25 g/1 oz/ ¼ cup cocoa powder
6 g sachet easy blend yeast
pinch of salt
15 g/½ oz/1 tbsp caster (superfine) sugar
40 g/1½ oz dark chocolate, grated
2 eggs
3 tbsp tepid milk
50 g/1¾ oz/4 tbsp butter, melted

SYRUP:
4 tbsp clear honey
2 tbsp water
4 tbsp rum

TO SERVE:
whipped cream
cocoa powder, to dust
fresh fruit (optional)

1 Lightly oil 4 individual ring tins (pans). In a large warmed mixing bowl, sieve (strain) the flour and cocoa powder together. Stir in the yeast, salt, sugar and grated chocolate. Beat the eggs together, add the milk and butter and beat until mixed.

2 Make a well in the centre of the dry ingredients and pour in the egg mixture, beating to mix to a batter. Beat for 10 minutes, ideally in a electric mixer with a dough hook. Divide the mixture between the tins (pans) – it should come halfway up the sides.

3 Place on a baking tray (cookie sheet) and cover with a damp tea towel. Leave in a warm place until the mixture rises almost to the tops of the tins (pans). Bake in a preheated oven, 200°C/ 400°F/ Gas Mark 6, for 15 minutes.

4 To make the syrup, gently heat all of the ingredients in a small pan. Turn out the babas and place on rack placed above a tray to catch the syrup. Drizzle the syrup over the babas and leave for at least 2 hours for the syrup to soak in. Once or twice, spoon the syrup that has dripped on to the tray over the babas.

5 Fill the centre of the babas with whipped cream and sprinkle a little cocoa powder over the top. Serve the babas with fresh fruit, if desired.

1

2

3

No-Bake Chocolate Squares

Makes 16

INGREDIENTS

275 g/9½ oz dark chocolate
175 g/6 oz/¾ cup butter
4 tbsp golden (light corn) syrup
2 tbsp dark rum (optional)
175 g/6 oz plain biscuits (cookies), such as Rich Tea
25 g/1 oz toasted rice cereal
50 g/1¾ oz/½ cup chopped walnuts or pecan nuts
100 g/3½ oz/½ cup glacé (candied) cherries, chopped roughly
25 g/1 oz white chocolate, to decorate

1 Place the dark chocolate in a large mixing bowl with the butter, syrup and rum, if using, and set over a saucepan of gently simmering water until melted, stirring until blended.

2 Break the biscuits (cookies) into small pieces and stir into the chocolate mixture along with the rice cereal, nuts and cherries.

3 Line an 18 cm/7inch square cake tin (pan) with baking parchment. Pour the mixture into the tin (pan) and level the top, pressing down well with the back of a spoon. Chill for 2 hours.

4 To decorate, melt the white chocolate and drizzle it over the top of the cake in a random pattern. Leave to set. To serve, carefully turn out of the tin (pan) and remove the baking parchment. Cut into 16 squares.

COOK'S TIP

Store in an airtight container in the refrigerator for up to 2 weeks.

VARIATIONS

For a coconut flavour, replace the rice cereal with desiccated (shredded) coconut and add a coconut flavoured liqueur.

VARIATIONS

Brandy or an orange-flavoured liqueur can be used instead of the rum, if you prefer. Cherry brandy also works well.

1

2

4

Chocolate Butterfly Cakes

Makes 12

INGREDIENTS

125 g/4½ oz/½ cup soft margarine
125 g/4½ oz/½ cup caster (superfine) sugar
150 g/5½ oz/1¼ cups self-raising flour
2 large eggs
2 tbsp cocoa powder
25 g/1 oz dark chocolate, melted

LEMON BUTTER CREAM:
100 g/3½ oz/ generous ⅓ cup unsalted butter, softened
225 g/8 oz/1⅓ cups icing (confectioners') sugar, sieved (strained)
grated rind of ½ lemon
1 tbsp lemon juice
icing (confectioners') sugar, to dust

1 Place 12 paper cases in a bun tray (sheet). Place all of the ingredients for the cakes, except for the melted chocolate, in a large mixing bowl and beat with electric beaters until the mixture is just smooth. Beat in the chocolate.

2 Spoon equal amounts of the cake mixture into each paper case, filling them three-quarters full. Bake in a preheated oven, 180°C/350°F/Gas Mark 4, for 15 minutes or until springy to the touch. Transfer the cakes to a wire rack and leave to cool.

3 To make the lemon butter cream, place the butter in a mixing bowl and beat until fluffy, then gradually beat in the icing (confectioners') sugar. Beat in the lemon rind and gradually add the lemon juice, beating well.

4 When cold, cut the top off each cake, using a serrated knife. Cut each top in half.

5 Spread or pipe the butter cream icing over the cut surface of each cake and push the 2 cut pieces of cake top into the icing to form wings. Sprinkle with icing (confectioners') sugar.

VARIATION

For a chocolate butter cream, beat the butter and icing (confectioners') sugar together, then beat in 25 g/ 1 oz melted dark chocolate.

Sticky Chocolate Brownies

Makes 9

INGREDIENTS

100 g/3½ oz/generous ⅓ cup unsalted butter
175 g/6 oz/¾ cup caster (superfine) sugar
75 g/2¾ oz/½ cup dark muscovado sugar
125 g/4½ oz dark chocolate
1 tbsp golden (light corn) syrup
2 eggs
1 tsp chocolate or vanilla flavouring (extract)
100 g/3½ oz/¾ cup plain (all-purpose) flour
2 tbsp cocoa powder
½ tsp baking powder

1 Lightly grease a 20 cm/8 inch shallow square cake tin (pan) and line the base.

2 Place the butter, sugars, dark chocolate and golden (light corn) syrup in a heavy-based saucepan and heat gently, stirring until the mixture is well blended and smooth. Remove from the heat and leave to cool.

3 Beat together the eggs and flavouring (extract). Whisk in the cooled chocolate mixture.

4 Sieve (strain) together the flour, cocoa powder and baking powder and fold carefully into the egg and chocolate mixture, using a metal spoon or a spatula.

5 Spoon the mixture into the prepared tin (pan) and bake in a preheated oven, 180°C/350°F/ Gas Mark 4, for 25 minutes until the top is crisp and the edge of the cake is beginning to shrink away from the tin (pan). The inside of the cake mixture will still be quite stodgy and soft to the touch.

6 Leave the cake to cool completely in the tin (pan), then cut it into squares to serve.

VARIATION

This cake can be well wrapped and frozen for up to 2 months. Defrost at room temperature for about 2 hours or overnight in the refrigerator.

Chocolate Fudge Brownies

Makes 16

INGREDIENTS

200 g/7 oz low-fat soft cheese
½ tsp vanilla flavouring (extract)
2 eggs
250 g/9 oz/generous 1 cup caster (superfine) sugar
100 g/3½ oz/generous ⅓ cup butter
3 tbsp cocoa powder
100 g/3½ oz/¾ cup self-raising flour, sieved (strained)
50 g/1¾ oz pecans, chopped

FUDGE ICING:
50 g/1¾ oz/1 tbsp butter
1 tbsp milk
100 g/3½ oz/½ cup icing (confectioners') sugar
2 tbsp cocoa powder
pecans, to decorate (optional)

1 Lightly grease a 20 cm/8 inch square shallow cake tin (pan) and line the base.

2 Beat together the cheese, vanilla flavouring (extract) and 25 g/1 oz/5 tsp of the caster (superfine) sugar until smooth, then set aside.

3 Beat the eggs and remaining caster (superfine) sugar together until light and fluffy. Place the butter and cocoa powder in a small pan and heat gently, stirring until the butter melts and the mixture combines, then stir it into the egg mixture. Fold in the flour and nuts.

4 Pour half of the brownie mixture into the tin (pan) and level the top. Carefully spread the soft cheese over it, then cover it with the remaining brownie mixture. Bake in a preheated oven, 180°C/350°F/Gas Mark 4, for 40–45 minutes. Cool in the tin (pan).

5 To make the icing, melt the butter in the milk. Stir in the icing (confectioners') sugar and cocoa powder. Spread the icing over the brownies and decorate with pecan nuts, if using. Leave the icing to set, then cut into squares to serve.

VARIATION

Omit the cheese layer if preferred. Use walnuts in place of the pecans.

Chocolate Chip Muffins

Makes 12

INGREDIENTS

100 g/$3\frac{1}{2}$ oz/generous $\frac{1}{3}$ cup soft margarine
225 g/8 oz/1 cup caster (superfine) sugar
2 large eggs
150 ml/ $\frac{1}{4}$ pint/$\frac{2}{3}$ cup whole milk natural yogurt
5 tbsp milk
275 g/$9\frac{1}{2}$ oz/2 cups plain (all-purpose) flour
1 tsp bicarbonate of soda (baking soda)
175 g/6 oz dark chocolate chips

1 Line 12 muffin tins (pans) with paper cases.

2 Place the margarine and sugar in a large mixing bowl and beat with a wooden spoon until light and fluffy. Beat in the eggs, yogurt and milk until combined.

3 Sieve (strain) the flour and bicarbonate of soda (baking soda) together and add to the mixture. Stir until just blended.

4 Stir in the chocolate chips, then spoon the mixture into the paper cases and bake in a preheated oven, 190°C/375°F/Gas Mark 5, for 25 minutes or until a fine skewer inserted into the centre comes out clean. Leave to cool in the tin (pan) for 5 minutes, then turn out on to a wire rack to cool completely.

VARIATION

For chocolate and orange muffins, add the grated rind of 1 orange and replace the milk with fresh orange juice.

VARIATION

The mixture can also be used to make 6 large or 24 mini muffins. Bake mini muffins for 10 minutes or until springy to the touch.

Chocolate Scones

Makes 9

INGREDIENTS

225 g/8 oz/2 cups self-raising flour sieved (strained)
60 g/2 oz/ 1/4 cup butter
1 tbsp caster (superfine) sugar
50 g/1 3/4 oz/1/3 cup chocolate chips
about 150 ml/ 1/4 pint/2/3 cup milk

1 Lightly grease a baking tray (cookie sheet). Place the flour in a mixing bowl. Cut the butter into small pieces and rub it into the flour with your fingertips until the scone mixture resembles fine breadcrumbs.

2 Stir in the caster (superfine) sugar and chocolate chips.

3 Mix in enough milk to form a soft dough.

4 On a lightly floured surface, roll out the dough to form a rectangle 10 x 15 cm/4 x 6 inches, about 2.5 cm/1 inch thick. Cut the dough into 9 squares.

5 Place the scones spaced well apart on the prepared baking tray (cookie sheet).

6 Brush with a little milk and bake in a preheated oven, 220°C/425°F/Gas Mark 7, for 10–12 minutes until the scones are risen and golden.

COOK'S TIP

To be at their best, all scones should be freshly baked and served warm. Split the warm scones and spread them with a little chocolate and hazelnut spread or a good dollop of whipped cream.

VARIATION

Use dark, milk or white chocolate chips or a mixture of all three. Use a 5 cm/2 inch biscuit (cookie) cutter to cut out round scones, if preferred.

Pain au Chocolate

Makes 12

INGREDIENTS

450 g/1 lb/4 cups strong plain (all-purpose) flour
$^1/_2$ tsp salt
6 g sachet of easy blend yeast
25 g/1 oz/2 tbsp white vegetable fat
1 egg, beaten lightly
225 ml/8 fl oz/1 cup tepid water
175 g/6 oz/$^3/_4$ cup butter, softened
100 g/3$^1/_2$ oz dark chocolate, broken into 12 squares
beaten egg, to glaze
icing (confectioners') sugar, to dust

1 Lightly grease a baking tray (cookie sheet). Sieve (strain) the flour and salt into a mixing bowl and stir in the yeast. Rub in the fat with your fingertips. Add the egg and enough of the water to mix to a soft dough. Knead it for about 10 minutes to make a smooth elastic dough.

2 Roll out to form a rectangle 37.5 x 20 cm/ 15 x 8 inches. Divide the butter into 3 portions and dot one portion over two-thirds of the rectangle, leaving a small border around the edge.

3 Fold the rectangle into 3 by first folding the plain part of the dough over and then the other side. Seal the edges of the dough by pressing with a rolling pin. Give the dough a quarter turn so the sealed edges are at the top and bottom. Re-roll and fold (without adding butter), then wrap the dough and chill for 30 minutes.

4 Repeat steps 2 and 3 until all of the butter has been used, chilling the dough each time. Re-roll and fold twice more without butter. Chill for a final 30 minutes.

5 Roll the dough to a rectangle 45 x 30 cm/18 x 12 inches, trim and halve lengthways. Cut each half into 6 rectangles and brush with beaten egg. Place a chocolate square at one end of each rectangle and roll up to form a sausage. Press the ends together and place, seamside down, on the baking tray (cookie sheet). Cover and leave to rise for 40 minutes in a warm place. Brush with egg and bake in a preheated oven, 220°C/425°F/Gas Mark 7, for 20–25 minutes until golden. Cool on a wire rack. Serve warm or cold.

Choc-Chip Tartlets

Makes 6

INGREDIENTS

50 g/1¾ oz toasted hazelnuts
150 g/5½ oz/1¾ cups plain (all-purpose) flour
1 tbsp icing (confectioners') sugar
75 g/2¾ oz/⅓ cup soft margarine

FILLING:
2 tbsp cornflour (cornstarch)
1 tbsp cocoa powder
1 tbsp caster (superfine) sugar
300 ml/½ pint/1¼ cups semi-skimmed milk
3 tbsp chocolate and hazelnut spread
25 g/1 oz/2½ tbsp dark chocolate chips
25 g/1 oz/2½ tbsp milk chocolate chips
25 g/1 oz/2½ tbsp white chocolate chips

1 Finely chop the nuts in a food processor. Add the flour, the 1 tbsp sugar and the margarine. Process for a few seconds until the mixture resembles breadcrumbs. Add 2–3 tbsp water and process to form a soft dough. Cover and chill in the freezer for 10 minutes.

2 Roll out the dough and use it to line six 10 cm/ 4 inch loose-bottomed tartlet tins (pans). Prick the bases with a fork and line them with loosely crumpled foil. Bake in a preheated oven, 200°C/ 400°F/Gas Mark 6, for 15 minutes. Remove the foil and bake for a further 5 minutes until the pastry cases (pie shells) are crisp and golden. Remove from the oven and leave to cool.

3 Mix together the cornflour (cornstarch), cocoa powder and sugar with enough milk to make a smooth paste. Stir in the remaining milk. Pour into a pan and cook gently over a low heat, stirring until thickened. Stir in the hazelnut and chocolate spread.

4 Mix together the chocolate chips and reserve a quarter. Stir half of the remaining chips into the custard. Cover with damp greaseproof paper and leave until almost cold, then stir in the second half of the chocolate chips. Spoon the mixture into the pastry cases (pie shells) and leave to cool. Decorate with the reserved chips, scattering them over the top.

Chocolate Eclairs

Makes about 10

INGREDIENTS

CHOUX PASTRY (PIE DOUGH):
- 150 ml/ ¼ pint/⅔ cup water
- 60 g/2 oz/ ¼ cup butter, cut into small pieces
- 90 g/3 oz/¾ cup strong plain (all-purpose) flour, sieved (strained)
- 2 eggs

PATISSERIE CREAM:
- 2 eggs, lightly beaten
- 50 g/1¾ oz/4 tbsp caster (superfine) sugar
- 2 tbsp cornflour (cornstarch)
- 300 ml/½ pint/1¼ cups milk
- ¼ tsp vanilla flavouring (extract)

ICING:
- 25 g/1 oz/2 tbsp butter
- 1 tbsp milk
- 1 tbsp cocoa powder
- 100 g/3½ oz/½ cup icing (confectioners') sugar
- a little white chocolate, melted

1 Lightly grease a baking tray (cookie sheet). Place the water in a saucepan, add the butter and heat gently until the butter melts. Bring to a rolling boil, then remove the pan from the heat and add the flour in one go, beating well until the mixture leaves the sides of the pan and forms a ball. Leave to cool slightly, then gradually beat in the eggs to form a smooth, glossy mixture. Spoon into a large piping bag fitted with a 1 cm/½ inch plain nozzle (tip).

2 Sprinkle the tray (sheet) with a little water. Pipe eclairs 7.5 cm/3 inches long, spaced well apart. Bake in a preheated oven, 200°C/ 400°F/Gas Mark 6, for 30–35 minutes or until crisp and golden. Make a small slit in each one to let the steam escape; cool on a rack.

3 To make the patisserie cream, whisk the eggs and sugar until thick and creamy, then fold in the cornflour (cornstarch). Heat the milk until almost boiling and pour on to the eggs, whisking. Transfer to the pan and cook over a low heat, stirring until thick. Remove the pan from the heat and stir in the flavouring (extract). Cover with baking parchment and cool. To make the icing, melt the butter with the milk in a pan, remove from the heat and stir in the cocoa and sugar. Split the eclairs lengthways and pipe in the patisserie cream. Spread the icing over the top of the eclair. Spoon over the white chocolate, swirl in and leave to set.

2

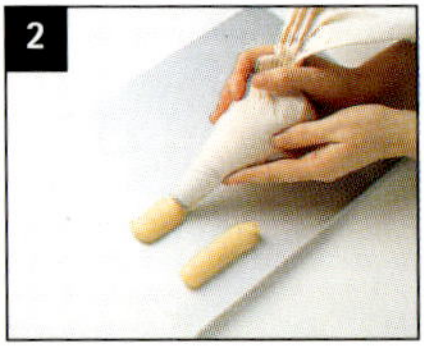
2

3

Chocolate Meringues

Makes 8

INGREDIENTS

4 egg whites
225 g/8 oz/1 cup caster (superfine) sugar
1 tsp cornflour (cornstarch)
40 g/1½ oz dark chocolate, grated

TO COMPLETE:
100 g/3½ oz dark chocolate
150 ml/ ¼ pint/⅔ cup double (heavy) cream
1 tbsp icing (confectioners') sugar
1 tbsp brandy (optional)

1 Line 2 baking trays (cookie sheets) with baking parchment. Whisk the egg whites until standing in soft peaks, then gradually whisk in half of the sugar. Continue whisking until the mixture is very stiff and glossy.

2 Carefully fold in the remaining sugar, cornflour (cornstarch) and grated chocolate with a metal spoon or spatula.

3 Spoon the mixture into a piping bag fitted with a large star or plain nozzle (tip). Pipe 16 large rosettes or mounds on the lined baking trays (cookie sheets).

4 Bake in a preheated oven, 140°C/275°F/Gas Mark 1, for about 1 hour, changing the position of the baking trays (cookie sheets) halfway through cooking. Without opening the oven door, turn off the oven and leave the meringues to cool in the oven. Once cold, carefully peel away the baking parchment.

5 Melt the dark chocolate and spread it over the base of the meringues. Stand them upside down on a wire rack until the chocolate has set. Whip the cream, icing (confectioners') sugar and brandy (if using), until the cream holds its shape. Spoon into a piping bag and use to sandwich the meringues together in pairs. Serve.

VARIATION

To make mini meringues, use a star shaped nozzle (tip) and pipe about 24 small rosettes. Bake for about 40 minutes until crisp.

1

2

3

Chocolate & Hazelnut Palmiers

Makes about 26

INGREDIENTS

375 g/13 oz ready-made puff pastry (pie dough)
8 tbsp chocolate hazelnut spread
50 g/1¾ oz/½ cup chopped toasted hazelnuts
25 g/1 oz/5 tsp caster (superfine) sugar

1 Lightly grease a baking tray (cookie sheet). On a lightly floured surface, roll out the puff pastry (pie dough) to a rectangle about 37.5 x 23 cm/15 x 9 inches in size.

2 Spread the chocolate hazelnut spread over the pastry (pie dough) using a palette knife, then scatter the chopped hazelnuts over the top.

3 Roll up one long side of the pastry (pie dough) to the centre, then roll up the other side so that they meet in the centre. Where the pieces meet, dampen the edges with a little water to join them. Using a sharp knife, cut into thin slices. Place each slice on to the prepared baking tray (cookie sheet) and flatten slightly with a palette knife. Sprinkle the slices with the caster (superfine) sugar.

4 Bake in a preheated oven, 20°C/425°F/Gas Mark 7, for about 10–15 minutes until golden. Transfer to a wire rack to cool.

VARIATION

For an extra chocolate flavour, dip the palmiers in melted dark chocolate to half-cover each biscuit.

COOK'S TIP

Palmiers can be served cold, but they are also delicious served warm.

The biscuits (cookies) can be frozen for up to 3 months in a rigid container.

Chocolate & Coconut Squares

Makes 9

INGREDIENTS

225 g/8 oz dark chocolate digestive biscuits (graham crackers)
75 g/2¾ oz/⅓ cup butter or margarine
170 g/6 oz can evaporated milk
1 egg, beaten
1 tsp vanilla flavouring (extract)
25 g/1 oz/5 tsp caster (superfine) sugar
50 g/1¾ oz/⅓ cup self-raising flour, sieved (strained)
125 g/4½ oz/1⅓ cups desiccated (shredded) coconut
50 g/1¾ oz dark chocolate (optional)

1 Grease a shallow 20 cm/ 8 inch square cake tin (pan) and line the base.

2 Crush the biscuits (crackers) in a polythene bag with a rolling pin or process them in a food processor.

3 Melt the butter or margarine in a saucepan and stir in the crushed biscuits (crackers) until well combined.

4 Press the mixture into the base of the cake tin (pan).

5 Beat together the evaporated milk, egg, vanilla and sugar until smooth. Stir in the flour and desiccated (shredded) coconut. Pour over the biscuit base and level the top.

6 Bake in a preheated oven, 190°C/375°F/Gas Mark 5, for 30 minutes or until the coconut topping is firm and just golden.

7 Leave to cool in the cake tin (pan) for about 5 minutes, then cut into squares. Leave to cool completely in the tin (pan).

8 Carefully remove the squares from the tin (pan) and place them on a board. Melt the dark chocolate (if using) and drizzle it over the squares to decorate them. Leave the chocolate to set before serving.

COOK'S TIP

Store the squares in an airtight tin for up to 4 days. They can be frozen, undecorated, for up to 2 months. Defrost at room temperature.

1

3

5

Chocolate & Coconut Cookies

Makes about 24

INGREDIENTS

125 g/4½ oz/⅓ cup soft margarine
1 tsp vanilla flavouring (extract)
90 g/3 oz/6 tbsp icing (confectioners') sugar, sieved (strained)
125 g/4½ oz/1 cup plain (all-purpose) flour
2 tbsp cocoa powder
50 g/1¾ oz/⅔ cup desiccated (shredded) coconut
25 g/1 oz/2 tbsp butter
100 g/3½ oz white marshmallows
25 g/1 oz/⅓ cup desiccated (shredded) coconut
a little dark chocolate, melted

1 Lightly grease a baking tray (cookie sheet). Beat together the margarine, vanilla flavouring (extract) and icing (confectioners') sugar in a mixing bowl until light and fluffy. Sift together the flour and cocoa powder and beat it into the mixture with the coconut.

2 Roll rounded teaspoons of the mixture into balls and place on the prepared baking tray (cookie sheet), allowing room for the biscuits (cookies) to spread during cooking.

3 Flatten the rounds slightly and bake in a preheated oven, 180°C/350°F/Gas Mark 4, for 12–15 minutes until just firm.

4 Leave to cool on the baking tray (cookie sheet) for a few minutes before transferring to a wire rack to cool completely.

5 Combine the butter and marshmallows in a small saucepan and heat gently, stirring until melted and well combined. Spread a little of the icing mixture over each biscuit and dip in the coconut. Leave to set. Decorate the biscuits (cookies) with a little melted chocolate and leave to set before serving.

COOK'S TIP

Store these biscuits (cookies) in an airtight container for about 1 week. Alternatively, they can be frozen, undecorated, for up to 2 months.

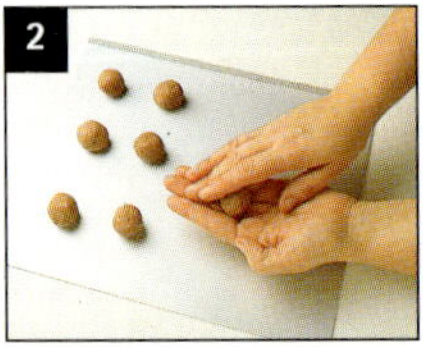

Chocolate Crispy Bites

Makes 16

INGREDIENTS

WHITE LAYER:
50 g/1¾ oz/4 tbsp butter
1 tbsp golden (light corn) syrup
150 g/5½ oz white chocolate
50 g/1¾ oz toasted rice cereal

DARK LAYER:
50 g/1¾ oz/4 tbsp butter
2 tbsp golden (light corn) syrup
125 g dark chocolate, broken into small pieces
75 g/2¾ oz toasted rice cereal

1 Grease a 20 cm/8 inch square cake tin (pan) and line with baking parchment.

2 To make the white chocolate layer, melt the butter, golden (light corn) syrup and chocolate in a bowl set over a pan of gently simmering water.

3 Remove from the heat and stir in the rice cereal until it is well combined.

4 Press into the prepared tin (pan) and level the surface.

5 To make the dark chocolate layer, melt the butter, golden (light corn) syrup and dark chocolate in a bowl set over a pan of gently simmering water.

6 Remove from the heat and stir in the rice cereal until it is well coated. Pour the dark chocolate layer over the hardened white chocolate layer and chill until the top layer has hardened.

7 Turn out of the cake tin (pan) and cut into small squares, using a sharp knife.

COOK'S TIP

These bites can be made up to 4 days ahead. Keep them covered in the refrigerator until ready to use.

3

6

7

Dutch Macaroons

Makes about 20

INGREDIENTS

rice paper
2 egg whites
225 g/8 oz/1 cup caster (superfine) sugar
175 g/6 oz/1⅔ cups ground almonds
225 g/8 oz dark chocolate

1 Cover 2 baking trays (cookie sheets) with rice paper. Whisk the egg whites in a large mixing bowl until stiff, then fold in the sugar and ground almonds.

2 Place the mixture in a large piping bag fitted with a 1 cm/½ inch plain nozzle (tip) and pipe fingers, about 7.5 cm/3 inches long, allowing space for the mixture to spread during cooking.

3 Bake in a preheated oven, 180°C/350°F/ Gas Mark 4, for 15–20 minutes until golden. Transfer to a wire rack and leave to cool. Remove the excess rice paper from around the edges.

4 Melt the chocolate and dip the base of each biscuit into the chocolate. Place the macaroons on a sheet of baking parchment and leave to set.

5 Drizzle any remaining chocolate over the top of the biscuits (cookies). Leave to set before serving.

COOK'S TIP

Rice paper is edible so you can break off the excess from around the edge of the biscuits (cookies). Remove it completely before dipping in the chocolate, if you prefer.

VARIATION

Almonds are most commonly used in macaroons, but they can be made with other ground nuts, such as hazelnuts.

Chocolate Orange Biscuits

Makes about 30

INGREDIENTS

75 g/2¾ oz/⅓ cup butter, softened
75 g/2¾ oz/⅓ cup caster (superfine) sugar
1 egg
1 tbsp milk
225 g/8 oz/2 cups plain (all-purpose) flour
25 g/1 oz/ ¼ cup cocoa powder

ICING:
175 g/6 oz/1 cup icing (confectioners') sugar, sifted
3 tbsp orange juice
a little dark chocolate, melted

1 Line 2 baking trays (cookie sheets) with sheets of baking parchment.

2 Beat together the butter and sugar until light and fluffy. Beat in the egg and milk until well combined. Sift together the flour and cocoa powder and gradually mix together to form a soft dough. Use your fingers to incorporate the last of the flour and bring the dough together.

3 Roll out the dough on to a lightly floured surface until 6 mm/¼ inch thick. Using a 5 cm/2 inch fluted round cutter, cut out as many cookies as you can. Re-roll the dough trimmings and cut out more cookies.

4 Place the cookies on the prepared baking tray (cookie sheet) and bake in a preheated oven, 180°C/350°F/Gas Mark 4, for 10–12 minutes or until golden.

5 Leave the cookies to cool on the baking tray (cookie sheet) for a few minutes, then transfer to a wire rack to cool completely.

6 To make the icing, place the icing (confectioners') sugar in a bowl and stir in enough orange juice to form a thin icing that will coat the back of a spoon. Spread the icing over the cookies and leave to set. Drizzle with melted chocolate. Leave the chocolate to set before serving.

Chocolate Caramel Squares

Makes 16

INGREDIENTS

100 g/3½ oz/generous ⅓ cup soft margarine
50 g/1¾ oz/4 tbsp light muscovado sugar
125 g/4½ oz/1 cup plain (all-purpose) flour
40 g/1½ oz/½ cup rolled oats

CARAMEL FILLING:
25 g/1 oz/2 tbsp butter
25 g/1 oz/2 tbsp light muscovado sugar
200 g/7 oz can condensed milk

TOPPING:
100 g/3½ oz dark chocolate
25 g/1 oz white chocolate (optional)

1 Beat together the margarine and muscovado sugar in a bowl until light and fluffy. Beat in the flour and the rolled oats. Use your fingertips to bring the mixture together, if necessary.

2 Press the mixture into the base of a shallow 20 cm/8 inch square cake tin (pan).

3 Bake in a preheated oven, 180°C/350°F/ Gas Mark 4, for 25 minutes or until just golden and firm. Cool in the tin (pan).

4 Place the ingredients for the caramel filling in a pan and heat gently, stirring until the sugar has dissolved and the ingredients combine. Bring slowly to the boil over a very low heat, then boil very gently for 3–4 minutes, stirring constantly until thickened.

5 Pour the caramel filling over the biscuit base in the tin (pan) and leave to set.

6 Melt the dark chocolate and spread it over the caramel. If using the white chocolate, melt it and pipe lines of white chocolate over the dark chocolate. Using a cocktail stick (toothpick) or a skewer, feather the white chocolate into the dark chocolate. Leave to set. Cut into squares to serve.

COOK'S TIP

If liked, you can line the tin (pan) with baking parchment so that the biscuit can be lifted out before cutting into pieces.

Chocolate Chip Flapjacks

Makes 12

INGREDIENTS

125 g/4½ oz/½ cup butter
75 g/2¾ oz/⅓ cup caster (superfine) sugar
1 tbsp golden (light corn) syrup
350 g/12 oz/4 cups rolled oats
75 g/2¾ oz/½ cup dark chocolate chips
50 g/1¾ oz/⅓ cup sultanas (golden raisins)

1 Lightly grease a shallow 20 cm/8 inch square cake tin (pan).

2 Place the butter, caster (superfine) sugar and golden (light corn) syrup in a saucepan and cook over a low heat, stirring until the butter and sugar melt and the mixture is well combined.

3 Remove the pan from the heat and stir in the rolled oats until they are well coated. Add the chocolate chips and the sultanas (golden raisins) and mix well to combine everything.

4 Turn into the prepared tin (pan) and press down well.

5 Bake in a preheated oven, 180°C/350°F/Gas Mark 4, for 30 minutes. Cool slightly, then mark into fingers. When almost cold cut into bars or squares and transfer to a wire rack until cold.

COOK'S TIP

The flapjacks will keep in an airtight container for up to 1 week, but they are so delicious they are unlikely to last that long!

VARIATION

For a really special flapjack, replace some of the oats with chopped nuts or sunflower seeds and a little extra dried fruit.

2

3

3

Chocolate Chip Cookies

Makes about 18

INGREDIENTS

175 g/6 oz/1½ cups plain (all-purpose) flour
1 tsp baking powder
125 g/4½ oz/½ cup soft margarine
90 g/3 oz/generous ½ cup light muscovado sugar
60 g/2 oz/ ¼ cup caster (superfine) sugar
½ tsp vanilla flavouring (extract)
1 egg
125 g/4½ oz/⅔ cup dark chocolate chips

1 Lightly grease 2 baking trays (cookie sheets).

2 Place all of the ingredients in a large mixing bowl and beat until well combined.

3 Place tablespoonfuls of the mixture on to the baking trays (cookie sheets), spacing them well apart to allow for spreading during cooking.

4 Bake in a preheated oven, 190°C/375°F/ Gas Mark 5, for 10–12 minutes or until the cookies are golden brown.

5 Using a palette knife (spatula), transfer the cookies to a wire rack to cool completely.

VARIATIONS

For Mixed Chocolate Chip Cookies, use a mixture of dark, milk and white chocolate chips in the basic mixture.

For Chocolate Chip & Coconut Cookies, add 25 g/ 1 oz/⅓ cup desiccated (shredded) coconut to the basic mixture.

VARIATIONS

For Choc & Nut Cookies, add 40 g/1½ oz/½ cup chopped hazelnuts to the basic mixture.

For Double Choc Cookies, beat in 40 g/1½ oz melted dark chocolate.

For White Chocolate Chip Cookies, use white chocolate chips instead of the dark chocolate chips.

For Chocolate Chip & Raisin Cookies, add 40 g/ 1½ oz/5 tbsp raisins to the basic mixture.

2

3

5

Chocolate Shortbread

Makes 12

INGREDIENTS

175 g/6 oz/1½ cups plain (all-purpose) flour
1 tbsp cocoa powder
50 g/1¾ oz/4 tbsp caster (superfine) sugar
150 g/5½ oz/⅔ cup butter, softened
50 g/1¾ oz dark chocolate, chopped finely

1 Lightly grease a baking tray (cookie sheet).

2 Place all of the ingredients in a large mixing bowl and beat together until they form a dough. Knead the dough lightly.

3 Place the dough on the prepared baking tray (cookie sheet) and roll or press out to form a 20 cm/8 inch circle.

4 Pinch the edges of the dough with your fingertips to form a decorative edge. Prick the dough all over with a fork and mark into 12 wedges, using a sharp knife.

5 Bake in a preheated oven, 160°C/325°F/ Gas Mark 3, for 40 minutes until firm and golden. Leave to cool slightly before cutting into wedges. Transfer to a wire rack to cool completely.

VARIATION

The shortbread dough can be pressed into a floured shortbread mould (mold) and turned out on to the baking tray (cookie sheet) before baking.

VARIATION

For round shortbread cookies, roll out the dough on a lightly floured surface to 8 mm/⅓ inch thick. Cut out 7.5 cm/3 inch rounds with a biscuit (cookie) cutter. Transfer to a greased baking tray (cookie sheet) and bake as above. If liked, coat half the biscuit in melted chocolate.

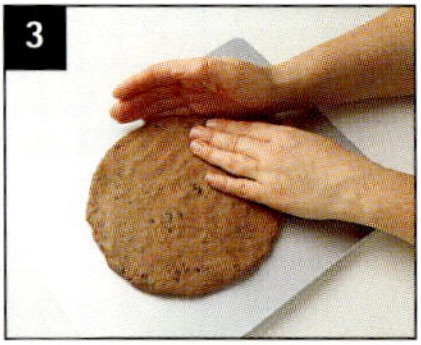

Malted Chocolate Wedges

Makes 16

INGREDIENTS

100 g/3½ oz/generous ⅓ cup butter
2 tbsp golden (light corn) syrup
2 tbsp malted chocolate drink
225 g/8 oz malted milk biscuits (cookies)
75 g/2¾ oz milk or dark chocolate, broken into pieces
25 g/1 oz/2 tbsp icing (confectioners') sugar
2 tbsp milk

1 Grease a shallow 18 cm/ 7 inch round cake tin (pan) or flan tin (pan) and line the base.

2 Place the butter, golden (light corn) syrup and malted chocolate drink in a small pan and heat gently, stirring all the time until the butter has melted and the mixture is well combined.

3 Crush the biscuits (cookies) in a plastic bag with a rolling pin, or process them in a food processor until they form crumbs. Stir the crumbs into the chocolate mixture and mix well.

4 Press the mixture into the prepared tin (pan) and chill in the refrigerator until firm.

5 Place the chocolate pieces in a small heatproof bowl with the icing (confectioners') sugar and the milk. Place the bowl over a pan of gently simmering water and stir until the chocolate melts and the mixture is combined.

6 Spread the chocolate icing over the biscuit (cookie) base and leave to set in the tin (pan). Using a sharp knife, cut into wedges to serve.

VARIATION

Add chopped pecan nuts to the biscuit (cookie) crumb mixture in step 3, if liked.

Chocolate Chequer-Board Cookies

Makes about 18

INGREDIENTS

175 g/6 oz/$\frac{3}{4}$ cup butter, softened
75 g/2$\frac{3}{4}$ oz/6 tbsp icing (confectioners') sugar
1 teaspoon vanilla flavouring (extract) or grated rind of $\frac{1}{2}$ orange
250 g/9 oz/2$\frac{1}{4}$ cups plain (all-purpose) flour
25 g/1 oz dark chocolate, melted
a little beaten egg white

1 Lightly grease a baking tray (cookie sheet). Beat the butter and icing (confectioners') sugar in a mixing bowl until light and fluffy. Beat in the vanilla flavouring (extract) or the grated orange rind.

2 Gradually beat in the flour to form a soft dough. Use your fingers to incorporate the last of the flour and bring the dough together.

3 Divide the dough into 2 equal pieces and beat the melted chocolate into one half. Keeping each half of the dough separate, cover and leave to chill for about 30 minutes.

4 Roll out each piece of dough to a rectangle about 7.5 x 20 cm/3 x 8 inches long and 3 cm/1$\frac{1}{2}$ inches thick. Brush one piece of dough with a little egg white and place the other on top.

5 Cut the block of dough in half lengthways and turn over one half. Brush the side of one strip with egg white and butt the other up to it, so that it resembles a chequer-board.

6 Cut the block into thin slices and place each slice flat on the baking tray (cookie sheet), allowing enough room for them to spread a little during cooking.

7 Bake in a preheated oven, 180°C/350°F/ Gas Mark 4, for about 10 minutes until just firm. Leave to cool on the baking trays (cookie sheets) for a few minutes, before carefully transferring to a wire rack with a palette knife (spatula). Leave to cool completely.

4

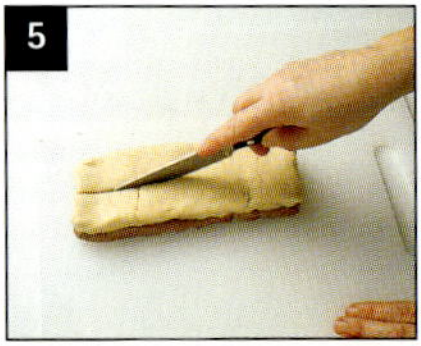
5

6

Viennese Chocolate Fingers

Makes about 18

INGREDIENTS

125 g/4½ oz/½ cup unsalted butter
75 g/2⅔ oz/6 tbsp icing (confectioners') sugar
175 g/6 oz/1½ cups self-raising flour, sieved (strained)
25 g/1 oz/3 tbsp cornflour (cornstarch)
200 g/7 oz dark chocolate

1 Lightly grease 2 baking trays (cookie sheets). Beat the butter and sugar in a mixing bowl until light and fluffy. Gradually beat in the flour and cornflour (cornstarch).

2 Melt 75 g/2¾ oz of the dark chocolate and beat into the biscuit dough.

3 Place in a piping bag fitted with a large star nozzle (tip) and pipe fingers about 5 cm/2 inches long on the baking trays (cookie sheets), slightly spaced apart to allow for spreading.

4 Bake in a preheated oven, 190°C/375°F/Gas Mark 5, for 12–15 minutes. Leave to cool slightly on the baking trays (cookie sheets), then transfer with a palette knife (spatula) to a wire rack and leave to cool completely.

5 Melt the remaining chocolate and dip one end of each biscuit (cookie) in the chocolate, allowing the excess to drip back into the bowl.

COOK'S TIP

If the biscuit (cookie) dough is too thick to pipe, beat in a little milk to thin it out a little.

VARIATION

Dip the base of each biscuit in melted chocolate and leave to set. Sandwich the biscuits (cookies) together in pairs with a little butter cream.

1

3

5

Chocolate Pretzels

Makes about 30

INGREDIENTS

100 g/3½ oz/generous ⅓ cup unsalted butter
100 g/3½ oz/7 tbsp caster (superfine) sugar
1 egg
225 g/8 oz/2 cups plain (all-purpose) flour
25 g/1 oz/ ¼ cup cocoa powder

TO FINISH:
15 g/½ oz/1 tbsp butter
100 g/3½ oz dark chocolate
icing (confectioners') sugar, to dust

1 Lightly grease a baking tray (cookie sheet). Beat together the butter and sugar in a mixing bowl until light and fluffy. Beat in the egg.

2 Sift together the flour and cocoa powder and gradually beat in to form a soft dough. Use your fingers to incorporate the last of the flour and bring the dough together. Chill for 15 minutes.

3 Break pieces from the dough and roll into thin sausage shapes about 10 cm/4 inches long and 6 mm/ ¼ inch thick. Twist into pretzel shapes by making a circle, then twist the ends through each other to form a letter 'B'.

4 Place on the prepared baking tray (cookie sheet), slightly spaced apart to allow for spreading during cooking.

5 Bake in a preheated oven, 190°C/375°F/Gas Mark 5, for 8–12 minutes. Leave the pretzels to cool slightly on the baking tray (cookie sheet), then transfer to a wire rack to cool completely.

6 Melt the butter and chocolate in a bowl set over a pan of gently simmering water, stirring to combine.

7 Dip half of each pretzel into the chocolate and allow the excess chocolate to drip back into the bowl. Place the pretzels on a sheet of baking parchment and leave to set.

8 When set, dust the non-chocolate coated side of each pretzel with icing (confectioners') sugar before serving.

2

3

7

Chocolate Wheatmeals

Makes about 20

INGREDIENTS

75 g/2¾ oz/⅓ cup butter
100 g/3½ oz/7 tbsp demerara (brown crystal) sugar
1 egg
25 g/1 oz wheatgerm
125 g/4½ oz/1 cup wholemeal (whole wheat) self-raising flour
60 g/2 oz/½ cup self raising flour, sieved (strained)
125 g/4½ oz chocolate

1 Lightly grease a baking tray (cookie sheet). Beat the butter and sugar until fluffy. Add the egg and beat well. Stir in the wheatgerm and flours. Bring the mixture together with your hands.

2 Roll rounded teaspoons of the mixture into balls and place on the prepared baking tray (cookie sheet), allowing room for the biscuits (cookies) to spread during cooking.

3 Flatten the biscuits (cookies) slightly with the prongs of a fork. Bake in a preheated oven, 180°C/350°F/Gas Mark 4, for 15–20 minutes until golden. Leave to cool on the tray (sheet) for a few minutes before transferring to a wire rack to cool completely.

4 Melt the chocolate, then dip each biscuit (cookie) in the chocolate to cover the bases and come a little way up the sides. Leave the excess to drip back into the bowl.

5 Place the biscuits (cookies) on a sheet of baking parchment and leave to set in a cool place.

COOK'S TIP

These biscuits (cookies) can be frozen very successfully. Freeze them at the end of step 3 for up to 3 months. Defrost and then dip them in melted chocolate.

Apricot Slices

Makes 12

INGREDIENTS

PASTRY:
225 g/8 oz/1¾ cups wholemeal (whole wheat) flour
50 g/1¾ oz finely ground mixed nuts
100 g/3½ oz/⅓ cup vegan margarine, cut into small pieces
4 tbsp water
soya milk, to glaze

FILLING:
225 g/8 oz dried apricots
grated rind of 1 orange
300 ml/½ pint/1⅓ cups apple juice
1 tsp ground cinnamon
50 g/1¾ oz/⅓ cup raisins

1 Lightly grease a 23 cm/9 inch square cake tin (pan). To make the pastry (pie dough), place the flour and nuts in a mixing bowl and rub in the margarine with your fingers until the mixture resembles breadcrumbs. Stir in the water and bring together to form a dough. Wrap and leave to chill for 30 minutes.

2 To make the filling, place the apricots, orange rind and apple juice in a pan and bring to the boil. Simmer for 30 minutes until the apricots are mushy. Cool slightly, then blend to a purée. Stir in the cinnamon and raisins.

3 Divide the pastry (pie dough) in half, roll out one half and use to line the base of the tin. Spread the apricot purée over the top and brush the edges of the pastry (pie dough) with water. Roll out the rest of the dough to fit over the top of the apricot purée. Press down and seal the edges.

4 Prick the top of the pastry (pie dough) with a fork and brush with soya milk. Bake in a preheated oven, 200°C/400°F/Gas Mark 6, for 20-25 minutes until the pastry is golden. Leave to cool slightly before cutting into 12 bars. Serve warm.

Apple Shortcakes

Makes 4

INGREDIENTS

150 g/5½ oz/1 ¼ cups plain (all-purpose) flour
½ tsp salt
1 tsp baking powder
1 tbsp caster (superfine) sugar
25 g/1 oz/6 tsp butter, cut into small pieces
50 ml/2 fl oz/ ¼ cup milk
icing (confectioners') sugar, for dusting

FILLING:
3 dessert apples, peeled, cored and sliced
100 g/3½ oz/½ cup caster (superfine) sugar
1 tbsp lemon juice
1 tsp ground cinnamon
300 ml/½ pint/1⅓ cups water
150 ml/ ¼ pint/⅔ cup double (heavy) cream, whipped lightly

1 Lightly grease a baking tray (cookie sheet).

2 Sieve (strain) the flour, salt and baking powder into a bowl. Stir in the sugar, then rub in the butter until the mixture resembles fine breadcrumbs. Pour in the milk and mix everything to a soft dough.

3 Knead the dough, then roll out to a thickness of 1 cm/½ inch. Stamp out 4 rounds, using a 5 cm/2 inch cutter. Transfer the rounds to the prepared baking tray (sheet). Bake in a preheated oven, 220°C/425°F/Gas Mark 7, for about 15 minutes until the shortcakes are well risen and lightly browned. Leave to cool.

4 To make the filling, place the apple slices, sugar, lemon juice and cinnamon in a saucepan. Add the water, bring to the boil and simmer uncovered for 5-10 minutes until the apples are tender. Leave to cool a little, then remove the apples from the pan.

5 To serve, split the shortcakes in half. Place each bottom half on an individual serving plate and spoon on a quarter of the apple slices, then the cream. Place the other half of the shortcake on top. Serve dusted with icing (confectioners') sugar, if wished.

2

3

4

Treacle Scones

Makes 8

INGREDIENTS

225 g/8 oz/2 cups self-raising flour
1 tbsp caster (superfine) sugar
pinch of salt
75 g/2 3/4 oz/1/3 cup butter, cut into small pieces
1 dessert apple, peeled, cored and chopped
1 egg, beaten
2 tbsp black treacle (molasses)
75 ml/2 1/2 fl oz/5 tbsp milk

1 Lightly grease a baking tray (cookie sheet).

2 Sieve (strain) the flour, sugar and salt into a mixing bowl.

3 Rub in the butter with your fingers until the mixture resembles fine breadcrumbs.

4 Stir the chopped apple into the mixture.

5 Mix the beaten egg, treacle (molasses) and milk together in a jug (pitcher). Add to the dry ingredients to form a soft dough.

6 On a lightly floured surface, roll out the dough to 2 cm/ 3/4 inches thick and cut out 8 scones, using a 5 cm/2 inch cutter.

7 Arrange the scones on the prepared baking tray (cookie sheet) and bake in a preheated oven, 220°C/425°F/Gas Mark 7, for 8-10 minutes.

8 Transfer the scones to a wire rack and leave to cool slightly.

9 Serve split in half and spread with butter.

COOK'S TIP

These scones can be frozen, but are best defrosted and eaten within 1 month.

4

5

6

Cherry Scones

Makes 8

INGREDIENTS

225 g/8 oz/2 cups self-raising flour
1 tbsp caster (superfine) sugar
pinch of salt
75 g/2¾ oz/⅓ cup butter, cut into small pieces
40 g/1½ oz//3 tbsp glacé (candied) cherries, chopped
40 g/1½ oz/3 tbsp sultanas (golden raisins)
1 egg, beaten
50 ml/2 fl oz/¼ cup milk

1 Lightly grease a baking tray (cookie sheet).

2 Sieve (strain) the flour, sugar and salt into a mixing bowl and rub in the butter with your fingers until the scone mixture resembles breadcrumbs.

3 Stir in the glacé (candied) cherries and sultanas (golden raisins). Add the beaten egg.

4 Reserve 1 tablespoon of the milk for glazing, then add the remainder to the mixture. Mix together to form a soft dough.

5 On a floured surface, roll out the dough to a thickness of 2 cm/¾ inches and cut out 8 scones, using a 5 cm/2 inch cutter.

6 Place the scones on to the baking tray (cookie sheet) and brush with the reserved milk.

7 Bake in a preheated oven, 220°C/425°F/Gas Mark 7, for 8-10 minutes or until the scones are golden brown.

8 Leave to cool on a wire rack, then serve split and buttered.

COOK'S TIP

These scones will freeze very successfully but they are best defrosted and eaten within 1 month.

Cranberry Muffins

Makes 18

INGREDIENTS

225 g/8 oz/2 cups plain (all-purpose) flour
2 tsp baking powder
½ tsp salt
50 g/1¾ oz/9 tsp caster (superfine) sugar
50 g/1¾ oz/10 tsp butter, melted
2 eggs, beaten
200 ml/7 fl oz/¾ cup milk
100 g/3½ oz fresh cranberries
2 tbsp freshly grated Parmesan cheese

1 Lightly grease 2 bun (patty) tins (pans).

2 Sieve (strain) the flour, baking powder and salt into a mixing bowl. Stir in the caster (superfine) sugar.

3 In a separate bowl, mix the butter, beaten eggs and milk together, then pour into the bowl of dry ingredients.

4 Mix lightly together until all of the ingredients are evenly combined, then stir in the fresh cranberries.

5 Divide the mixture between the prepared tins (pans).

6 Sprinkle the grated Parmesan cheese over the top of each muffin mixture.

7 Bake in a preheated oven, 200°C/400°F/ Gas Mark 6, for about 20 minutes or until the muffins are well risen and a golden brown colour.

8 Leave the muffins to cool in the tins (pans). Transfer the muffins to a wire rack and leave to cool completely before serving.

VARIATION

For a sweet alternative to this recipe, replace the Parmesan cheese with demerara (brown crystal) sugar in step 6, if you prefer.

Spiced Biscuits

Makes about 24

INGREDIENTS

175 g/6 oz/¾ cup unsalted butter
175 g/6 oz/1 cup dark muscovado sugar
225 g/8 oz/2 cups plain (all-purpose) flour
pinch of salt
½ tsp bicarbonate of soda (baking soda)
1 tsp ground cinnamon
½ tsp ground coriander
½ tsp ground nutmeg
¼ tsp ground cloves
2 tbsp dark rum

1 Lightly grease 2 baking trays (cookie sheets).

2 Cream together the butter and sugar in a mixing bowl and whisk until light and fluffy.

3 Sieve (strain) the flour, salt, bicarbonate of soda (baking soda), cinnamon, coriander, nutmeg and cloves into the creamed mixture and combine well.

4 Stir the dark rum into the creamed mixture.

5 Using 2 teaspoons, place small mounds of the mixture, on to the baking trays (cookie sheets), placing them 7 cm/3 inch apart to allow for spreading during cooking. Flatten each one slightly with the back of a spoon.

6 Bake in a preheated oven, 180°C/350°F/Gas Mark 4, for 10-12 minutes until golden.

7 Leave the biscuits (cookies) to cool and crispen on wire racks before serving.

COOK'S TIP

Use the back of a fork to flatten the biscuits (cookies) slightly before baking.

2

3

5

Cinnamon & Sunflower Squares

Makes 12

INGREDIENTS

250 g/9 oz/1 cup butter, softened
250 g/9 oz/1 ¼ cups caster (superfine) sugar
3 eggs, beaten
250 g/9 oz/2 cups self-raising flour
1/2 tsp bicarbonate of soda (baking soda)
1 tbsp ground cinnamon
150 ml/ ¼ pint/⅔ cup soured cream
100 g/3½ oz sunflower seeds

1 Grease a 23 cm/9 inch square cake tin (pan) and line the base with baking parchment.

2 In a large mixing bowl, cream together the butter and caster (superfine) sugar until the mixture is light and fluffy.

3 Gradually add the beaten eggs to the mixture, beating well after each addition.

4 Sieve (strain) the self-raising flour, bicarbonate of soda (baking soda) and ground cinnamon into the creamed mixture and fold in gently, using a metal spoon.

5 Spoon in the soured cream and sunflower seeds and gently mix until well combined.

6 Spoon the mixture into the prepared cake tin (pan) and level the surface with the back of a spoon or a knife.

7 Bake in a preheated oven, 180°C/350°F/Gas Mark 4, for 45 minutes until the mixture is firm to the touch when pressed with a finger.

8 Loosen the edges with a round-bladed knife, then turn out on to a wire rack to cool completely. Slice into 12 squares.

COOK'S TIP

These moist squares will freeze well and will keep for up to 1 month.

Gingernuts

Makes 30

INGREDIENTS

350 g/12 oz/3 cups self-raising (self-rising) flour
pinch of salt
200 g/7 oz/1 cup caster (superfine) sugar
1 tbsp ground ginger
1 tsp bicarbonate of soda (baking soda)
125 g/4½ oz/½ cup butter
75 g/2¾ oz/¼ cup golden (light corn) syrup
1 egg, beaten
1 tsp grated orange rind

1 Lightly grease several baking trays (cookie sheets).

2 Sieve (strain) the flour, salt, sugar, ginger and bicarbonate of soda (baking soda) into a large mixing bowl.

3 Heat the butter and golden (light corn) syrup together in a saucepan over a very low heat until the butter has melted.

4 Leave the butter mixture to cool slightly, then pour it on to the dry ingredients.

5 Add the egg and orange rind and mix well.

6 Using your hands, carefully shape the dough into 30 even-sized balls.

7 Place the balls well apart on the prepared baking trays (cookie sheets), then flatten them slightly with your fingers.

8 Bake in a preheated oven, 160°C/325°F/ Gas Mark 3, for 15-20 minutes, then transfer them to a wire rack to cool.

VARIATION

If you like your gingernuts crunchy, bake them in the oven for a few minutes longer.

Caraway Biscuits

Makes about 36

INGREDIENTS

225 g/8 oz/2 cups plain (all-purpose) flour
pinch of salt
100 g/31/2 oz/1/3 cup butter, cut into small pieces
225 g/8 oz/1 1/4 cups caster (superfine) sugar
1 egg, beaten
2 tbsp caraway seeds
demerara (brown crystal) sugar, for sprinkling (optional)

1 Lightly grease several baking trays (cookie sheets).

2 Sieve (strain) the flour and salt into a mixing bowl. Rub in the butter with your fingers until the mixture resembles fine breadcrumbs. Stir in the caster (superfine) sugar.

3 Reserve 1 tbsp beaten egg for brushing the biscuits (cookies). Add the rest of the egg and the caraway seeds to the mixture and bring together to form a soft dough.

4 On a lightly floured surface, roll out the biscuit (cookie) dough thinly and then cut out about 36 rounds with a 6 cm/2 1/2 inch biscuit (cookie) cutter.

5 Transfer the rounds to the prepared baking trays (cookie sheets), brush with the reserved egg and sprinkle with demerara (brown crystal) sugar.

6 Bake in a preheated oven, 160°C/325°F/ Gas 3, for 15 minutes until lightly golden and crisp.

7 Leave the biscuits (cookies) to cool on a wire rack and store in an airtight container.

VARIATION

Caraway seeds have a nutty, delicate anise flavour. If you don't like their flavour, replace the caraway seeds with the milder-flavoured poppy seeds.

Peanut Butter Cookies

Makes 20

INGREDIENTS

125 g/4½ oz/½ cup butter, softened
150 g/5½ oz/½ cup chunky peanut butter
225 g/8 oz/1 cup granulated sugar
1 egg, lightly beaten
150 g/5½ oz/1¼ cup plain (all-purpose) flour
½ tsp baking powder
pinch of salt
75 g/2¾ oz unsalted natural peanuts, chopped

1 Lightly grease 2 baking trays (cookie sheets).

2 In a large mixing bowl, beat together the butter and peanut butter.

3 Gradually add the sugar and beat well.

4 Add the beaten egg a little at a time until it is thoroughly combined.

5 Sieve (strain) the flour, baking powder and salt into the peanut butter mixture.

6 Add the peanuts and bring all of the ingredients together to form a soft dough. Wrap and leave to chill for about 30 minutes.

7 Form the dough into 20 balls and place them on to the prepared baking trays (cookie sheets) about 5 cm/2 inches apart to allow for spreading. Flatten them slightly with your hand.

8 Bake in a preheated oven, 190°C/375°F/ Gas Mark 5, for 15 minutes until golden brown. Transfer the biscuits (cookies) to a wire rack and leave to cool.

COOK'S TIP

For a crunchy bite and sparkling appearance, sprinkle the biscuits (cookies) with demerara (brown crystal) sugar before baking.

2

6

7

Hazelnut Squares

Makes 16

INGREDIENTS

150 g/5½ oz/1¼ cups plain (all-purpose) flour
pinch of salt
1 tsp baking powder
100 g/3½ oz/⅓ cup butter, cut into small pieces
150 g/5½ oz/1 cup soft brown sugar
1 egg, beaten
4 tbsp milk
100 g/3½ oz/1 cup hazelnuts, halved
demerara (brown crystal) sugar, for sprinkling (optional)

1 Grease a 23 cm/9 inch square cake tin (pan) and line the base with baking parchment.

2 Sieve (strain) the flour, salt and baking powder into a large mixing bowl.

3 Rub in the butter with your fingers until the mixture resembles fine breadcrumbs. Stir in the brown sugar.

4 Add the egg, milk and nuts to the mixture and mix well.

5 Spoon the mixture into the prepared cake tin (pan) and level the surface. Sprinkle with demerara (brown crystal) sugar, if using.

6 Bake in a preheated oven, 180°C/350°F/Gas Mark 4, for about 25 minutes or until the mixture is firm to the touch when pressed with a finger.

7 Leave to cool for 10 minutes, then loosen the edges with a round-bladed knife and turn out on to a wire rack. Cut into squares.

VARIATION

For a coffee time biscuit (cookie), replace the milk with the same amount of cold strong black coffee, the stronger the better!

3

4

5

Coconut Flapjacks

Makes 16 squares

INGREDIENTS

200 g/7 oz/1 cup butter
200 g /7 oz/1⅓ cups demerara (brown crystal) sugar
2 tbsp golden (light corn) syrup
275 g/9½ oz/3½ cups porridge oats
100 g/3½ oz/1 cup desiccated (shredded) coconut
75 g/2¾ oz/⅓ cup glacé (candied) cherries, chopped

1 Lightly grease a 30 × 23 cm/12 × 9 inch baking tray (cookie sheet).

2 Heat the butter, demerara (brown crystal) sugar and golden (light corn) syrup in a large saucepan until just melted.

3 Stir in the oats, desiccated (shredded) coconut and glacé (candied) cherries and mix until evenly combined.

4 Spread the mixture on to the baking tray (cookie sheet) and press down with the back of a palette knife (spatula) to make a smooth surface.

5 Bake in a preheated oven, 170°C/325°F/ Gas Mark 3, for about 30 minutes.

6 Remove from the oven and leave to cool on the baking tray (cookie sheet) for 10 minutes.

7 Cut the mixture into squares using a sharp knife.

8 Carefully transfer the flapjacks to a wire rack and leave to cool completely.

COOK'S TIP

The flapjacks are best stored in an airtight container and eaten within 1 week. They can also be frozen for up to 1 month.

Oat & Raisin Biscuits

Makes 10

INGREDIENTS

50 g/1¾ oz/10 tsp butter
125 g/4½ oz/½ cup caster (superfine) sugar
1 egg, beaten
50 g/1¾/½ cup plain (all-purpose) flour
½ tsp salt
½ tsp baking powder
175 g/6 oz/2 cups porridge oats
125 g/4½ oz/¾ cup raisins
2 tbsp sesame seeds

1 Lightly grease 2 baking trays (cookie sheets).

2 In a large mixing bowl, cream together the butter and sugar until light and fluffy.

3 Add the beaten egg gradually and beat until well combined.

4 Sieve (strain) the flour, salt and baking powder into the creamed mixture. Mix well.

5 Add the porridge oats, raisins and sesame seeds and mix well.

6 Place spoonfuls of the mixture well apart on the prepared baking trays (cookie sheets) and flatten them slightly with the back of a spoon.

7 Bake in a preheated oven, 180°C/350°F/Gas Mark 4, for 15 minutes.

8 Leave the biscuits (cookies) to cool slightly on the baking trays (cookie sheets).

9 Transfer the biscuits (cookies) to a wire rack and leave to cool completely before serving.

VARIATION

Substitute chopped ready-to-eat dried apricots for the raisins, if you prefer.

COOK'S TIP

To enjoy these biscuits (cookies) at their best, store them in an airtight container.

Rosemary Biscuits

Makes about 25

INGREDIENTS

50 g/$1^3/_4$ oz/10 tsp butter, softened
4 tbsp caster (superfine) sugar
grated rind of 1 lemon
4 tbsp lemon juice
1 egg, separated
2 tsp finely chopped fresh rosemary
200 g/7 oz/$1^3/_4$ cups plain (all-purpose) flour, sieved (strained)
caster (superfine) sugar, for sprinkling (optional)

1 Lightly grease 2 baking trays (cookie sheets).

2 In a large bowl, cream together the butter and sugar until pale and fluffy.

3 Add the lemon rind and juice, then the egg yolk and beat until they are thoroughly combined. Stir in the chopped fresh rosemary.

4 Add the sieved (strained) flour, mixing well until a soft dough is formed. Wrap and chill for 30 minutes.

5 On a lightly floured surface, roll out the dough thinly and stamp out about 25 circles with a 6 cm/$2^1/_2$ inch biscuit (cookie) cutter. Arrange the dough circles on the prepared baking trays (cookie sheets).

6 In a bowl, lightly whisk the egg white. Gently brush the egg white over the surface of each biscuit, then sprinkle with a little caster (superfine) sugar.

7 Bake in a preheated oven, 180°C/350°F/Gas Mark 4, for about 15 minutes.

8 Transfer the biscuits (cookies) to a wire rack and leave to cool before serving.

VARIATION

In place of the fresh rosemary, use $1^1/_2$ teaspoons of dried rosemary, if you prefer.

Citrus Crescents

Makes about 25

INGREDIENTS

100 g/3½ oz/⅓ cup butter, softened
75 g/2¾ oz/⅓ cup caster (superfine) sugar
1 egg, separated
200 g/7 oz/1¾ cups plain (all-purpose) flour
grated rind of 1 orange
grated rind of 1 lemon
grated rind of 1 lime
2-3 tbsp orange juice
caster (superfine) sugar, for sprinkling (optional)

1 Lightly grease 2 baking trays (cookie sheets).

2 In a mixing bowl, cream together the butter and sugar until light and fluffy, then gradually beat in the egg yolk.

3 Sieve (strain) the flour into the creamed mixture and mix well. Add the orange, lemon and lime rinds with enough of the orange juice to make a soft dough.

4 Roll out the dough on a lightly floured surface. Stamp out rounds using a 7.5 cm/3 inch biscuit (cookie) cutter. Make crescent shapes out of the rounds by cutting away a quarter of each round. Re-roll the trimmings to make about 25 crescents.

5 Place the crescents on to the prepared baking trays (cookie sheets). Prick the surface of each crescent with a fork.

6 Lightly whisk the egg white and brush it over the biscuits (cookies). Dust with extra caster (superfine) sugar, if using.

7 Bake in a preheated oven, 200°C/400°F/ Gas Mark 6, for about 12-15 minutes. Leave the biscuits (cookies) to cool before serving.

COOK'S TIP

Store the citrus crescents in an airtight container or freeze them for up to 1 month.

Lemon Jumbles

Makes about 50

INGREDIENTS

100 g/3½ oz/⅓ cup butter, softened
125 g/4½ oz/½ cup caster (superfine) sugar
grated rind of 1 lemon
1 egg, beaten
4 tbsp lemon juice
350 g/12 oz/3 cups plain (all-purpose) flour
1 tsp baking powder
1 tbsp milk
icing (confectioners') sugar, for dredging

1 Lightly grease several baking trays (cookie sheets).

2 Cream together the butter, caster sugar and lemon rind until pale and fluffy.

3 Add the beaten egg and lemon juice a little at a time, beating well after each addition.

4 Sieve (strain) the flour and baking powder into the creamed mixture and mix together. Add the milk, mixing to form a dough.

5 Turn the dough out on to a lightly floured work surface and divide into about 50 equal-sized pieces.

6 Roll each piece into a sausage shape with your hands and twist in the middle to make an 'S' shape.

7 Place on the prepared baking trays (cookie sheets) and bake in a preheated oven, 170°C/325°F/Gas Mark 3, for 15-20 minutes. Leave to cool completely on a wire rack. Dredge with icing (confectioners') sugar to serve.

VARIATION

If you prefer, shape the dough into other shapes – letters of the alphabet or geometric shapes – or just make into round biscuits (cookies).

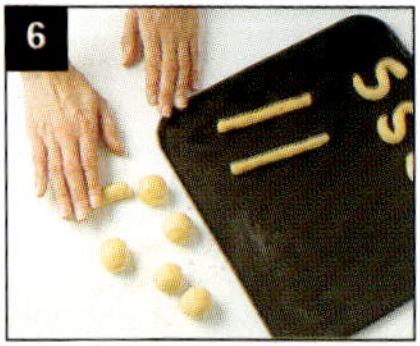

Chocolate & Lemon Pinwheels

Makes about 40

INGREDIENTS

175 g/6 oz/¾ cup butter, softened
300 g/10½ oz/1⅓ cups caster (superfine) sugar
1 egg, beaten
350 g/12 oz/3 cups plain (all-purpose) flour
25 g/1 oz dark chocolate, melted and cooled slightly
grated rind of 1 lemon

1 Grease and flour several baking trays (cookie sheets).

2 In a large bowl, cream together the butter and sugar until light and fluffy.

3 Gradually add the beaten egg to the creamed mixture, beating well after each addition.

4 Sieve (strain) the flour into the creamed mixture and mix until a soft dough forms.

5 Transfer half of the dough to another bowl and beat in the cooled melted chocolate.

6 Stir the grated lemon rind into the other half of the plain dough.

7 On a lightly floured surface, roll out the 2 pieces of dough to form rectangles of the same size.

8 Lay the lemon dough on top of the chocolate dough. Roll up the dough tightly into a sausage shape, using a sheet of baking parchment to guide you. Leave the dough to chill in the refrigerator.

9 Cut the roll into about 40 slices, place them on the baking trays (cookie sheets) and bake in a preheated oven, 190°C/375°F/Gas Mark 5, for 10-12 minutes or until lightly golden. Transfer the pinwheels to a wire rack and leave to cool completely before serving.

White Chocolate Cookies

Makes 24

INGREDIENTS

125 g/4½ oz/½ cup butter, softened
125 g/4½ oz/¾ cup soft brown sugar
1 egg, beaten
200 g/7 oz/1¾ cups self-raising flour
pinch of salt
125 g/4½ oz white chocolate, chopped roughly
50 g/1¾ oz brazil nuts, chopped

1 Lightly grease several baking trays (cookie sheets).

2 In a large bowl, cream together the butter and sugar until light and fluffy.

3 Gradually add the beaten egg, beating well after each addition.

4 Sieve (strain) the flour and salt into the creamed mixture and blend well.

5 Stir in the chocolate and brazil nuts.

6 Place heaped teaspoons of the mixture on to the prepared baking trays (cookie sheets). Do not put more than 6 teaspoons of the mixture on to each baking tray (cookie sheet) as the cookies will spread during cooking.

7 Bake in a preheated oven, 190°C/375°F/ Gas Mark 5, for about 10-12 minutes or until just golden brown.

8 Transfer the cookies to wire racks. Leave to cool before serving.

VARIATION

Use plain or milk chocolate instead of white chocolate, if you prefer.

3

5

6

Shortbread Fantails

Makes 8

INGREDIENTS

125 g/4½ oz/½ cup butter, softened
40 g/1½ oz/8 tsp granulated sugar
25 g/1 oz/8 tsp icing (confectioners') sugar
225 g/8 oz/2 cups plain (all-purpose) flour
pinch of salt
2 tsp orange flower water
caster (superfine) sugar, for sprinkling

1 Lightly grease a 20 cm/8 inch shallow round cake tin (pan).

2 In a large mixing bowl, cream together the butter, the granulated sugar and the icing (confectioners') sugar until light and fluffy.

3 Sieve (strain) the flour and salt into the creamed mixture. Add the orange flower water, combine well and bring the mixture together to form a soft dough.

4 On a lightly floured surface, roll out the dough to a 20 cm/8 inch round and place in the tin (pan). Prick the dough well and score into 8 triangles with a round-bladed knife.

5 Bake in a preheated oven, 160°C/300°F/Gas Mark 2, for 30-35 minutes or until the biscuit (cookie) is pale golden and crisp.

6 Sprinkle with caster (superfine) sugar, then cut along the marked lines to make the fantails.

7 Leave the shortbread to cool before removing the pieces from the tin (pan). Store in an airtight container.

COOK'S TIP

For a crunchy addition, sprinkle 2 tablespoons of chopped mixed nuts over the top of the fantails before baking.

4

4

4

Millionaire's Shortbread

Makes 12 bars

INGREDIENTS

175 g/6 oz/1½ cups plain (all-purpose) flour
125 g/4½ oz/½ cup butter, cut into small pieces
50 g/1¾ oz/3 tbsp soft brown sugar, sieved (strained)

TOPPING:
50 g/1¾ oz/10 tsp butter
50 g/1¾ oz/3 tbsp soft brown sugar
400 g/14 oz can condensed milk
150 g/5½ oz milk chocolate

1 Grease a 23 cm/9 inch square cake tin (pan).

2 Sieve (strain) the flour into a mixing bowl and rub in the butter with your fingers until the mixture resembles fine breadcrumbs. Add the sugar and mix to form a firm dough.

3 Press the dough into the prepared tin (pan) and prick with a fork.

4 Bake in a preheated oven, 190°C/375°F/ Gas Mark 5, for 20 minutes until lightly golden. Leave to cool in the tin (pan).

5 To make the topping, place the butter, sugar and condensed milk in a non-stick saucepan and cook over a gentle heat, stirring constantly, until the mixture comes to the boil.

6 Reduce the heat and cook for 4-5 minutes until the caramel is pale golden and thick and is coming away from the sides of the pan. Pour the topping over the shortbread base and leave to cool.

7 When the caramel topping is firm, melt the milk chocolate in a heatproof bowl set over a saucepan of simmering water. Spread the melted chocolate over the topping, leave to set in a cool place, then cut the shortbread into squares or fingers to serve.

2

3

6

Vanilla Hearts

Makes about 16

INGREDIENTS

225 g/8 oz/2 cups plain (all-purpose) flour
150 g/5½ oz/⅔ cup butter, cut into small pieces
125 g/4½ oz/½ cup caster (superfine) sugar
1 tsp vanilla flavouring (extract)
caster (superfine) sugar, for dusting

1 Lightly grease a baking tray (cookie sheet).

2 Sieve (strain) the flour into a large mixing bowl and rub in the butter with your fingers until the mixture resembles fine breadcrumbs.

3 Stir in the caster (superfine) sugar and vanilla flavouring (extract) and bring the mixture together with your hands to make a firm dough.

4 On a lightly floured surface, roll out the dough to a thickness of 2.5 cm/1 inch. Stamp out 12 hearts with a heart-shaped biscuit cutter measuring about 5 cm/2 inches across and 2.5 cm/1 inch deep.

5 Arrange the hearts on the prepared baking tray (cookie sheet). Bake in a preheated oven, 180°C/350°F/Gas Mark 4, for 15-20 minutes until the hearts are a light golden colour.

6 Transfer the vanilla hearts to a wire rack and leave to cool. Dust with a little caster (superfine) sugar just before serving.

COOK'S TIP

Place a fresh vanilla pod in your caster (superfine) sugar and keep it in a storage jar for several weeks to give the sugar a delicious vanilla flavour.

Rock Drops

Makes 8

INGREDIENTS

200 g/7 oz/1$\frac{3}{4}$ cups plain (all-purpose) flour
2 tsp baking powder
100 g/3$\frac{1}{2}$ oz/$\frac{1}{3}$ cup butter, cut into small pieces
75 g/2$\frac{3}{4}$ oz/$\frac{1}{3}$ cup demerara (brown crystal) sugar
100 g/3$\frac{1}{2}$ oz/$\frac{1}{2}$ cup sultanas (golden raisins)
25 g/1 oz/2 tbsp glacé (candied) cherries, chopped finely
1 egg, beaten
2 tbsp milk

1 Lightly grease a baking tray (cookie sheet).

2 Sieve (strain) the flour and baking powder into a mixing bowl. Rub in the butter with your fingers until the mixture resembles breadcrumbs.

3 Stir in the sugar, sultanas (golden raisins) and chopped glacé (candied) cherries.

4 Add the beaten egg and the milk to the mixture and bring together to form a soft dough.

5 Spoon 8 mounds of the mixture on to the baking tray (cookie sheet). Make sure they are spaced well apart as they will spread during cooking.

6 Bake in a preheated oven, 200°C/400°F/Gas Mark 6, for about 15-20 minutes until firm to the touch when pressed with a finger.

7 Remove the rock drops from the baking tray (cookie sheet). Either serve piping hot from the oven or transfer to a wire rack and leave to cool before serving.

COOK'S TIP

For convenience, prepare the dry ingredients in advance and just before cooking stir in the liquid.

Chocolate Chip Brownies

Makes 12

INGREDIENTS

150 g/5½ oz dark chocolate, broken into pieces
225 g/8 oz/1 cup butter, softened
225 g/8 oz/2 cups self-raising flour
125 g/4½ oz/½ cup caster (superfine) sugar
4 eggs, beaten
75 g/2¾ oz pistachio nuts, chopped
100 g/3½ oz white chocolate, chopped roughly
icing (confectioners') sugar, for dusting

1 Lightly grease a 23 cm/9 inch baking tin (pan) and line with greaseproof paper.

2 Melt the dark chocolate and butter in a heatproof bowl set over a saucepan of simmering water. Leave to cool.

3 Sieve (strain) the flour into a separate mixing bowl and stir in the caster (superfine) sugar.

4 Stir the eggs into the melted chocolate mixture, then pour this mixture into the flour and sugar mixture, beating well. Stir in the pistachio nuts and white chocolate, then pour the mixture into the tin (pan).

5 Bake in a preheated oven, 180°C/350°/Gas Mark 4, for 30-35 minutes until firm to the touch. Leave to cool in the tin (pan) for 20 minutes, then turn out on to a wire rack.

6 Dust the brownie with icing (confectioners') sugar and cut into 12 pieces when cold.

COOK'S TIP

The brownie won't be completely firm in the middle when it is removed from the oven, but it will set when it has cooled.

4

4

4

Chocolate Biscotti

Makes 16

INGREDIENTS

1 egg
100 g/3½ oz/⅓ cup caster (superfine) sugar
1 tsp vanilla flavouring (extract)
125 g/4½ oz/1 cup (all-purpose) plain flour
½ tsp baking powder
1 tsp ground cinnamon
50 g/1¾ oz dark chocolate, chopped roughly
50 g/1¾ oz toasted flaked (slivered) almonds
50 g/1¾ oz pine kernels (nuts)

1 Grease a large baking tray (cookie sheet).

2 Whisk the egg, sugar and vanilla flavouring (extract) in a mixing bowl with an electric mixer until it is thick and pale – ribbons of mixture should trail from the whisk as you lift it.

3 Sieve (strain) the flour, baking powder and cinnamon into a separate bowl, then sieve (strain) into the egg mixture and fold in gently. Stir in the chocolate, almonds and pine kernels (nuts).

4 Turn out on to a lightly floured surface and shape into a flat log about 23 cm/9 inches long and 1.5 cm/¾ inch wide. Transfer to the prepared baking tray (cookie sheet).

5 Bake in a preheated oven, 180°C/350°F/ Gas Mark 4, for 20-25 minutes or until golden. Remove from the oven and leave to cool for 5 minutes or until firm.

6 Transfer the log to a cutting board. Using a serrated bread knife, cut the log on the diagonal into slices about 1 cm/ ½ inch thick and arrange them on the baking tray (cookie sheet). Cook for 10-15 minutes, turning halfway through the cooking time.

7 Leave to cool for about 5 minutes, then transfer to a wire rack to cool completely.

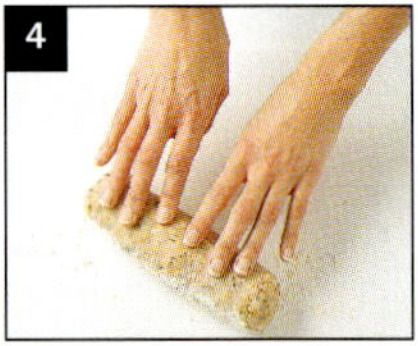

Chocolate Macaroons

Makes 18

INGREDIENTS

75 g/2¾ oz dark chocolate, broken into pieces
2 egg whites
pinch of salt
200 g/7 oz/1 cup caster (superfine) sugar
125 g/4½ oz/1¼ cups ground almonds
desiccated (shredded) coconut, for sprinkling (optional)

1 Grease 2 baking trays (cookie sheets) and line with baking parchment or rice paper.

2 Melt the dark chocolate in a small heatproof bowl set over a saucepan of simmering water. Leave to cool slightly.

3 In a mixing bowl, whisk the egg whites with the salt until they form soft peaks.

4 Gradually whisk the caster (superfine) sugar into the egg whites, then fold in the almonds and cooled melted chocolate.

5 Place heaped teaspoonfuls of the mixture spaced well apart on the prepared baking trays (cookie sheets) and spread into circles about 6 cm/2½inches across. Sprinkle with desiccated (shredded) coconut, if using.

6 Bake in a preheated oven, 150°C/300°F/ Gas Mark 2, for about 25 minutes or until firm to the touch.

7 Leave to cool before carefully lifting from the baking trays (cookie sheets). Transfer to a wire rack and leave to cool completely before serving.

COOK'S TIP

Store the macaroons in an airtight container and eat within 1 week.

Florentines

Makes 8–10

INGREDIENTS

50 g/1¾ oz/ 10 tsp butter
50 g/1¾ oz/ ¼ cup caster (superfine) sugar
25 g/1 oz/ ¼ cup plain (all-purpose) flour, sieved (strained)
50 g/1¾ oz/⅓ cup almonds, chopped
50 g/1¾ oz/⅓ cup chopped mixed peel
25 g/1 oz/ ¼ cup raisins, chopped
25 g/1 oz/2 tbsp glacé (candied) cherries, chopped
finely grated rind of ½ lemon
125 g/4½ oz dark chocolate, melted

1 Line 2 large baking trays (cookie sheets) with baking parchment.

2 Heat the butter and caster (superfine) sugar in a small saucepan until the butter has just melted and the sugar dissolved. Remove the pan from the heat.

3 Stir in the flour and mix well. Stir in the chopped almonds, mixed peel, raisins, cherries and lemon rind. Place teaspoonfuls of the mixture well apart on the baking trays (cookie sheets).

4 Bake in a preheated oven, 180°C/350°F/Gas Mark 4, for 10 minutes or until lightly golden.

5 As soon as the florentines are removed from the oven, press the edges into neat shapes while still on the baking trays (cookie sheets), using a biscuit (cookie) cutter. Leave to cool on the baking trays (cookie sheets) until firm, then transfer to a wire rack to cool completely.

6 Spread the melted chocolate over the smooth side of each florentine. As the chocolate begins to set, mark wavy lines in it with a fork. Leave the florentines until set, chocolate side up.

Meringues

Makes about 13

INGREDIENTS

4 egg whites
pinch of salt
125 g/4½ oz/½ cup granulated sugar

125 g/4½ oz/½ cup caster (superfine) sugar

300 ml/½ pint/1¼ cups double (heavy) cream, whipped lightly

1 Line 3 baking trays (cookie sheets) with baking parchment.

2 In a large clean bowl, whisk together the egg whites and salt until they are stiff, using an electric hand-held whisk or a balloon whisk. (You should be able to turn the bowl upside down without any movement from the egg whites.)

3 Whisk in the granulated sugar a little at a time; the meringue should start to look glossy at this stage.

4 Sprinkle in the caster (superfine) sugar a little at a time and continue whisking until all the sugar has been incorporated and the meringue is thick, white and stands in tall peaks.

5 Transfer the meringue mixture to a piping (pastry) bag fitted with a 2 cm/¾ inch star nozzle (tip). Pipe about 26 small whirls on to the prepared baking trays (cookie sheets).

6 Bake in a preheated oven, 120°C/250°F/Gas Mark ½, for 1½ hours or until the meringues are pale golden in colour and can be easily lifted off the paper. Leave them to cool in the turned-off oven overnight.

7 Just before serving, sandwich the meringues together in pairs with the cream and arrange on a serving plate.

VARIATION

For a finer texture, replace the granulated sugar with caster (superfine) sugar.

2

3
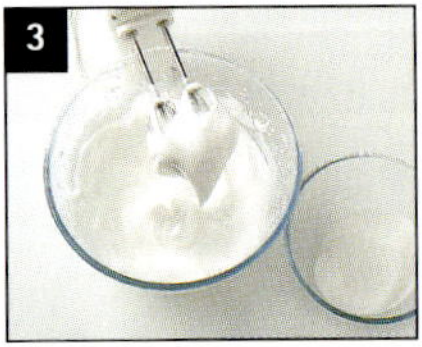

5

Puddings & Desserts

No true meal is really complete without a pudding and this chapter indulges the reader with a hearty and wholesome collection of some of best-loved family favourites. Fruit puddings, chocolate puddings, lemon puddings and crumbly puddings–they are all fun, easy to make and deliciously delightful to eat. This chapter also offers some new surprises for old-fashioned puddings, leaving you with the difficult decision of which to try first.

Chocolate is comforting at anytime but no more so than when served in a steaming hot pudding. It is hard to think of anything more warming, comforting and homely than tucking into a steamed hot chocolate pudding on a cold day. The child in us will love the chocolate addition to nursery favourites such as Bread & Butter Pudding. In fact, there are several old favourites that have been given the chocolate treatment, bringing them bang up to-date and putting them on the chocolate lover's map.

Chocolate Queen of Puddings

Serves 4

INGREDIENTS

50 g/1¾ oz dark chocolate
450 ml/16 fl oz/2 cups chocolate-flavoured milk
100 g/3½ oz/1¾ cups fresh white or wholemeal (whole wheat) breadcrumbs
125 g/4½ oz/½ cup caster (superfine) sugar
2 eggs, separated
4 tbsp black cherry jam

1 Break the chocolate into small pieces and place in a saucepan with the chocolate-flavoured milk. Heat gently, stirring until the chocolate melts. Bring almost to the boil, then remove the pan from the heat.

2 Place the breadcrumbs in a large mixing bowl with 25 g/1 oz/5 tsp of the sugar. Pour over the chocolate milk and mix well. Beat in the egg yolks.

3 Spoon into a 1.1 litre/2 pint/5 cup pie dish and bake in a preheated oven, 180°C/350°F/ Gas Mark 4, for 25–30 minutes or until set and firm to the touch.

4 Whisk the egg whites in a large grease-free bowl until standing in soft peaks. Gradually whisk in the remaining caster (superfine) sugar and whisk until you have a glossy, thick meringue.

5 Spread the black cherry jam over the surface of the chocolate mixture and pile or pipe the meringue on top. Return the pudding to the oven for 15 minutes or until the meringue is crisp and golden.

VARIATION

If you prefer, add 40 g/1½ oz/½ cup desiccated (shredded) coconut to the breadcrumbs and omit the jam.

Chocolate Eve's Pudding with Bitter Chocolate Sauce

Serves 4

INGREDIENTS

225 g/8 oz fresh or frozen raspberries
2 eating apples, peeled, cored and sliced thickly
4 tbsp seedless raspberry jam
2 tbsp port (optional)

SPONGE TOPPING:
50 g/1$^3/_4$ oz/4 tbsp soft margarine
50 g/1$^3/_4$ oz/4 tbsp caster (superfine) sugar
75 g/2$^3/_4$ oz/$^2/_3$ cup self-raising flour, sieved (strained)
50 g/1$^3/_4$ oz white chocolate, grated
1 egg
2 tbsp milk

BITTER CHOCOLATE SAUCE:
90 g/3 oz dark chocolate
150 ml/$^1/_4$ pint/$^2/_3$ cup single (light) cream

1 Place the apple slices and raspberries in a shallow 1.1 litre/2 pint/5 cup ovenproof dish.

2 Place the raspberry jam and port (if using) in a small pan and heat gently until the jam melts and combines with the port. Pour the mixture over the fruit.

3 Place all of the ingredients for the sponge topping in a large mixing bowl and beat until the mixture is smooth.

4 Spoon the sponge mixture over the fruit and level the top. Bake in a preheated oven, 180°C/350°F/Gas Mark 4, for 40–45 minutes or until the sponge is springy to the touch.

5 To make the sauce, break the chocolate into small pieces and place in a heavy-based saucepan with the cream. Heat gently, beating until a smooth sauce is formed. Serve warm with the pudding.

VARIATION

Use dark chocolate in the sponge and top with apricot halves, covered with peach schnapps and apricot conserve.

Mini Chocolate Ginger Puddings with Chocolate Custard

Serves 4

INGREDIENTS

100 g/3½ oz/generous ⅓ cup soft margarine
100 g/3½ oz/¾ cup self-raising flour, sieved (strained)
100 g/3½ oz/7 tbsp caster (superfine) sugar
2 eggs
25 g/1 oz/¼ cup cocoa powder, sieved (strained)
25 g/1 oz dark chocolate
50 g/1¾ oz stem ginger

CHOCOLATE CUSTARD:
2 egg yolks
1 tbsp caster (superfine) sugar
1 tbsp cornflour (cornstarch)
300 ml/½ pint/1¼ cups milk
100 g/3½ oz dark chocolate, broken into pieces
icing (confectioners') sugar, to dust

1 Lightly grease 4 individual pudding basins. Place the margarine, flour, sugar, eggs and cocoa powder in a mixing bowl and beat until well combined and smooth. Chop the chocolate and ginger and stir into the mixture.

2 Spoon the cake mixture into the prepared basins and level the top. The mixture should three-quarters fill the basins. Cover the basins with discs of baking parchment and cover with a pleated sheet of foil. Steam for 45 minutes until the puddings are cooked and springy to the touch.

3 Meanwhile, make the custard. Beat together the egg yolks, sugar and cornflour (cornstarch) to form a smooth paste. Heat the milk until boiling and pour over the egg mixture. Return to the pan and cook over a very low heat stirring until thick. Remove from the heat and beat in the chocolate. Stir until the chocolate melts.

4 Lift the puddings from the steamer, run a knife around the edge of the basins and turn out on to serving plates. Dust with sugar and drizzle some chocolate custard over the top. Serve the remaining custard separately.

2

2

3

Chocolate Bread & Butter Pudding

Serves 4

INGREDIENTS

225 g/8 oz brioche
15 g/½ oz/1 tbsp butter
50 g/1¾ oz dark chocolate chips
1 egg
2 egg yolks
50 g/1¾ oz/4 tbsp caster (superfine) sugar
410 g/15 oz can light evaporated milk

1 Cut the brioche into thin slices. Lightly butter one side of each slice.

2 Place a layer of brioche, buttered-side down, in the bottom of a shallow ovenproof dish. Sprinkle a few chocolate chips over the top.

3 Continue layering the brioche and chocolate chips, finishing with a layer of bread on top.

4 Whisk together the egg, egg yolks and sugar until well combined. Heat the milk in a small saucepan until it just begins to simmer. Gradually add to the egg mixture, whisking well.

5 Pour the custard over the pudding and leave to stand for 5 minutes. Press the brioche down into the milk.

6 Place in a roasting tin (pan) and fill with boiling water to come halfway up the side of the dish (this is known as a bain-marie).

7 Bake in a preheated oven, 180°C/350°F/Gas Mark 4, for 30 minutes or until the custard has set.

VARIATION

For a double-chocolate pudding, heat the milk with 1 tbsp of cocoa powder, stirring until well dissolved then continue from step 4.

COOK'S TIP

The pudding can be made a few hours ahead and baked when required. It also tastes good cold.

Chocolate French Toasties

Serves 4–6

INGREDIENTS

50 g/1¾ oz dark chocolate
150 ml/¼ pint/⅔ cup milk
1 egg
4 tbsp seedless raspberry jam
2 tbsp rum (optional)
8 thick slices white bread
butter or oil, for shallow-frying
½ tsp ground cinnamon
40 g/1½ oz/3 tbsp caster (superfine) sugar
a little whipped cream, to serve

1 Break the chocolate into small pieces and place in a small pan with the milk. Heat gently, stirring until the chocolate melts. Leave to cool slightly.

2 Beat the egg in a large mixing bowl and whisk in the warm chocolate milk.

3 Heat the raspberry jam gently and stir in the rum, if using. Set aside and keep warm.

4 Remove the crusts from the bread, cut into triangles and dip each one into the chocolate mixture. Heat the butter or oil in a frying pan (skillet) and shallow-fry the bread triangles for 2–3 minutes until just crispy, turning once.

5 Mix together the cinnamon and caster (superfine) sugar and sprinkle it over the toasties. Serve with the hot jam sauce and a little whipped cream.

VARIATION

If you wish, try this recipe using brioche or fruit bread for a tasty variation.

COOK'S TIP

Young children adore this dessert. Cut the bread into fingers to make it easer for them to handle.

Chocolate Fudge Pudding

Serves 6

INGREDIENTS

150 g/5½ oz/generous ⅓ cup soft margarine
150 g/5½ oz/1¼ cups self-raising flour
150 g/5½ oz/½ cup golden (light corn) syrup
3 eggs
25 g/1 oz/¼ cup cocoa powder

CHOCOLATE FUDGE SAUCE:
100 g/3½ oz dark chocolate
125 ml/4 fl oz/½ cup sweetened condensed milk
4 tbsp double (heavy) cream

1 Lightly grease a 1.2 litre/2 pint/5 cup pudding basin.

2 Place the ingredients for the sponge in a mixing bowl and beat until well combined and smooth.

3 Spoon into the prepared basin and level the top. Cover with a disc of baking parchment and tie a pleated sheet of foil over the basin. Steam for 1½–2 hours until the pudding is cooked and springy to the touch.

4 To make the sauce, break the chocolate into small pieces and place in a small pan with the condensed milk. Heat gently, stirring until the chocolate melts.

5 Remove the pan from the heat and stir in the double (heavy) cream.

6 To serve the pudding, turn it out on to a serving plate and pour over a little of the chocolate fudge sauce. Serve the remaining sauce separately.

COOK'S TIP

To cook the cake in the microwave, cook it, uncovered, on High for 4 minutes, turning the basin once. Leave to stand for at least 5 minutes before turning out. Whilst the pudding is standing, make the sauce. Break the chocolate into pieces and place in a microwave-proof bowl with the milk. Cook on high for 1 minute, then stir until the chocolate melts. Stir in the double (heavy) cream and serve.

2

3

5

Chocolate Fruit Crumble

Serves 4

INGREDIENTS

400 g/14 oz can apricots, in natural juice
450 g/1 lb cooking apples, peeled and sliced thickly
100 g/3½ oz/¾ cup plain (all-purpose) flour
75 g/2¾ oz/⅓ cup butter
50 g/1¾ oz/⅔ cup porridge oats
50 g/1¾ oz/4 tbsp caster (superfine) sugar
100 g/3½ oz/⅔ cup chocolate chips

1 Lightly grease an ovenproof dish with a little butter or margarine.

2 Drain the apricots, reserving 4 tbsp of the juice. Place the apples and apricots in the prepared ovenproof dish with the reserved apricot juice and toss to mix.

3 Sieve (strain) the flour into a mixing bowl. Cut the butter into small cubes and rub in with your fingertips until the mixture resembles fine breadcrumbs. Stir in the porridge oats, sugar and chocolate chips.

4 Sprinkle the crumble mixture over the apples and apricots and level the top roughly. Do not press the crumble into the fruit.

5 Bake in a preheated oven, 350°F/180°C/Gas Mark 4, for 40–45 minutes or until the topping is golden. Serve hot or cold.

VARIATION

For a double chocolate crumble, replace 1–2 tablespoons of flour with cocoa powder.

COOK'S TIP

You can use dark, milk or white chocolate chips in this recipe or a mixture of all three.

VARIATION

Other fruits can be used to make this crumble – fresh pears mixed with fresh or frozen raspberries work well. If you do not use canned fruit, add 4 tablespoons of orange juice to the fresh fruit.

2

3

4

Poached Pears with Mascarpone Chocolate Sauce

Serves 6

INGREDIENTS

6 firm ripe pears
100 g/3½ oz/7 tbsp caster (superfine) sugar
2 cinnamon sticks
rind of 1 orange
2 cloves
1 bottle rosé wine

CHOCOLATE SAUCE:
175 g/6 oz dark chocolate
250 g/9 oz mascarpone cheese
2 tbsp orange-flavoured liqueur

1 Carefully peel the pears, leaving the stalk intact.

2 Place the sugar, cinnamon sticks, orange rind, cloves and wine in a saucepan that will hold the 6 pears snugly.

3 Heat gently until the sugar has dissolved, then add the pears to the liquid and bring to a simmer. Cover and poach gently for 20 minutes. If serving them cold, leave the pears to cool in the liquid, then chill until required. If serving hot, leave the pears in the hot liquid whilst preparing the chocolate sauce.

4 To make the sauce, melt the chocolate. Beat together the cheese and the orange-flavoured liqueur. Beat the cheese mixture into the chocolate.

5 Remove the pears from the poaching liquid and place on a serving plate. Add a generous spoonful of sauce on the side and serve the remainder separately.

COOK'S TIP

There is no need to waste the tasty poaching liquid. Boil it rapidly in a clean pan for about 10 minutes to reduce to a syrup. Use the syrup to sweeten a fresh fruit salad or spoon it over ice cream.

COOK'S TIP

Rosettes of cream can be piped on to the dessert, if liked.

Saucy Chocolate Pudding

Serves 4

INGREDIENTS

300 ml/½ pint/1¼ cups milk
75 g/2¾ oz dark chocolate
½ tsp vanilla flavouring (extract)
100 g/3½ oz/7 tbsp caster (superfine) sugar
100 g/3½ oz/generous ⅓ cup butter
150 g/5½ oz/1¼ cups self-raising flour
2 tbsp cocoa powder
icing (confectioners') sugar, to dust

FOR THE SAUCE:
3 tbsp cocoa powder
50 g/1¾ oz/4 tbsp light muscovado sugar
300 ml/½ pint/1¼ cups boiling water

1 Lightly grease an 850 ml/1½ pint/3¾ cup ovenproof dish.

2 Place the milk in a small pan. Break the chocolate into pieces and add to the milk. Heat gently, stirring until the chocolate melts. Leave to cool slightly. Stir in the vanilla flavouring (extract).

3 Beat together the caster (superfine) sugar and butter in a bowl until light and fluffy. Sieve (strain) the flour and cocoa powder together. Add to the bowl with the chocolate milk and beat until smooth, using an electric whisk if you have one. Pour the mixture into the prepared dish.

4 To make the sauce, mix together the cocoa powder and sugar. Add a little boiling water and mix to a smooth paste, then stir in the remaining water. Pour the sauce over the pudding but do not mix in.

5 Place the dish on to a baking tray (cookie sheet) and bake in a preheated oven, 180°C/350°F/Gas Mark 4, for 40 minutes or until dry on top and springy to the touch. Leave to stand for about 5 minutes, then dust with a little icing (confectioners') sugar just before serving.

VARIATION

For a mocha sauce, add 1 tbsp instant coffee to the cocoa powder and sugar in step 4, before mixing to a paste with the boiling water.

2

3

4

Pecan & Chocolate Fudge Ring

Serves 6

INGREDIENTS

FUDGE SAUCE:
40 g/1½ oz/3 tbsp butter
40 g/1½ oz/3 tbsp light muscovado sugar
4 tbsp golden (light corn) syrup
2 tbsp milk
1 tbsp cocoa powder
40 g/1½ oz dark chocolate
50 g/1¾ oz pecan nuts, finely chopped

CAKE:
100 g/3½ oz/generous ⅓ cup soft margarine
100 g/3½ oz/7 tbsp light muscovado sugar
125 g/4½ oz/1 cup self-raising flour
2 eggs
2 tbsp milk
1 tbsp golden (light corn) syrup

1 Lightly grease a 20 cm/8 inch ring tin (pan).

2 To make the fudge sauce, place the butter, sugar, syrup, milk and cocoa powder in a small pan and heat gently, stirring until combined.

3 Break the chocolate into pieces, add to the mixture and stir until melted. Stir in the chopped nuts. Pour into the base of the tin (pan) and leave to cool.

4 To make the cake, place all of the ingredients in a mixing bowl and beat until smooth. Carefully spoon the cake mixture over the chocolate fudge sauce.

5 Bake in a preheated oven, 180°C/350°F/Gas Mark 4, for 35 minutes or until the cake is springy to the touch.

6 Leave to cool in the tin (pan) for 5 minutes, then turn out on to a serving dish and serve.

COOK'S TIP

To make in the microwave, place the butter, sugar, syrup, milk and cocoa powder for the sauce in a microwave-proof bowl. Cook on high for 2 minutes, stirring twice. Stir in the chocolate until melted, then add the nuts. Pour into a 1.1 litre/2 pint/5 cup microwave-proof ring mould (mold). Make the cake and cook on high for 3–4 minutes until just dry on top; stand for 5 minutes.

2

3

4

Chocolate Meringue Pie

Serves 6

INGREDIENTS

225 g/8 oz dark chocolate digestive biscuits (graham crackers)
50 g/1¾ oz/4 tbsp butter

FILLING:
3 egg yolks
50 g/1¾ oz/4 tbsp caster (superfine) sugar
4 tbsp cornflour (cornstarch)
600 ml/1 pint/2½ cups milk
100 g/3½ oz dark chocolate, melted

MERINGUE:
2 egg whites
100 g/3½ oz/7 tbsp caster (superfine) sugar
¼ tsp vanilla flavouring (extract)

1 Place the digestive biscuits (graham crackers) in a plastic bag and crush with a rolling pin. Pour into a mixing bowl. Melt the butter and stir it into the biscuit (cracker) crumbs until well mixed. Press the biscuit mixture firmly into the base and up the sides of a 23 cm/9 inch flan tin (pan) or dish.

2 To make the filling, beat the egg yolks, caster (superfine) sugar and cornflour (cornstarch) in a large bowl until they form a smooth paste, adding a little of the milk if necessary. Heat the milk until almost boiling, then slowly pour it on to the egg mixture, whisking well.

3 Return the mixture to the saucepan and cook gently, whisking constantly until it thickens. Remove from the heat. Whisk in the melted chocolate, then pour it on to the digestive biscuit (graham cracker) base.

4 To make the meringue, whisk the egg whites in a large mixing bowl until standing in soft peaks. Gradually whisk in about two-thirds of the sugar until the mixture is stiff and glossy. Fold in the remaining sugar and vanilla flavouring (extract).

5 Spread the meringue over the filling, swirling the surface with the back of a spoon to give it an attractive finish. Bake in the centre of a preheated oven, 170°C/ 375°F/Gas Mark 3, for 30 minutes or until the meringue is golden. Serve hot or just warm.

Chocolate Apple Pie

Serves 6

INGREDIENTS

CHOCOLATE PASTRY:
4 tbsp cocoa powder
200 g/7 oz/1¾ cups plain (all-purpose) flour
2 egg yolks
100 g/3½ oz/¾ cup softened butter
50 g/1¾ oz/4 tbsp caster (superfine) sugar
few drops of vanilla flavouring (extract)
cold water, to mix

FILLING:
750 g/1 lb/10 oz cooking apples
25 g/1 oz/2 tbsp butter
½ tsp ground cinnamon
50 g/1¾ oz/¾ cup dark chocolate chips
a little egg white, beaten
½ tsp caster (superfine) sugar
whipped cream or vanilla ice cream, to serve

1 To make the pastry, sieve (strain) the cocoa powder and flour into a mixing bowl and rub in the butter until the mixture resembles fine breadcrumbs. Stir in the sugar. Add the egg yolk, vanilla flavouring (extract) and enough water to mix to a dough.

2 Roll out the dough on a lightly floured surface and use to line a deep 20 cm/8 inch flan or cake tin (pan). Chill for 30 minutes. Roll out any trimmings and cut out some pastry leaves to decorate the top of the pie.

3 Peel, core and thickly slice the apples. Place half of the apple slices in a saucepan with the butter and cinnamon and cook over a gently heat, stirring occasionally until the apples soften.

4 Stir in the uncooked apple slices, leave to cool slightly, then stir in the chocolate chips. Prick the base of the pastry case (pie shell) and pile the apple mixture into it. Arrange the pastry leaves on top. Brush the leaves with a little egg white and sprinkle with caster (superfine) sugar.

5 Bake in a preheated oven, 180°C/350°F/Gas Mark 4, for 35 minutes until the pastry is crisp. Serve warm or cold, with whipped cream or vanilla ice cream.

3

4

4

Chocolate Pear & Almond Flan

Serves 6

INGREDIENTS

100 g/3½ oz/¾ cup plain (all-purpose) flour
25 g/1 oz/¼ cup ground almonds
60 g/2 oz/¼ cup block margarine
about 3 tbsp water

FILLING:
400 g/14 oz can pear halves, in natural juice
50 g/1¾ oz/4 tbsp butter
50 g/1¾ oz/4 tbsp caster (superfine) sugar
2 eggs, beaten
100 g/3½ oz/1 cup ground almonds
2 tbsp cocoa powder
few drops of almond flavouring (extract)
icing (confectioners') sugar, to dust

CHOCOLATE SAUCE:
50 g/1¾ oz/4 tbsp caster (superfine) sugar
3 tbsp golden (light corn) syrup
100 ml/3 fl oz/⅓ cup water
175 g/6 oz dark chocolate, broken into pieces
25 g/1 oz/2 tbsp butter

1 Lightly grease a 20 cm/8 inch flan tin (pan). Sieve (strain) the flour into a mixing bowl and stir in the almonds. Rub in the margarine with your fingertips until the mixture resembles breadcrumbs. Add enough water to mix to a soft dough. Cover, chill in the freezer for 10 minutes, then roll out and use to line the tin (pan). Prick the base and chill.

2 To make the filling, drain the pears well. Beat the butter and sugar until light and fluffy. Beat in the eggs. Fold in the almonds, cocoa powder and flavouring (extract). Spread the chocolate mixture in the pastry case (pie shell) and arrange the pears on top, pressing down lightly. Bake in the centre of a preheated oven, 200°C/400°F/Gas Mark 6, for 30 minutes or until the filling has risen. Cool slightly and transfer to a serving dish, if wished. Dust with sugar.

3 To make the sauce, place the sugar, syrup and water in a pan and heat gently, stirring until the sugar dissolves. Boil gently for 1 minute. Remove from the heat, add the chocolate and butter and stir until melted. Serve with the flan.

Chocolate & Banana Pancakes

Serves 4

INGREDIENTS

3 large bananas
6 tbsp orange juice
grated rind of 1 orange
2 tbsp orange- or banana-flavoured liqueur

HOT CHOCOLATE SAUCE:
1 tbsp cocoa powder
2 tsp cornflour (cornstarch)
3 tbsp milk
40 g/1½ oz dark chocolate
15 g/½ oz/1 tbsp butter
175 g/6 oz/½ cup golden (light corn) syrup
¼ tsp vanilla flavouring (extract)

PANCAKES:
100 g/3½ oz/1 cup plain (all-purpose) flour
1 tbsp cocoa powder
1 egg
1 tsp sunflower oil
300 ml/½ pint/1¼ cups milk
oil, for frying

1 Peel and slice the bananas and arrange them in a dish with the orange juice and rind and the liqueur. Set aside.

2 Mix the cocoa powder and cornflour (cornstarch) in a bowl, then stir in the milk. Break the dark chocolate into pieces and place in a pan with the butter and golden (light corn) syrup. Heat gently, stirring until well blended. Add the cocoa mixture and bring to the boil over a gentle heat, stirring. Simmer for 1 minute, then remove from the heat and stir in the vanilla flavouring (extract).

3 To make the pancakes, sieve (strain) the flour and cocoa into a mixing bowl and make a well in the centre. Add the egg and oil. Gradually whisk in the milk to form a smooth batter. Heat a little oil in a heavy-based frying pan (skillet) and pour off any excess. Pour in a little batter and tilt the pan to coat the base. Cook over a medium heat until the underside is browned. Flip over and cook the other side. Slide the pancake out of the pan and keep warm. Repeat until all the batter has been used.

4 To serve, reheat the chocolate sauce for 1–2 minutes. Fill the pancakes with the bananas and fold in half or into triangles. Pour over a little chocolate sauce and serve.

Chocolate Apple Pancake Stack

Serves 4–6

INGREDIENTS

225 g/8 oz/2 cups plain (all-purpose) flour
$1\frac{1}{2}$ tsp baking powder
50 g/$1\frac{3}{4}$ oz/4 tbsp caster (superfine) sugar
1 egg
1 tbsp butter, melted
300 ml/$\frac{1}{2}$ pint/$1\frac{1}{4}$ cups milk
1 eating apple
50 g/$1\frac{3}{4}$ oz dark chocolate chips
Hot Chocolate Sauce or maple syrup, to serve

1 Sieve (strain) the flour and baking powder into a mixing bowl. Stir in the caster (superfine) sugar. Make a well in the centre and add the egg and melted butter. Gradually whisk in the milk to form a smooth batter.

2 Peel, core and grate the apple and stir it into the batter with the chocolate chips.

3 Heat a griddle or heavy-based frying pan (skillet) over a medium heat and grease it lightly. For each pancake, place about 2 tablespoons of the batter on to the griddle or pan (skillet) and spread to make a 7.5 cm/3 inch round.

4 Cook for a few minutes until you see bubbles appear on the surface of the pancake. Turn over and cook for a further 1 minute. Remove from the pan and keep warm. Repeat with the remaining batter to make about 12 pancakes.

5 To serve, stack 2 or 3 pancakes on an individual serving plate and serve with the hot chocolate sauce or maple syrup.

COOK'S TIP

To keep the cooked pancakes warm, pile them on top of each other with baking parchment in between to prevent them sticking to each other.

VARIATION

Milk chocolate chips can be used instead of the dark ones, if preferred.

Chocolate Fondue

Serves 6–8

INGREDIENTS

CHOCOLATE FONDUE:
225 g/8 oz dark chocolate
200 ml/7 fl oz/¾ cup double (heavy) cream
2 tbsp brandy

TO SERVE:
selection of fruit
white and pink marshmallows
sweet biscuits (cookies)

1 Break the chocolate into small pieces and place in a small saucepan with the double (heavy) cream.

2 Heat the mixture gently, stirring constantly until the chocolate has melted and blended with the cream.

3 Remove the pan from the heat and stir in the brandy.

4 Pour into a fondue pot or a small flameproof dish and keep warm, preferably over a small burner.

5 Serve with a selection of fruit, marshmallows and biscuits (cookies) for dipping. The fruit and marshmallows can be spiked on fondue forks, wooden skewers or ordinary forks for dipping into the chocolate fondue.

COOK'S TIP

To prepare the fruit for dipping, cut larger fruit into bite-size pieces. Fruit which discolours, such as bananas, apples and pears, should be dipped in a little lemon juice as soon as it is cut.

COOK'S TIP

It is not essential to use a special fondue set. Dish warmers which use a night light are just as good for keeping the fondue warm. If you do not have one, stand the fondue dish in a larger dish and pour in enough boiling water to come halfway up the fondue dish. Whichever method you use to keep your fondue warm, place it on a heatproof stand to protect the table.

Hot Chocolate Soufflé

Serves 4

INGREDIENTS

100 g/3½ oz dark chocolate
300 ml/½ pint/1¼ cups milk
25 g/1 oz/2 tbsp butter
4 large eggs, separated
1 tbsp cornflour (cornstarch)
50 g/1¾ oz/4 tbsp caster (superfine) sugar
½ tsp vanilla flavouring (extract)
100 g/3½ oz/⅔ cup dark chocolate chips
caster (superfine) and icing (confectioners') sugar, to dust

CHOCOLATE CUSTARD:
2 tbsp cornflour (cornstarch)
1 tbsp caster (superfine) sugar
450 ml/¾ pint/2 cups milk
50 g/1¾ oz dark chocolate

1 Grease an 850 ml/1½ pint/5 cup soufflé dish and sprinkle with caster (superfine) sugar. Break the chocolate into pieces.

2 Heat the milk with the butter in a pan until almost boiling. Mix the egg yolks, cornflour (cornstarch) and caster (superfine) sugar in a bowl and pour on some of the hot milk, whisking. Return it to the pan and cook gently, stirring constantly until thickened. Add the chocolate and stir until melted. Remove from the heat and stir in the flavouring (extract).

3 Whisk the egg whites until standing in soft peaks. Fold half of the egg whites into the chocolate mixture. Fold in the rest with the chocolate chips. Pour into the dish and bake in a preheated oven, 180°C/350°F/ Gas Mark 4, for 40–45 minutes until well risen.

4 Meanwhile, make the custard. Put the cornflour (cornstarch) and sugar in a small bowl and mix to a smooth paste with a little of the milk. Heat the remaining milk until almost boiling.
Pour a little of the hot milk on to the cornflour (cornstarch), mix well, then pour back into the pan. Cook gently, stirring until thickened. Break the chocolate into pieces and add to the custard, stirring until melted.

5 Dust the soufflé with sugar and serve immediately with the chocolate custard.

Chocolate Zabaglione

Serves 2

INGREDIENTS

4 egg yolks
50 g/1^3/4 oz/4 tbsp caster (superfine) sugar
50 g/1^3/4 oz dark chocolate
125 ml/4 fl oz/1 cup Marsala wine
cocoa powder, to dust

1 In a large glass mixing bowl, whisk together the egg yolks and caster (superfine) sugar until you have a very pale mixture, using electric beaters.

2 Grate the chocolate finely and fold into the egg mixture. Fold in the wine.

3 Place the mixing bowl over a saucepan of gently simmering water and set the beaters on the lowest speed or swop to a balloon whisk. Cook gently, whisking continuously until the mixture thickens; take care not to overcook or the mixture will curdle.

4 Spoon the hot mixture into warmed individual glass dishes and dust lightly with cocoa powder. Serve the zabaglione as soon as possible so that it is warm, light and fluffy.

COOK'S TIP

For an up-to-the minute serving idea, spoon the zabaglione into coffee cups and serve with amaretti biscuits to the side of the saucer.

COOK'S TIP

Make the dessert just before serving as the mixture will separate if left to stand.If it begins to curdle, you may be able to save it if you remove it from the heat immediately and place it in a bowl of cold water to stop the cooking. Whisk furiously until the mixture comes together.

1

2

3

Chocolate Mint Swirl

Serves 6

INGREDIENTS

300 ml/½ pint/1¼ cups double (heavy) cream
150 ml/¼ pint/⅔ cup creamy fromage frais
25 g/1 oz/2 tbsp icing (confectioners') sugar
1 tbsp crème de menthe
175 g/6 oz dark chocolate
chocolate, to decorate

1 Place the cream in a large mixing bowl and whisk until standing in soft peaks.

2 Fold in the fromage frais and icing (confectioners') sugar, then place about one-third of the mixture in a smaller bowl. Stir the crème de menthe into the smaller bowl. Melt the dark chocolate and stir it into the remaining mixture.

3 Place alternate spoonfuls of the 2 mixtures into serving glasses, then swirl the mixture together to give a decorative effect. Leave to chill until required.

4 To make the piped chocolate decorations, melt a small amount of chocolate and place in a paper piping bag.

5 Place a sheet of baking parchment on a board and pipe squiggles, stars or flower shapes with the melted chocolate. Alternatively, to make curved decorations, pipe decorations on to a long strip of baking parchment, then carefully place the strip over a rolling pin, securing with sticky tape. Leave the chocolate to set, then carefully remove from the baking parchment.

6 Decorate each dessert with piped chocolate decorations and serve. The desserts can be decorated and then chilled, if preferred.

COOK'S TIP

Pipe the patterns freehand or draw patterns on to baking parchment first, turn the parchment over and then pipe the chocolate, following the drawn outline.

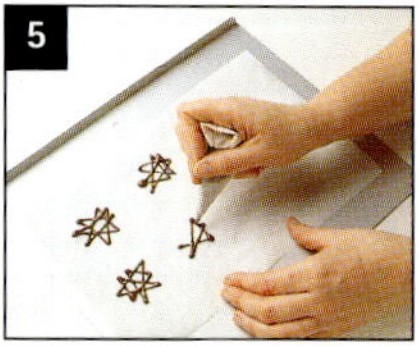

Chocolate Rum Pots

Serves 6

INGREDIENTS

225 g/8 oz dark chocolate
4 eggs, separated
75 g/2¾ oz/⅓ cup caster (superfine) sugar
4 tbsp dark rum
4 tbsp double (heavy) cream

TO DECORATE:
a little whipped cream
chocolate shapes

1 Melt the chocolate and leave to cool slightly.

2 Whisk the egg yolks with the caster (superfine) sugar in a bowl until very pale and fluffy; this will take about 5 minutes with electric beaters, a little longer with a balloon whisk.

3 Drizzle the chocolate into the mixture and fold in together with the rum and the double (heavy) cream.

4 Whisk the egg whites in a grease-free bowl until standing in soft peaks. Fold the egg whites into the chocolate mixture in 2 batches. Divide the mixture between 6 ramekins (custard pots), or other individual dishes, and leave to chill for at least 2 hours.

5 To serve, decorate with a little whipped cream and small chocolate shapes.

VARIATION

These delicious little pots can be flavoured with brandy instead of rum, if preferred.

COOK'S TIP

Make sure you use a perfectly clean and grease-free bowl for whisking the egg whites. They will not aerate if any grease is present as the smallest amount breaks down the bubbles in the whites, preventing them from trapping and holding air.

1
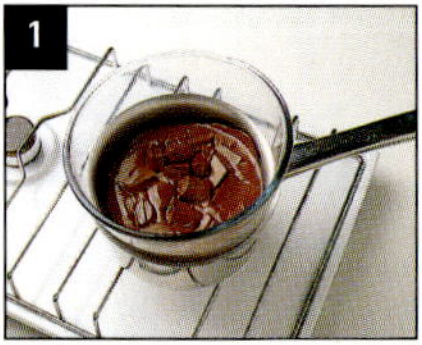

3

4

Chocolate & Vanilla Creams

Serves 4

INGREDIENTS

450 ml/16 fl oz/2 cups double (heavy) cream
75 g/2¾ oz/⅓ cup caster (superfine) sugar
1 vanilla pod
200 ml/7 fl oz/¾ cup crème fraîche
2 tsp gelatine
3 tbsp water
50 g/1¾ oz dark chocolate

MARBLED CHOCOLATE SHAPES:
a little melted white chocolate
a little melted dark chocolate

1 Place the cream and sugar in a saucepan. Cut the vanilla pod into 2 pieces and add to the cream. Heat gently, stirring until the sugar has dissolved, then bring to the boil. Reduce the heat and leave to simmer for 2–3 minutes.

2 Remove the pan from the heat and take out the vanilla pod. Stir in the crème fraîche.

3 Sprinkle the gelatine over the water in a small heatproof bowl and leave to go spongy, then place over a pan of hot water and stir until dissolved. Stir into the cream mixture. Pour half of this mixture into another mixing bowl.

4 Melt the dark chocolate and stir it into one half of the cream mixture. Pour the chocolate mixture into 4 individual glass serving dishes and chill for 15–20 minutes until just set. While it is chilling, keep the vanilla mixture at room temperature.

5 Spoon the vanilla mixture on top of the chocolate mixture and chill until the vanilla is set.

6 Meanwhile, make the shapes for the decoration. Spoon the melted white chocolate into a paper piping bag and snip off the tip. Spread some melted dark chocolate on a piece of baking parchment. Whilst still wet, pipe a fine line of white chocolate in a scribble over the top. Use the tip of a cocktail stick (toothpick)to marble the white chocolate into the dark. When firm but not too hard, cut into shapes with a small shaped cutter or a sharp knife. Chill the shapes until firm, then use to decorate the desserts.

1

6

6

Chocolate Hazelnut Pots

Serves 6

INGREDIENTS

2 eggs
2 egg yolks
15 g/½ oz/1 tbsp caster (superfine) sugar
1 tsp cornflour (cornstarch)
600 ml/1 pint/2½ cups milk
75 g/3 oz dark chocolate
4 tbsp chocolate and hazelnut spread

TO DECORATE:
grated chocolate or large chocolate curls

1 Beat together the eggs, egg yolks, caster (superfine) sugar and cornflour (cornstarch) until well combined. Heat the milk until almost boiling.

2 Gradually pour the milk on to the eggs, whisking as you do so. Melt the chocolate and hazelnut spread in a bowl set over a pan of gently simmering water, then whisk the melted chocolate mixture into the eggs.

3 Pour into 6 small ovenproof dishes and cover the dishes with foil. Place them in a roasting tin (pan). Fill the tin (pan) with boiling water to come halfway up the sides of the dishes.

4 Bake in a preheated oven, 170°C/325°F/Gas Mark 3, for 35–40 minutes until the custard is just set. Remove from the tin (pan) and cool, then chill until required. Serve decorated with grated chocolate or chocolate curls.

COOK'S TIP

This dish is traditionally made in little pots called pots de crème, which are individual ovenproof dishes with a lid. Ramekins (custard pots) are fine. The dessert can also be made in one large dish; cook for about 1 hour or until set.

COOK'S TIP

The foil lid prevents a skin forming on the surface of the custards.

2

3

3

Mocha Creams

Serves 4

INGREDIENTS

225 g/8 oz dark chocolate
1 tbsp instant coffee
300 ml/½ pint/1¼ cups boiling water
1 sachet (envelope) gelatine
3 tbsp cold water
1 tsp vanilla flavouring (extract)
1 tbsp coffee-flavoured liqueur (optional)
300 ml/½ pint/1¼ cups double (heavy) cream
4 chocolate coffee beans
8 amaretti biscuits (cookies)

1 Break the chocolate into small pieces and place in a saucepan with the coffee. Stir in the boiling water and heat gently, stirring until the chocolate melts.

2 Sprinkle the gelatine over the cold water and leave to go spongy, then whisk it into the hot chocolate mixture to dissolve it.

3 Stir in the vanilla flavouring (extract) and coffee-flavoured liqueur, if using. Leave to stand in a cool place until just beginning to thicken; whisk from time to time.

4 Whisk the cream until it is standing in soft peaks, then reserve a little for decorating the desserts and fold the remainder into the chocolate mixture. Spoon into serving dishes and leave to set.

5 Decorate with the reserved cream and coffee beans and serve with the biscuits (cookies).

COOK'S TIP

If preferred, the puddings can be made in one large serving dish.

VARIATION

To add a delicious almond flavour to the dessert, replace the coffee-flavoured liqueur with almond-flavoured (amaretto) liqueur.

Layered Chocolate Mousse

Serves 8

INGREDIENTS

3 eggs
1 tsp cornflour (cornstarch)
50 g/1¾ oz/4 tbsp caster (superfine) sugar
300 ml/½ pint/1¼ cups milk
1 sachet (envelope) gelatine
3 tbsp water
300 ml/½ pint/1¼ cups double (heavy) cream
75 g/2¾ oz dark chocolate
75 g/2¾ oz white chocolate
75 g/2¾ oz milk chocolate
chocolate caraque, to decorate

1 Line a 450 g/1 lb loaf tin (pan) with baking parchment. Separate the eggs, putting each egg white in a separate bowl. Place the egg yolks and sugar in a large mixing bowl and whisk until well combined. Place the milk in a pan and heat gently, stirring until almost boiling. Pour the milk on to the egg yolks, whisking.

2 Set the bowl over a pan of gently simmering water and cook, stirring until the mixture thickens enough to thinly coat the back of a wooden spoon.

3 Sprinkle the gelatine over the water in a small heatproof bowl and leave to go spongy. Place over a pan of hot water and stir until dissolved. Stir into the hot mixture. Leave to cool.

4 Whip the cream until just holding its shape. Fold into the egg custard, then divide the mixture into 3. Melt the 3 types of chocolate separately. Fold the dark chocolate into one egg custard portion. Whisk one egg white until standing in soft peaks and fold into the dark chocolate custard until combined. Pour into the prepared tin (pan) and level the top. Chill in the coldest part of the refrigerator until just set. Leave the remaining mixtures at room temperature.

5 Fold the white chocolate into another portion of the egg custard. Whisk another egg white and fold in. Pour on top of the dark chocolate layer and chill quickly. Repeat with the remaining milk chocolate and egg white. Chill until set. To serve, carefully turn out on to a serving dish and decorate with chocolate caraque.

Chocolate Marquise

Serves 6

INGREDIENTS

200 g/7 oz dark chocolate
100 g/3½ oz/generous ⅓ cup butter
3 egg yolks
75 g/2¾ oz/⅓ cup caster (superfine) sugar
1 tsp chocolate flavouring (extract) or 1 tbsp chocolate-flavoured liqueur
300 ml/½ pint/1¼ cups double (heavy) cream

TO SERVE:
crème fraîche
chocolate-dipped fruits
cocoa powder, to dust

1 Break the chocolate into pieces. Place the chocolate and butter in a bowl over a pan of gently simmering water and stir until melted and well combined. Remove from the heat and leave to cool.

2 Place the egg yolks in a mixing bowl with the sugar and whisk until pale and fluffy. Using an electric whisk running on low speed, slowly whisk in the cool chocolate mixture. Stir in the chocolate flavouring (extract) or chocolate-flavoured liqueur.

3 Whip the cream until just holding its shape. Fold into the chocolate mixture. Spoon into 6 small ramekins (custard pots), or individual metal moulds (molds). Leave to chill for at least 2 hours.

4 To serve, turn out the desserts on to individual serving dishes. If you have difficulty turning them out, dip the moulds (molds) into a bowl of warm water for a few seconds to help the marquise to slip out. Serve with chocolate-dipped fruit and crème fraîche and dust with cocoa powder.

COOK'S TIP

The slight tartness of the crème fraîche contrasts well with this very rich dessert. Dip the fruit in white chocolate to give a good colour contrast.

Iced White Chocolate Terrine

Serves 8–10

INGREDIENTS

2 tbsp granulated sugar
5 tbsp water
300 g/10½ oz white chocolate
3 eggs, separated
300 ml/½ pint/1¼ cups double (heavy) cream

1 Line a 450 g/1 lb loaf tin (pan) with foil or cling film (plastic wrap), pressing out as many creases as you can.

2 Place the granulated sugar and water in a heavy-based pan and heat gently, stirring until the sugar has dissolved. Bring to the boil and boil for 1–2 minutes until syrupy, then remove the pan from the heat.

3 Break the white chocolate into small pieces and stir it into the syrup, continuing to stir until the chocolate has melted and combined with the syrup. Leave to cool slightly.

4 Beat the egg yolks into the chocolate mixture. Leave to cool completely.

5 Lightly whip the cream until just holding its shape and fold it into the chocolate mixture.

6 Whisk the egg whites in a grease-free bowl until they are standing in soft peaks. Fold into the chocolate mixture. Pour into the prepared loaf tin (pan) and freeze overnight.

7 To serve, remove from the freezer about 10–15 minutes before serving. Turn out of the tin (pan) and cut into slices to serve.

COOK'S TIP

To make a coulis, place 225 g/8 oz soft fruit of your choice – strawberries, black or red currants, mango or raspberries are ideal – in a food processor or blender. Add 1–2 tbsp icing (confectioners') sugar and blend to form a purée. If the fruit contains seeds, push the purée through a sieve to remove them. Leave to chill until required.

1

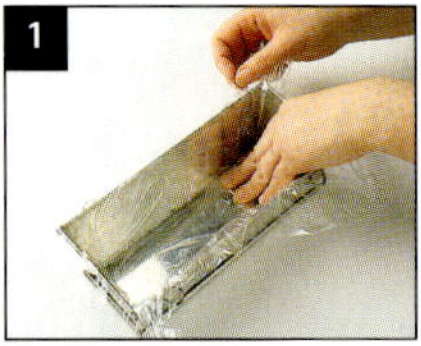

2

3

Chocolate Banana Sundae

Serves 4

INGREDIENTS

GLOSSY CHOCOLATE SAUCE:
60 g/2 oz dark chocolate
4 tbsp golden (light corn) syrup
15 g/½ oz/1 tbsp butter
1 tbsp brandy or rum (optional)

SUNDAE:
4 bananas
150 ml/¼ pint/⅔ cup double (heavy) cream
8–12 scoops of good quality vanilla ice cream
75 g/2¾ oz/⅔ cup flaked (slivered) or chopped almonds, toasted
grated or flaked chocolate, to sprinkle
4 fan wafer biscuits (cookies)

1 To make the chocolate sauce, break the chocolate into small pieces and place in a heatproof bowl with the syrup and butter. Heat over a pan of hot water until melted, stirring until well combined. Remove the bowl from the heat and stir in the brandy or rum, if using.

2 Slice the bananas and whip the cream until just holding its shape. Place a scoop of ice cream in the bottom of 4 tall sundae dishes. Top with slices of banana, some chocolate sauce, a spoonful of cream and a good sprinkling of nuts.

3 Repeat the layers, finishing with a good dollop of cream, sprinkled with nuts and a little grated or flaked chocolate. Serve with fan wafer biscuits (cookies).

VARIATION

Use half vanilla ice cream and half chocolate ice cream, if you like.

VARIATION

For a traditional banana split, halve the bananas lengthways and place on a plate with two scoops of ice cream between. Top with cream and sprinkle with nuts. Serve with the glossy chocolate sauce poured over the top.

1

2

2

Rich Chocolate Ice Cream

Serves 6–8

INGREDIENTS

ICE CREAM:
1 egg
3 egg yolks
90 g/3 oz/6 tbsp caster (superfine) sugar
300 ml/½ pint/1¼ cups full cream milk
250 g/9 oz dark chocolate
300 ml/½ pint/1¼ cups double (heavy) cream

TRELLIS CUPS:
100 g/3½ oz dark chocolate

1 Beat together the egg, egg yolks and caster (superfine) sugar in a mixing bowl until well combined. Heat the milk until almost boiling.

2 Gradually pour the hot milk on to the eggs, whisking as you do so. Place the bowl over a pan of gently simmering water and cook, stirring until the mixture thickens sufficiently to thinly coat the back of a wooden spoon.

3 Break the dark chocolate into small pieces and add to the hot custard. Stir until the chocolate has melted. Cover with a sheet of dampened baking parchment and leave to cool.

4 Whip the cream until just holding its shape, then fold into the cooled chocolate custard. Transfer to a freezer container and freeze for 1–2 hours until the mixture is frozen 2.5 cm/1 inch from the sides.

5 Scrape the ice cream into a chilled bowl and beat again until smooth. Re-freeze until firm.

6 To make the trellis cups, invert a muffin tray (pan) and cover 6 alternate mounds with cling film (plastic wrap). Melt the chocolate, place it in a paper piping bag and snip off the end.

7 Pipe a circle around the base of the mound, then pipe chocolate back and forth over it to form a trellis; carefully pipe a double thickness. Pipe around the base again. Chill until set, then lift from the tray (pan) and remove the cling film (plastic wrap). Serve the ice cream in the trellis cups.

3

7

7

Baked Chocolate Alaska

Serves 6

INGREDIENTS

2 eggs
50 g/1¾ oz/4 tbsp caster (superfine) sugar
40 g/1½ oz/generous ¼ cup plain (all-purpose) flour
15 g/½ oz/2 tbsp cocoa powder
3 egg whites
150 g/5½ oz/⅔ cup caster (superfine) sugar
1 litre/1¾ pint/4½ cups good quality chocolate ice cream

1 Grease an 18 cm/7 inch round cake tin (pan) and line the base with baking parchment.

2 Whisk the egg and the 4 tbsp sugar in a mixing bowl until very thick and pale. Sieve (strain) the flour and cocoa powder together and carefully fold in.

3 Pour into the prepared tin (pan) and bake in a preheated oven, 220°C/425°F/Gas Mark 7, for 7 minutes or until springy to the touch. Transfer to a wire rack to cool completely.

4 Whisk the egg whites in a grease-free bowl until they are standing in soft peaks. Gradually add the sugar, whisking until you have a thick, glossy meringue.

5 Place the sponge on a baking tray (cookie sheet) and pile the ice cream on to the centre in a heaped dome.

6 Pipe or spread the meringue over the ice cream, making sure the ice cream is completely enclosed. (At this point the dessert can be frozen, if wished.)

7 Return it to the oven, for 5 minutes until the meringue is just golden. Serve immediately.

COOK'S TIP

This dessert is delicious served with a blackcurrant coulis. Cook a few blackcurrants in a little orange juice until soft, purée and push through a sieve, then sweeten to taste with a little icing (confectioners') sugar.

White Chocolate Ice Cream in a Biscuit Cup

Serves 6

INGREDIENTS

ICE CREAM:
1 egg
1 egg yolk
40 g/1½ oz/3 tbsp caster (superfine) sugar
150 g/5½ oz white chocolate
300 ml/½ pint/1¼ cups milk
150 ml/¼ pint/⅔ cup double (heavy) cream

BISCUIT (COOKIE) CUPS:
1 egg white
50 g/1¾ oz/4 tbsp caster (superfine) sugar
15 g/½ oz/2 tbsp plain (all-purpose) flour, sieved (strained)
15 g/½ oz/2 tbsp cocoa powder, sieved (strained)
25 g/1 oz/2 tbsp butter, melted

1 Place baking parchment on 2 baking trays (cookie sheets). To make the ice cream, beat the egg, egg yolks and sugar. Break the chocolate into pieces, place in a bowl with 3 tbsp milk and melt over a pan of hot water. Heat the milk until almost boiling and pour on to the eggs, whisking. Place over a pan of simmering water and cook, stirring until the mixture thickens enough to coat the back of a wooden spoon. Whisk in the chocolate. Cover with dampened baking parchment and let cool.

2 Whip the cream until just holding its shape and fold into the custard. Transfer to a freezer container and freeze the mixture for 1–2 hours until frozen 2.5 cm/1 inch from the sides. Scrape into a bowl and beat again until smooth. Re-freeze until firm.

3 To make the cups, beat the egg white and sugar together. Beat in the flour and cocoa, then the butter. Place 1 tbsp of mixture on one tray (sheet); spread out to a 12.5 cm/5 inch circle. Bake in a preheated oven, 200°C/400°F/Gas Mark 6, for 4–5 minutes. Remove and mould over an upturned cup. Leave to set, then cool on a wire rack. Repeat to make 6 cups. Serve the ice cream in the cups.

Chocolate Horns with Ginger Cardamom Cream

Serves 6

INGREDIENTS

1 egg white
50 g/1¾ oz/4 tbsp caster (superfine) sugar
15 g/½ oz/2 tbsp plain (all-purpose) flour
15 g/½ oz/2 tbsp cocoa powder
25 g/1 oz/2 tbsp butter, melted
50 g/1¾ oz dark chocolate

CARDAMOM CREAM:
150 ml/¼ pint/⅓ cup double (heavy) cream
1 tbsp icing (confectioners') sugar
¼ tsp ground cardamom
pinch of ground ginger
25 g/1 oz stem ginger, chopped finely

1 Place a sheet of baking parchment on 2 baking trays (cookie sheets). Lightly grease 6 cream horn moulds (molds). To make the horns, beat the egg white and sugar in a mixing bowl until well combined. Sieve (strain) the flour and cocoa powder together, then beat into the egg followed by the melted butter.

2 Place 1 tablespoon of the mixture on to 1 baking tray (cookie sheet) and spread out to form a 12.5 cm/5 inch circle. Bake in a preheated oven, 200°C/400°F/Gas Mark 6, for 4–5 minutes.

3 Working quickly, remove the biscuit (cookie) with a palette knife (spatula) and wrap around the cream horn mould (mold) to form a cone. Leave to set, then remove from the mould (mold). Repeat with the remaining mixture to make 6 cones.

4 Melt the chocolate and dip the open edges of the horn in the chocolate. Place on a piece of baking parchment and leave to set.

5 To make the cardamom cream, place the cream in a bowl and sieve (strain) the icing (confectioners') sugar and ground spices over the surface. Whisk the cream until standing in soft peaks. Fold in the chopped ginger and use to fill the chocolate cones.

Chocolate Charlotte

Serves 8

INGREDIENTS

about 22 boudoir biscuits (lady-fingers)
4 tbsp orange-flavoured liqueur
250 g/9 oz dark chocolate
150 ml/¼ pint double (heavy) cream
4 eggs
150 g/5½ oz/⅔ cup caster (superfine) sugar

TO DECORATE:
150 ml/¼ pint/⅔ cup whipping cream
2 tbsp caster (superfine) sugar
½ tsp vanilla flavouring (extract)
large dark chocolate curls, chocolate leaves or chocolate shapes

1 Line the base of a Charlotte mould (mold) or a deep 18 cm/7 inch round cake tin (pan) with a piece of baking parchment.

2 Place the boudoir biscuits (lady-fingers) on a tray and sprinkle with half of the orange-flavoured liqueur. Use to line the sides of the mould (mold) or tin (pan), trimming if necessary to make a tight fit.

3 Break the chocolate into small pieces, place in a bowl and melt over a pan of hot water. Remove from the heat and stir in the double (heavy) cream.

4 Separate the eggs and place the whites in a large grease-free bowl. Beat the egg yolks into the chocolate mixture.

5 Whisk the egg whites until standing in stiff peaks, then gradually add the caster (superfine) sugar, whisking until stiff and glossy. Carefully fold the egg whites into the chocolate mixture in 2 batches, taking care not to knock out all of the air. Pour into the centre of the mould (mold). Trim the biscuits (lady-fingers) so that they are level with the chocolate mixture. Leave to chill for at least 5 hours.

6 To decorate, whisk the cream, sugar and vanilla flavouring (extract) until standing in soft peaks. Turn out the Charlotte on to a serving dish. Pipe cream rosettes around the base and decorate with chocolate curls and leaves.

2

3

5

Marble Cheesecake

Serves 10–12

INGREDIENTS

BASE:
225 g/8 oz toasted oat cereal
50 g/1¾ oz/½ cup toasted hazelnuts, chopped
50 g/1¾ oz/4 tbsp butter
25 g/1 oz dark chocolate

FILLING:
350 g/12 oz full fat soft cheese
100 g/3½ oz/7 tbsp caster (superfine) sugar
200 ml/7 fl oz/¾ cup thick yogurt
300 ml/½ pint/1¼ cups double (heavy) cream
1 sachet (envelope) gelatine
3 tbsp water
175 g/6 oz dark chocolate, melted
175 g/6 oz white chocolate, melted

1 Place the toasted oat cereal in a plastic bag and crush with a rolling pin. Pour the crushed cereal into a mixing bowl and stir in the hazelnuts.

2 Melt the butter and chocolate together over a low heat and stir into the cereal mixture, stirring until well coated.

3 Using the bottom of a glass, press the mixture into the base and up the sides of a 20 cm/8 inch springform tin (pan).

4 Beat together the cheese and sugar with a wooden spoon until smooth. Beat in the yogurt. Whip the cream until just holding its shape and fold into the mixture. Sprinkle the gelatine over the water in a heatproof bowl and leave to go spongy. Place over a pan of hot water and stir until dissolved. Stir into the mixture.

5 Divide the mixture in half and beat the dark chocolate into one half and the white chocolate into the other half.

6 Place alternate spoonfuls of mixture on top of the cereal base. Swirl the filling together with the tip of a knife to give a marbled effect. Level the top with a scraper or a palette knife (spatula). Leave to chill until set before serving.

COOK'S TIP

For a lighter texture, fold in 2 egg whites whipped to soft peaks before folding in the cream in step 4.

Banana & Coconut Cheesecake

Serves 10

INGREDIENTS

225 g/8 oz chocolate chip cookies
50 g/1¾ oz/4 tbsp butter
350 g/12 oz medium-fat soft cheese
75 g/2¾ oz/⅓ cup caster (superfine) sugar
50 g/1¾ oz fresh coconut, grated
2 tbsp coconut-flavoured liqueur
2 ripe bananas
125 g/4½ oz dark chocolate
1 sachet (envelope) gelatine
3 tbsp water
150 ml/¼ pint/⅔ cup double (heavy) cream

TO DECORATE:
1 banana
lemon juice
a little melted chocolate

1 Place the biscuits (cookies) in a plastic bag and crush with a rolling pin. Pour into a mixing bowl. Melt the butter and stir into the biscuit (cookie) crumbs until well coated. Firmly press the biscuit (cookie) mixture into the base and up the sides of a 20 cm/8 inch springform tin (pan).

2 Beat together the soft cheese and caster (superfine) sugar until well combined, then beat in the grated coconut and coconut-flavoured liqueur. Mash the 2 bananas and beat them in. Melt the dark chocolate and beat in until well combined.

3 Sprinkle the gelatine over the water in a heatproof bowl and leave to go spongy. Place over a pan of hot water and stir until dissolved. Stir into the chocolate mixture. Whisk the cream until just holding its shape and stir into the chocolate mixture. Spoon over the biscuit base and chill until set.

4 To serve, carefully transfer to a serving plate. Slice the banana, toss in the lemon juice and arrange around the edge of the cheesecake. Drizzle with melted chocolate and leave to set.

COOK'S TIP

To crack the coconut, pierce 2 of the 'eyes' and drain off the liquid. Tap hard around the centre with a hammer until it cracks; lever apart.

Chocolate Brandy Torte

Serves 12

INGREDIENTS

BASE:
250 g/9 oz gingernut biscuits
75 g/2¾ oz dark chocolate
100 g/3½ oz/generous ⅓ cup butter

FILLING:
225 g/8 oz dark chocolate
250 g/9 oz mascarpone cheese
2 eggs, separated
3 tbsp brandy
300 ml/½ pint/1¼ cups double (heavy) cream
50 g/1¾ oz/4 tbsp caster (superfine) sugar

TO DECORATE:
100 ml/3½ fl oz/½ cup double (heavy) cream
chocolate coffee beans

1 Crush the biscuits in a bag with a rolling pin or in a food processor. Melt the chocolate and butter together and pour over the biscuits. Mix well, then use to line the base and sides of a 23 cm/9 inch loose-bottomed fluted flan tin (pan) or springform tin (pan). Leave to chill whilst preparing the filling.

2 To make the filling, melt the dark chocolate in a pan, remove from the heat and beat in the mascarpone cheese, egg yolks and brandy.

3 Lightly whip the cream until just holding its shape and fold in the chocolate mixture.

4 Whisk the egg whites in a grease-free bowl until standing in soft peaks. Add the caster (superfine) sugar a little at a time and whisk until thick and glossy. Fold into the chocolate mixture, in 2 batches, until just mixed.

5 Spoon the mixture into the prepared base and chill for at least 2 hours. Carefully transfer to a serving plate. To decorate, whip the cream and pipe on to the cheesecake and add the chocolate coffee beans.

VARIATION

If chocolate coffee beans are unavailable, use chocolate-coated raisins to decorate.

1

3

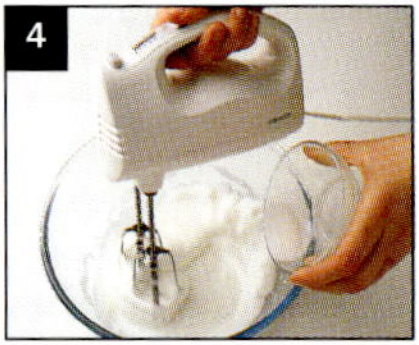
4

Chocolate Shortcake Towers

Serves 6

INGREDIENTS

SHORTCAKE:
225 g/8 oz/1 cup butter
75 g/2¾ oz/½ cup light muscovado sugar
50 g/1¾ oz dark chocolate, grated
275 g/10½ oz/2½ cups plain (all-purpose) flour

TO FINISH:
350 g/12 oz fresh raspberries
25 g/1 oz/2 tbsp icing (confectioners') sugar
3 tbsp milk
300 ml/½ pint/1¼ cups double (heavy) cream
100 g/3 oz white chocolate, melted
icing (confectioners') sugar, to dust

1 Lightly grease a baking tray (cookie sheet). To make the shortcake, beat together the butter and sugar until light and fluffy. Beat in the dark chocolate. Mix in the flour to form a stiff dough.

2 Roll out the dough on a lightly floured surface and stamp out eighteen 7.5 cm/3 inch rounds with a fluted biscuit (cookie) cutter. Place the rounds on the baking tray (cookie sheet) and bake in a preheated oven, 200°C/400°F/Gas Mark 6, for 10 minutes until crisp and golden. Leave to cool on the tray (sheet).

3 To make the coulis, set aside about 100 g/3½ oz of the raspberries. Purée the remainder in a food processor with the icing (confectioners') sugar, then push through a sieve to remove the seeds. Chill. Set aside 2 teaspoons of the cream. Whip the remainder until just holding its shape. Fold in the milk and the melted chocolate.

4 For each tower, spoon a little coulis on to a serving plate. Drop small dots of the reserved cream into the coulis around the edge of the plate and use a skewer to drag through the cream to make an attractive pattern.

5 Place a shortcake circle on the plate and spoon on a little of the chocolate cream. Top with 2 or 3 raspberries, top with another shortcake and repeat. Place a third biscuit on top. Dust with sugar.

Black Forest Trifle

Serves 6–8

INGREDIENTS

6 thin slices chocolate butter cream Swiss roll
2 x 400 g/14 oz can black cherries
2 tbsp kirsch
1 tbsp cornflour (cornstarch)
2 tbsp caster (superfine) sugar
425 ml/$^3/_4$ pint/1$^3/_4$ cups milk
3 egg yolks
1 egg
75 g/2$^3/_4$ oz dark chocolate
300 ml/$^1/_2$ pint/1$^1/_4$ cups double (heavy) cream, lightly whipped

TO DECORATE:
dark chocolate, melted
maraschino cherries (optional)

1 Place the slices of chocolate Swiss roll in the bottom of a glass serving bowl.

2 Drain the black cherries, reserving 6 tbsp of the juice. Place the cherries and the reserved juice on top of the cake. Sprinkle with the kirsch.

3 In a bowl, mix the cornflour (cornstarch) and caster (superfine) sugar. Stir in enough of the milk to mix to a smooth paste. Beat in the egg yolks and the whole egg.

4 Heat the remaining milk in a small saucepan until almost boiling, then gradually pour it on to the egg mixture, whisking well until it is combined.

5 Place the bowl over a pan of hot water and cook over a low heat until the custard thickens, stirring. Add the chocolate and stir until melted.

6 Pour the chocolate custard over the cherries and cool. When cold, spread the cream over the custard, swirling with the back of a spoon. Chill before decorating.

7 To make chocolate caraque, spread the melted dark chocolate on a marble or acrylic board. As it begins to set, pull a knife through the chocolate at a 45°C angle, working quickly. Remove each caraque as you make it and chill firmly before using.

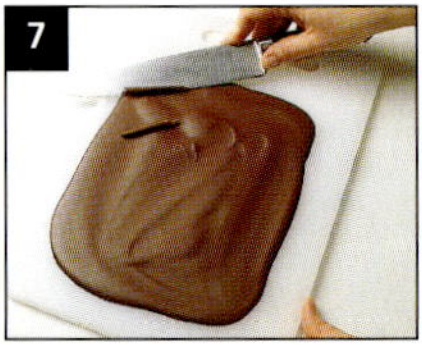

Champagne Mousse

Serves 4

INGREDIENTS

SPONGE:
4 eggs
100 g/3½ oz/7 tbsp caster (superfine) sugar
75 g/2¾ oz/⅔ cup self-raising flour
15 g/¼ oz/2 tbsp cocoa powder
25 g/1 oz/2 tbsp butter, melted

MOUSSE:
1 sachet (envelope) gelatine
3 tbsp water
300 ml/½ pint/1¼ cups champagne
300 ml/½ pint/1¼ cups double (heavy) cream
2 egg whites
75 g/2¾ oz/⅓ cup caster (superfine) sugar

TO DECORATE:
50 g/2 oz dark chocolate-flavoured cake covering, melted
fresh strawberries

1 Line a 37.5 x 25 cm/15 x 10 inch Swiss roll tin (pan) with greased baking parchment. Place the eggs and sugar in a bowl and whisk with electric beaters until the mixture is very thick and the whisk leaves a trail when lifted. If using a balloon whisk, stand the bowl over a pan of hot water whilst whisking. Sieve (strain) the flour and cocoa together and fold into the egg mixture. Fold in the butter. Pour into the tin (pan) and bake in a preheated oven, 200°C/ 400°F/Gas Mark 6, for 8 minutes or until springy to the touch. Cool for 5 minutes, then turn out on to a wire rack until cold. Line four 10 cm/4 inch baking rings with baking parchment. Line the sides with 2.5 cm/1 inch strips of cake and the base with circles.

2 To make the mousse, sprinkle the gelatine over the water and leave to go spongy. Place the bowl over a pan of hot water; stir until dissolved. Stir in the champagne.

3 Whip the cream until just holding its shape. Fold in the champagne mixture. Leave in a cool place until on the point of setting, stirring. Whisk the egg whites until standing in soft peaks, add the sugar and whisk until glossy. Fold into the setting mixture. Spoon into the sponge cases, allowing the mixture to go above the sponge. Chill for 2 hours. Pipe the cake covering in squiggles on a piece of parchment; leave to set. Decorate the mousses.

1

3

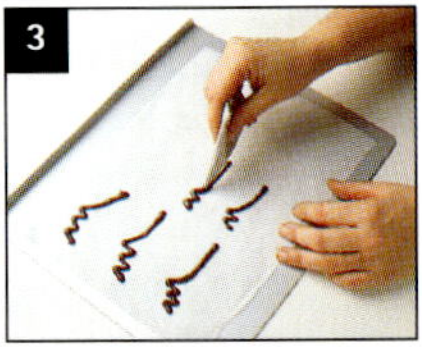
3

Chocolate Freezer Cake

Serves 8–10

INGREDIENTS

4 eggs
175 g/6 oz/¾ cup caster (superfine) sugar
100 g/3½ oz/¾ cup self-raising flour
40 g/1½ oz/3 tbsp cocoa powder
500 ml/½ litre/2¼ cups chocolate and mint ice cream
Glossy Chocolate Sauce

1 Lightly grease a 23 cm/9 inch ring tin (pan). Place the eggs and sugar in a large mixing bowl. Using an electric whisk if you have one, whisk the mixture until it is very thick and the whisk leaves a trail. If using a balloon whisk, stand the bowl over a pan of hot water whilst whisking.

2 Sieve (strain) the flour and cocoa together and fold into the egg mixture. Pour into the prepared tin (pan) and bake in a preheated oven, 180°C/350°F/Gas Mark 4, for 30 minutes or until springy to the touch. Leave to cool in the tin (pan) before turning out on to a wire rack to cool completely.

3 Rinse the cake tin (pan) and line with a strip of cling film (plastic wrap), overhanging slightly. Cut the top off the cake about 1 cm/½ inch thick and set aside.

4 Return the cake to the tin (pan). Using a spoon, scoop out the centre of the cake leaving a shell about 1 cm/½ inch thick .

5 Remove the ice cream from the freezer and leave to stand for a few minutes, then beat with a wooden spoon until softened a little. Fill the centre of the cake with the ice cream, levelling the top. Replace the top of the cake.

6 Cover with the overhanging cling film (plastic wrap) and freeze for at least 2 hours.

7 To serve, turn the cake out on to a serving dish and drizzle over some of the chocolate sauce in an attractive pattern, if you wish. Cut the cake into slices and serve the remaining sauce separately.

Mississippi Mud Pie

Serves 8–10

INGREDIENTS

225 g/8 oz/2 cups plain (all-purpose) flour
25 g/1 oz/¼ cup cocoa powder
150 g/5½ oz/⅔ cup butter
25 g/1 oz/5 tsp caster (superfine) sugar
about 2 tbsp cold water

FILLING:
175 g/6 oz/¾ cup butter
350 g/12 oz dark muscovado sugar
4 eggs, lightly beaten
4 tbsp cocoa powder, sieved (strained)
150 g/5½ oz dark chocolate
300 ml/½ pt single (light) cream
1 tsp chocolate flavouring (extract)

TO DECORATE:
425 ml/¾ pint/1¾ cups double (heavy) cream, whipped
thick bar of chocolate

1 To make the pastry (pie dough), sieve (strain) the flour and cocoa powder into a mixing bowl. Rub in the butter until the mixture resembles fine breadcrumbs. Stir in the sugar and enough cold water to mix to a soft dough. Chill for 15 minutes.

2 Roll out the dough on a lightly floured surface and use to line a deep 23 cm/ 9 inch loose-bottomed flan tin (pan) or ceramic flan dish. Line with foil or baking parchment and baking beans. Bake blind in a preheated oven, 190°C/375°F/ Gas Mark 5, for 15 minutes. Remove the beans and foil or paper and cook for a further 10 minutes until crisp.

3 To make the filling, beat the butter and sugar in a bowl and gradually beat in the eggs with the cocoa powder. Melt the chocolate and beat it into the mixture with the single (light) cream and the chocolate flavouring (extract).

4 Pour the mixture into the cooked pastry case and bake at 170°C/ 325°F/ Gas Mark 3 for 45 minutes or until the filling is set.

5 Leave to cool completely, then transfer the pie to a serving plate, if preferred. Cover with the whipped cream and leave to chill.

6 To make small chocolate curls, use a potato peeler to remove curls from the bar of chocolate. Decorate the pie and leave to chill.

Chocolate Fruit Tartlets

Serves 6

INGREDIENTS

250 g/9 oz/1¼ cups plain (all-purpose) flour
3 tbsp cocoa powder
150 g/5½ oz/⅔ cup butter
40 g/1½ oz/3 tbsp caster (superfine) sugar
2-3 tbsp water
50 g/1¾ oz dark chocolate
50 g/1¾ oz/½ cup chopped mixed nuts, toasted
350 g/12 oz prepared fruit
3 tbsp apricot jam or redcurrant jelly

1 Sieve (strain) the flour and cocoa powder into a mixing bowl. Cut the butter into small pieces and rub into the flour with your fingertips until the mixture resembles fine breadcrumbs.

2 Stir in the sugar. Add enough of the water to mix to a soft dough, about 1–2 tablespoons. Cover and chill for 15 minutes.

3 Roll out the pastry (pie dough) on a lightly floured surface and use to line six 10 cm/4 inch tartlet tins (pans). Prick the pastry (pie dough) with a fork and line the pastry cases (pie shells) with a little crumpled foil. Bake in a preheated oven, 190°C/375°F/Gas Mark 5, for 10 minutes.

4 Remove the foil and bake for a further 5–10 minutes until the pastry (pie dough) is crisp. Place the tins (pans) on a wire rack to cool completely.

5 Melt the chocolate. Spread out the chopped nuts on a plate. Remove the pastry cases (pie shells) from the tins (pans). Spread melted chocolate on the rims, then dip in the nuts. Leave to set.

6 Arrange the fruit in the tartlet cases (shells). Melt the apricot jam or redcurrant jelly with the remaining 1 tablespoon of water and brush it over the fruit. Chill the tartlets until required.

VARIATION

If liked, you can fill the cases with a little sweetened cream before topping with the fruit. For a chocolate-flavoured filling, blend 225 g/8 oz chocolate hazelnut spread with 5 tablespoons of thick yogurt or whipped cream.

Profiteroles with Banana Cream

Serves 4–6

INGREDIENTS

CHOUX PASTRY (PIE DOUGH):
150 ml/¼ pint/⅔ cup water
60 g/2 oz/¼ cup butter
90 g/3 oz/¾ cup strong plain (all-purpose) flour, sieved (strained)
2 eggs

CHOCOLATE SAUCE:
100 g/3½ oz dark chocolate, broken into pieces
2 tbsp water
50 g/1¾ oz/4 tbsp icing (confectioners') sugar
25 g/1 oz/2 tbsp unsalted butter

FILLING:
300 ml/½ pint/1¼ cups double (heavy) cream
1 banana
25 g/1 oz/2 tbsp icing (confectioners') sugar
2 tbsp banana-flavoured liqueur

1 Lightly grease a baking tray (cookie sheet) and sprinkle with a little water. To make the pastry, place the water in a pan. Cut the butter into small pieces and add to the pan. Heat gently until the butter melts, then bring to a rolling boil. Remove the pan from the heat and add the flour in one go, beating well until the mixture leaves the sides of the pan and forms a ball. Leave to cool slightly, then gradually beat in the eggs to form a smooth, glossy mixture. Spoon the paste into a large piping bag fitted with a 1 cm/½ inch plain nozzle (tip).

2 Pipe about 18 small balls of the paste on to the baking tray (cookie sheet), allowing enough room for them to expand during cooking. Bake in a preheated oven, 220°C/425°F/Gas Mark 7, for 15–20 minutes until crisp and golden. Remove from the oven and make a small slit in each one for steam to escape. Cool on a wire rack.

3 To make the sauce, place all the ingredients in a heatproof bowl, set over a pan of simmering water and heat until combined to make a smooth sauce, stirring.

4 To make the filling, whip the cream until standing in soft peaks. Mash the banana with the sugar and liqueur. Fold into the cream. Place in a piping bag fitted with a 1 cm/½ inch plain nozzle (tip) and pipe into the profiteroles. Serve with the sauce poured over.

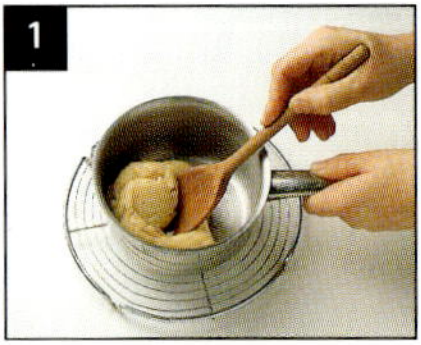
1

1

2

Chocolate Mousse

Serves 8

INGREDIENTS

100 g/3½ oz dark chocolate, melted
300 ml/½ pint/1 ¼ cups natural (unsweetened) yogurt
150 ml/ ¼ pint/ ⅔ cup quark
4 tbsp caster (superfine) sugar
1 tbsp orange juice
1 tbsp brandy
1½ tsp gelozone
9 tbsp cold water
2 large egg whites
coarsely grated dark and white chocolate and orange zest, to decorate

1 Put the melted chocolate, natural (unsweetened) yogurt, quark, caster (superfine) sugar, orange juice and brandy in a food processor and blend for 30 seconds. Transfer the mixture to a large bowl.

2 Sprinkle the gelozone over the water and stir until dissolved.

3 In a small saucepan, bring the gelozone and water to the boil for 2 minutes. Leave to cool slightly, then stir into the chocolate mixture.

4 Whisk the egg whites until stiff peaks form and fold into the chocolate mixture using a metal spoon.

5 Line a 850 ml/1½ pint loaf tin (pan) with cling film (plastic wrap). Spoon the mousse into the tin (pan). Chill for 2 hours in the refrigerator until set. Turn the mousse out on to a plate, decorate and serve.

COOK'S TIP

For a quick fruit sauce, blend a can of mandarin segments in natural juice in a food processor and press through a sieve. Stir in 1 tbsp clear honey and serve with the mousse.

Tiramisu

Serves 6

INGREDIENTS

300 g/10½ oz dark chocolate
400 g/14 oz mascarpone cheese
150 ml/5 fl oz/⅔ cup double (heavy) cream, whipped until it just holds its shape
400 ml/14 fl oz black coffee with 50 g/1¾ oz caster (superfine) sugar, cooled
6 tbsp dark rum or brandy
36 sponge fingers (lady-fingers), about 400 g/14 oz
cocoa powder, to dust

1 Melt the chocolate in a bowl set over a saucepan of simmering water, stirring occasionally. Leave the chocolate to cool slightly, then stir it into the mascarpone and cream.

2 Mix the coffee and rum together in a bowl. Dip the sponge fingers (lady-fingers) into the mixture briefly so that they absorb the liquid but do not become soggy.

3 Place 3 sponge fingers (lady-fingers) on 3 serving plates.

4 Spoon a layer of the mascarpone and chocolate mixture over the sponge fingers (lady-fingers).

5 Place 3 more sponge fingers (lady-fingers) on top of the mascarpone layer. Spread another layer of mascarpone and chocolate mixture and place 3 more sponge fingers (lady-fingers) on top.

6 Leave the tiramisu to chill in the refrigerator for at least 1 hour. Dust with a little cocoa powder just before serving.

COOK'S TIP

Tiramisu can also be served semi-frozen, like icecream. Freeze the tiramisu for 2 hours and serve immediately as it defrosts very quickly.

VARIATION

Try adding 50 g/1¾ oz toasted, chopped hazelnuts to the chocolate cream mixture in step 1, if you prefer.

1

1

2

Rich Chocolate Loaf

Makes 16 Slices

INGREDIENTS

150 g/5½ oz dark chocolate
75 g/2¾ oz/6 tbsp butter, unsalted
1 x 210 g/7¼ oz tin condensed milk
2 tsp cinnamon
75 g/2¾ oz almonds
75 g/2¾ oz amaretti biscuits, broken
50 g/1¾ oz dried no-need-to-soak apricots, roughly chopped

1 Line a 675 g/1½ lb loaf tin (pan) with a sheet of kitchen foil.

2 Using a sharp knife, roughly chop the almonds.

3 Place the chocolate, butter, milk and cinnamon in a heavy-based saucepan. Heat gently over a low heat for 3–4 minutes, stirring with a wooden spoon, until the chocolate has melted. Beat the mixture well.

4 Stir the almonds, biscuits and apricots into the chocolate mixture in the pan, stirring with a wooden spoon, until well mixed.

5 Pour the mixture into the prepared tin (pan) and leave to chill in the refrigerator for about 1 hour or until set.

6 Cut the rich chocolate loaf into slices to serve.

COOK'S TIP

To melt chocolate, first break it into manageable pieces. The smaller the pieces, the quicker it will melt.

COOK'S TIP

When baking or cooking with fat, butter has the finest flavour. If possible, it is best to use unsalted butter as an ingredient in puddings and desserts, unless stated otherwise in the recipe. 'Low-fat' spreads are not suitable for cooking.

1

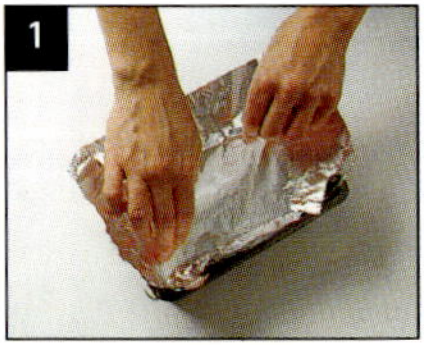

2

3

Chocolate & Tofu (Bean Curd) Cheesecake

Serves 12

INGREDIENTS

100 g/3½ oz/¾ cup plain (all-purpose) flour
100 g/3½ oz/¾ cup ground almonds
200 g/7 oz/¾ cup demerara (brown crystal) sugar
150 g/5½ oz/10 tbsp vegetarian margarine
675 g/1½ lb firm tofu (bean curd)
175 ml/6 fl oz/¾ cup vegetable oil
125 ml/4 fl oz/½ cup orange juice
175 ml/6 fl oz/¾ cup brandy
50 g/1¾ oz/6 tbsp cocoa powder, plus extra to decorate
2 tsp almond essence (extract)
icing (confectioners') sugar and Cape gooseberries, to decorate

1 Put the flour, ground almonds and 1 tablespoon of the sugar in a bowl and mix well. Rub the margarine into the mixture to form a dough.

2 Lightly grease and line the base of a 23 cm/9 inch spring-form tin (pan). Press the dough into the base of the tin (pan) to cover, pushing the dough right up to the edge of the tin (pan).

3 Roughly chop the tofu (bean curd) and put in a food processor with all of the remaining ingredients and blend until smooth and creamy. Pour over the base in the tin (pan) and cook in a preheated oven, 160°C/325°F/ Gas Mark 3, for 1–1¼ hours or until set.

4 Leave to cool in the tin (pan) for 5 minutes, then remove from the tin (pan) and chill in the refrigerator. Dust with icing (confectioners') sugar and cocoa powder. Decorate and serve.

Eve's Pudding

Serves 6

INGREDIENTS

450 g/1 lb cooking apples, peeled, cored and sliced
75 g/2¾ oz/⅓ cup granulated sugar
1 tbsp lemon juice
50 g/1¾ oz/⅓ cup sultanas (golden raisins)
75 g/2¾ oz/⅓ cup butter
75 g/2¾ oz/⅓ cup caster (superfine) sugar
1 egg, beaten
150 g/5½ oz/1¼ cups self-raising flour
3 tbsp milk
25 g/1 oz/¼ cup flaked (slivered) almonds
custard or double (heavy) cream, to serve

1 Grease an 850 ml/ 1½ pint/3½ cup ovenproof dish.

2 Mix the apples with the sugar, lemon juice and sultanas (golden raisins). Spoon the mixture into the greased dish.

3 Cream the butter and caster (superfine) sugar together until pale. Gradually add the egg.

4 Carefully fold in the self-raising flour and stir in the milk to give a soft, dropping consistency.

5 Spread the mixture over the apples and sprinkle with the flaked (slivered) almonds.

6 Bake in a preheated oven, 180°C/350°F/Gas Mark 4, for 40-45 minutes until the sponge is golden brown.

7 Serve the pudding hot, with custard or double (thick) cream.

COOK'S TIP

To increase the almond flavour of this pudding, add 25 g/1 oz/¼ cup ground almonds with the flour in step 4.

Queen of Puddings

Serves 8

INGREDIENTS

600 ml/1 pint/2½ cups milk
25 g/1 oz/6 tsp butter
225 g/ 8 oz/1¼ cups caster (superfine) sugar
finely grated rind of 1 orange
4 eggs, separated
75 g/2¾ oz/¾ cup fresh breadcrumbs
pinch of salt
6 tbsp orange marmalade

1 Grease a 1.5 litre/ 2¾ pint/6 cup ovenproof dish.

2 To make the custard, heat the milk in a pan with the butter, 50 g/ 1¾ oz/¼ cup of the caster (superfine) sugar and the grated orange rind until just warm.

3 Whisk the egg yolks in a bowl. Gradually pour the warm milk over the eggs, stirring.

4 Stir the breadcrumbs into the pan, then transfer the mixture to the prepared dish and leave to stand for 15 minutes.

5 Bake in a preheated oven, 180°C/350°F/Gas Mark 4, for 20-25 minutes until the custard has just set. Remove the custard from the oven but do not turn the oven off.

6 To make the meringue, whisk the egg whites with a pinch of salt until they stand in soft peaks. Whisk in the remaining sugar, a little at a time.

7 Spread the orange marmalade over the cooked custard. Top with the meringue, spreading it right to the edges of the dish.

8 Return the pudding to the oven and bake for a further 20 minutes until the meringue is crisp and golden.

3

6

7

Bread & Butter Pudding

Serves 6

INGREDIENTS

200 g/7 oz white bread, sliced
50 g/1¾ oz/10 tsp butter, softened
25 g/1 oz/2 tbsp sultanas (golden raisins)
25 g/1 oz mixed (candied) peel
600 ml/1 pint/2½ cups milk
4 egg yolks
75 g /2¾ oz/⅓ cup caster (superfine) sugar
½ tsp ground mixed spice (allspice)

1 Grease a 1.2 litre/ 2 pint/5⅓ cup ovenproof dish.

2 Remove the crusts from the bread (optional) and spread with butter. Cut into quarters.

3 Arrange half of the buttered bread slices in the prepared ovenproof dish. Sprinkle half of the sultanas (golden raisins) and mixed (candied) peel over the top of the bread.

4 Place the remaining bread slices over the fruit, and then sprinkle over the reserved fruit.

5 To make the custard, bring the milk almost to the boil. Whisk together the egg yolks and the sugar in a bowl, then pour in the warm milk.

6 Strain the warm custard through a sieve. Pour the custard over the bread slices.

7 Leave to stand for 30 minutes, then sprinkle with the ground mixed spice (allspice).

8 Place the ovenproof dish in a roasting tin (pan) half-filled with hot water.

9 Bake in a preheated oven, 200°C/400°F/ Gas Mark 6, for 40-45 minutes until the pudding has just set. Serve warm.

2

5

6

Plum Cobbler

Serves 6

INGREDIENTS

1 kg/2 1/4 lb plums, stones removed and sliced
100 g/3 1/2 oz/1/3 cup caster (superfine) sugar
1 tbsp lemon juice
250 g/9 oz/2 1/4 cups plain (all-purpose) flour
75 g/2 3/4 oz/1/3 cup granulated sugar
2 tsp baking powder
1 egg, beaten
150 ml/1/4 pint/2/3 cup buttermilk
75 g/2 3/4 oz/1/3 cup butter, melted and cooled
double (heavy) cream, to serve

1 Lightly grease a 2 litre/3 1/2 pint/8 cup ovenproof dish.

2 Mix together the plums, caster (superfine) sugar, lemon juice and 25 g/1 oz/1/4 cup of the plain (all-purpose) flour.

3 Spoon the mixture into the prepared dish.

4 Combine the remaining flour, granulated sugar and baking powder in a bowl.

5 Add the beaten egg, buttermilk and cooled melted butter. Mix gently to form a soft dough.

6 Place spoonfuls of the dough on top of the fruit mixture until it is almost covered.

7 Bake in a preheated oven, 190°C/375°F/Gas Mark 5, for 35-40 minutes until golden brown.

8 Serve the pudding piping hot, with double (heavy) cream.

COOK'S TIP

If you cannot find buttermilk, try using soured cream.

3

5

6

Blackberry Pudding

Serves 4

INGREDIENTS

450 g/1 lb blackberries
75 g/2¾ oz/⅓ cup caster (superfine) sugar
1 egg
75 g/2¾ oz/⅓ cup soft brown sugar
75 g/2¾ oz/⅓ cup butter, melted
8 tbsp milk
125 g/4 ½ oz self-raising flour

1 Grease an 850 ml/ 1½ pint/3½ cup ovenproof dish.

2 In a large bowl, gently mix the blackberries and caster (superfine) sugar until well combined.

3 Transfer the blackberry mixture to the prepared ovenproof dish.

4 Beat the egg and soft brown sugar in a separate bowl. Stir in the melted butter and milk.

5 Sieve (strain) the flour into the egg and butter mixture and fold together lightly to form a smooth batter.

6 Carefully spread the batter over the blackberry and sugar mixture in the ovenproof dish, covering the fruit.

7 Bake the pudding in a preheated oven, 180°C/350°F/Gas Mark 4, for about 25-30 minutes until the topping is firm and golden.

8 Sprinkle the pudding with a little sugar and serve hot.

VARIATION

You can add 2 tablespoons of cocoa powder to the batter in step 5, if you prefer a chocolate flavour.

Raspberry Shortcake

Serves 8

INGREDIENTS

175 g/6 oz/1½ cups self-raising flour
100 g/3½ oz/⅓ cup butter, cut into cubes
75 g/2 ¾ oz/⅓ cup caster (superfine) sugar
1 egg yolk
1 tbsp rose water
600 ml/1 pint/2 ½ cups whipping cream, whipped lightly
225 g/8 oz raspberries, plus a few for decoration

TO DECORATE:
icing (confectioners') sugar
mint leaves

1 Lightly grease 2 baking trays (cookie sheets).

2 To make the shortcakes, sieve (strain) the flour into a bowl.

3 Rub the butter into the flour with your fingers until the mixture resembles breadcrumbs.

4 Stir the sugar, egg yolk and rose water into the mixture and bring together to form a soft dough. Divide the dough in half.

5 Roll each piece of dough to a 20 cm/ 8 inch round and lift each one on to a prepared baking tray (cookie sheet). Crimp the edges of the dough.

6 Bake in a preheated oven, 190°C/375°F/Gas Mark 5, for 15 minutes until lightly golden. Transfer the shortcakes to a wire rack and leave to cool.

7 Mix the cream with the raspberries and spoon on top of one of the shortcakes. Top with the other shortcake round, dust with a little icing (confectioners') sugar and decorate with the extra raspberries and mint leaves.

COOK'S TIP

The shortcake can be made a few days in advance and stored in an airtight container until required.

Pavlova

Serves 6

INGREDIENTS

3 egg whites
pinch of salt
175 g/6 oz/¾ cup caster (superfine) sugar
300 ml/½ pint/1 ¼ cups double (heavy) cream, lightly whipped
fresh fruit of your choice (raspberries, strawberries, peaches, passion fruit, cape gooseberries)

1 Line a baking sheet (cookie sheet) with a sheet of baking parchment.

2 Whisk the egg whites with the salt in a large bowl until soft peaks form.

3 Whisk in the sugar a little at a time, whisking well after each addition until all of the sugar has been incorporated.

4 Spoon three-quarters of the meringue on to the baking sheet (cookie sheet), forming a round 20 cm/8 inches in diameter.

5 Place spoonfuls of the remaining meringue all around the edge of the round so they join up to make a nest shape.

6 Bake in a preheated oven, 140°C/275°F/Gas Mark 1, for 1¼ hours.

7 Turn the heat off, but leave the pavlova in the oven until completely cold.

8 To serve, place the pavlova on a serving dish. Spread with the lightly whipped cream, then arrange the fresh fruit on top.

COOK'S TIP

It is a good idea to make the pavlova in the evening and leave it in the turned-off oven overnight.

2

3

5

Sticky Chocolate Pudding

Serves 6

INGREDIENTS

125 g/4½ oz/½ cup butter, softened
150 g/5½ oz/¾ cup soft brown sugar
3 eggs, beaten
pinch of salt
25 g/1 oz cocoa powder
125 g/4½ oz/1 cup self-raising flour
25 g/1 oz dark chocolate, chopped finely
75 g/2¾ oz white chocolate, chopped finely

SAUCE:
150 ml/5 fl oz/⅔ cup double (heavy) cream
75 g/2¾ oz/⅓ cup soft brown sugar
25 g/1 oz/6 tsp butter

1 Lightly grease 6 individual 175 ml/ 6 fl oz/¾ cup pudding basins (molds).

2 Cream together the butter and sugar until pale and fluffy. Beat in the eggs a little at a time.

3 Sieve (strain) the salt, cocoa powder and flour into the creamed mixture and fold through the mixture. Stir the chopped chocolate evenly into the mixture.

4 Divide the mixture between the prepared pudding basins (molds). Lightly grease 6 squares of foil and use them to cover the basins (molds). Press around the edges to seal.

5 Place the basins (molds) in a roasting tin (pan) and add boiling water to come halfway up the sides of the basins (molds).

6 Bake in a preheated oven, 180°/350°F/Gas Mark 4, for 50 minutes, or until a skewer inserted into the centre comes out clean. Remove the basins (molds) from the tin and set aside.

7 To make the sauce, put the cream, sugar and butter into a pan and bring to the boil over a gentle heat. Simmer gently until the sugar has dissolved.

8 Turn the puddings out on to serving plates, pour the sauce over the top and serve immediately.

3

3

5

Chocolate Brownie Roulade

Serves 8

INGREDIENTS

150 g/5½ oz dark chocolate, broken into pieces
3 tbsp water
175 g/6 oz/¾ cup caster (superfine) sugar
5 eggs, separated
25 g/1 oz/2 tbsp raisins, chopped
25 g/1 oz pecan nuts, chopped
pinch of salt
300 ml/½ pint/1¼ cups double (heavy) cream, whipped lightly
icing (confectioners') sugar, for dusting

1 Grease a 30 × 20 cm/ 12 × 8 inch swiss roll tin (pan) and line with greased baking parchment.

2 Melt the chocolate with the water in a small saucepan over a low heat until the chocolate has just melted. Leave to cool.

3 Whisk the sugar and egg yolks for 2-3 minutes until thick. Fold in the cooled chocolate, raisins and pecan nuts.

4 Whisk the egg whites with the salt. Fold a quarter of the egg whites into the chocolate mixture, then lightly fold in the rest.

5 Transfer the mixture to the prepared tin (pan) and bake in a preheated oven, 180°C/350°F/ Gas Mark 4, for 25 minutes until risen and just firm to the touch. Leave to cool before covering with a sheet of non-stick baking parchment and a damp clean tea towel (dish cloth). Leave to cool completely.

6 Turn the roulade out on to another piece of baking parchment dusted with icing (confectioners') sugar and remove the lining paper.

7 Spread the cream over the roulade. Starting from a short end, roll the sponge away from you using the paper to guide you. Trim the ends of the roulade to make a neat finish and transfer to a serving plate. Leave to chill in the refrigerator until ready to serve. Dust with a little icing (confectioners') sugar before serving, if wished.

3

4

4

One Roll Fruit Pie

Serves 8

INGREDIENTS

PASTRY (PIE DOUGH):
175 g/6 oz/1½ cups plain (all-purpose) flour
100 g/3½ oz/⅓ cup butter, cut into small pieces
1 tbsp water
1 egg, separated
sugar cubes, crushed, for sprinkling

FILLING:
600 g/1½ lb prepared fruit (rhubarb, gooseberries, plums, damsons)
75 g/3 oz/6 tbsp soft brown sugar
1 tbsp ground ginger

1 Grease a large baking sheet (cookie sheet).

2 To make the pastry (pie dough), place the flour and butter in a mixing bowl and rub in the butter with your fingers. Add the water and work the mixture together until a soft pastry (pie dough) has formed. Wrap and leave to chill in the refrigerator for 30 minutes.

3 Roll out the chilled pastry (pie dough) to a round about 35 cm/14 inches in diameter.

4 Transfer the round to the centre of the greased baking sheet (cookie sheet). Brush the pastry (pie dough) with the egg yolk.

5 To make the filling, mix the prepared fruit with the brown sugar and ginger and pile it into the centre of the pastry.

6 Turn in the edges of the pastry (pie dough) all the way around. Brush the surface of the pastry (pie dough) with the egg white and sprinkle evenly with the crushed sugar cubes.

7 Bake in a preheated 200°C/400°F/ Gas Mark 6 oven for 35 minutes, or until golden brown. Serve warm.

2

4

6

Fruit Crumble Tart

Serves 8

INGREDIENTS

PASTRY (PIE DOUGH):
- 150 g/5 oz/1¼ cups plain (all-purpose) flour
- 25 g/1 oz/5 tsp caster (superfine) sugar
- 125 g/4½ oz/½ cup butter, cut into small pieces
- 1 tbsp water

FILLING:
- 250 g/9 oz raspberries
- 450 g/1 lb plums, halved, stoned and chopped roughly
- 3 tbsp demerara (brown crystal) sugar

TO SERVE:
- single (light) cream

TOPPING:
- 125 g/4½ oz/1 cup plain (all-purpose) flour
- 75 g/2¾ oz/⅓ cup demerara (brown crystal) sugar
- 100 g/3½ oz/⅓ cup butter, cut into small pieces
- 100 g/3½ oz chopped mixed nuts
- 1 tsp ground cinnamon

1 To make the pastry (pie dough), place the flour, sugar and butter in a bowl and rub in the butter with your fingers. Add the water and work the mixture together until a soft pastry (pie dough) has formed. Wrap and leave to chill for 30 minutes.

2 Roll out the pastry (pie dough) to line the base of a 24 cm/9½ inch loose-bottomed quiche/flan tin (pan). Prick the base of the pastry (pie dough) with a fork and leave to chill for about 30 minutes.

3 To make the filling, toss the raspberries and plums together with the sugar and spoon into the pastry case (pie shell).

4 To make the crumble topping, combine the flour, sugar and butter. Work the butter into the flour with your fingers until the mixture resembles coarse breadcrumbs. Stir in the nuts and cinnamon.

5 Sprinkle the topping over the fruit and bake in a preheated oven, 200°C/400°F/Gas Mark 6, for 20-25 minutes until golden. Serve the tart with single (light) cream.

Cheese & Apple Tart

Serves 8

INGREDIENTS

175 g/6 oz/1½ cups self-raising flour
1 tsp baking powder
pinch of salt
75 g/2¾ oz/⅓ cup soft brown sugar
100 g/3½ oz stoned dates, chopped
500 g/1lb 2 oz dessert apples, cored and chopped
50 g /1¾ oz/¼ cup walnuts, chopped
50 ml/2 fl oz/¼ cup sunflower oil
2 eggs
175 g/6 oz Red Leicester cheese, grated

1 Grease a 23 cm/9½ inch loose-bottomed quiche/flan tin (pan) and line with baking parchment.

2 Sieve (strain) the flour, baking powder and salt into a bowl. Stir in the brown sugar and the chopped dates, apples and walnuts. Mix together until well combined.

3 Beat the oil and eggs together and add the mixture to the dry ingredients. Stir until well combined.

4 Spoon half of the mixture into the tin (pan) and level the surface.

5 Sprinkle with the cheese, then spoon over the remaining cake mix, spreading it to the edges of the tin (pan).

6 Bake in a preheated oven, 180°C/350°F/Gas Mark 4, for 45-50 minutes or until golden and firm to the touch.

7 Leave to cool slightly in the tin. Serve warm.

COOK'S TIP

This is a deliciously moist tart. Any leftovers should be stored in the refrigerator and heated to serve.

Apple Tart Tatin

Serves 8

INGREDIENTS

125 g/4½ oz/½ cup butter
125 g/4½ oz/½ cup caster (superfine) sugar
4 dessert apples, cored and quartered
250 g/9 oz fresh ready-made shortcrust pastry (pie dough)
crème fraîche, to serve

1 Heat the butter and sugar in a 23 cm/9 inch ovenproof frying pan (skillet) over a medium heat for 5 minutes until the mixture begins to caramelize. Remove from the heat.

2 Arrange the apple quarters, skin side down, in the pan, taking care as the butter and sugar are very hot. Return the pan (skillet) to the heat and simmer for 2 minutes.

3 On a lightly floured surface, roll out the pastry (pie dough) to form a circle just a little larger than the pan.

4 Place the pastry (pie dough) over the apples, press down and tuck in the edges to seal the apples under the layer of pastry.

5 Bake in a preheated oven, 200°C/400°F/Gas Mark 6, for 20-25 minutes until golden. Remove from the oven and leave to cool for about 10 minutes.

6 Place a serving plate over the frying pan (skillet) and invert so that the pastry forms the base of the turned-out tart. Serve warm with crème fraîche.

VARIATION

Replace the apples with pears, if you prefer. Leave the skin on the pears, cut them into quarters and then remove the core.

Treacle Tart

Serves 8

INGREDIENTS

- 250 g/ 9 oz fresh ready-made shortcrust pastry
- 350 g/12 oz/1 cup golden (light corn) syrup
- 125 g/4½ oz/2 cups fresh white breadcrumbs
- 125 ml/4 fl oz/½ cup double (heavy) cream
- finely grated rind of ½ lemon or orange
- 2 tbsp lemon or orange juice
- custard, to serve

1 Roll out the pastry (pie dough) to line a 20 cm/8 inch loose-bottomed quiche/flan tin (pan), reserving the pastry (pie dough) trimmings. Prick the base of the pastry (pie dough) with a fork and leave to chill in the refrigerator.

2 Using a shaped pastry cutter or a sharp knife, cut out small shapes from the reserved pastry (pie dough) trimmings, such as leaves, stars or hearts, to decorate the top of the tart.

3 In a bowl, mix together the golden (light corn) syrup, breadcrumbs, cream and grated lemon or orange rind and lemon or orange juice.

4 Pour the mixture into the pastry case (pie shell) and decorate the edges of the tart with the pastry (pie dough) cut-outs.

5 Bake in a preheated oven, 190°C/375°F/Gas Mark 5, for 35-40 minutes or until the filling is just set.

6 Leave the tart to cool slightly in the tin. Turn out and serve with custard.

VARIATION

Use the pastry (pie dough) trimmings to create a lattice pattern on top of the tart, if preferred.

Apple & Mincemeat Tart

Serves 8

INGREDIENTS

PASTRY (PIE DOUGH):
150 g/5 oz/1¼ cups plain (all-purpose) flour
25 g/1 oz/5 tsp caster (superfine) sugar
125 g/4½ oz/½ cup butter, cut into small pieces
1 tbsp water

FILLING:
411 g/14½ oz jar mincemeat
3 dessert apples, cored
1 tbsp lemon juice
40 g/1½ oz/6 tsp golden (light corn) syrup
40 g/1½ oz/9 tsp butter

1 To make the pastry (pie dough), place the flour and caster (superfine) sugar in a large mixing bowl and rub in the butter with your fingertips.

2 Add the water and work the mixture together until a soft pastry (pie dough) has formed. Wrap and leave to chill in the refrigerator for 30 minutes.

3 On a lightly floured surface, roll out the dough and line a 24 cm/ 9½ inch loose-bottomed quiche/flan tin (pan). Prick the dough with a fork and leave to chill for 30 minutes.

4 Line the pastry case (pie shell) with foil and baking beans. Bake the case (shell) in a preheated oven, 190°C/375°F/ Gas Mark 5, for 15 minutes. Remove the foil and beans and cook for 15 minutes.

5 Grate the apples and mix with the lemon juice and mincemeat. Spoon into the baked pastry case (pie shell).

6 Melt the syrup and butter together and pour it over the mincemeat mixture.

7 Return the tart to the oven and bake for about 20 minutes or until firm. Serve warm.

VARIATION

Add 2 tbsp sherry to spice up the mincemeat, if you wish.

4

5

6

Custard Tart

Serves 8

INGREDIENTS

PASTRY (PIE DOUGH):
150 g/5½ oz plain (all-purpose) flour
25 g/1 oz/5 tsp caster (superfine) sugar
125 g/4½ oz/½ cup butter, cut into small pieces
1 tbsp water

FILLING:
3 eggs
150 ml /¼ pint/⅔ cup single (light) cream
150 ml/¼ pint/⅔ cup milk
freshly grated nutmeg

TO SERVE:
whipping cream

1 To make the pastry (pie dough), place the flour and sugar in a mixing bowl and rub in the butter.

2 Add the water and mix together until a soft pastry (pie dough) has formed. Wrap and leave to chill in the refrigerator for about 30 minutes.

3 Roll out the dough to form a round slightly larger than a 24 cm/ 9½ inch loose-bottomed quiche/flan tin (pan).

4 Line the tin (pan) with the dough, trimming off the edges. Prick the dough with a fork and leave to chill in the refrigerator for 30 minutes.

5 Line the pastry case (pie shell) with foil and baking beans.

6 Bake the tart in a preheated oven, 190°C/375°F/ Gas Mark 5, for 15 minutes. Remove the foil and baking beans and bake the pastry case (pie shell) for a further 15 minutes.

7 To make the filling, whisk together the eggs, cream, milk and nutmeg. Pour the filling into the prepared pastry case (pie shell). Transfer the tart to the oven and cook for 25-30 minutes or until just set. Serve with whipping cream, if wished.

Lemon Tart

Serves 8

INGREDIENTS

PASTRY (PIE DOUGH):
150 g/5½ oz/1¼ cups plain (all-purpose) flour
25 g/1 oz/5 tsp caster (superfine) sugar
125 g/4½ oz/½ cup butter, cut into small pieces
1 tbsp water

FILLING:
150 ml/¼ pint/⅔ cup double (heavy) cream
100 g/3½ oz/½ cup caster (superfine) sugar
4 eggs
grated rind of 3 lemons
12 tbsp lemon juice
icing (confectioners') sugar, for dusting

1 To make the pastry (pie dough), place the flour and sugar in a bowl and rub in the butter. Add the water and mix until a soft pastry (pie dough) has formed. Wrap and leave to chill for 30 minutes.

2 On a lightly floured surface, roll out the dough and line a 24 cm/9½ inch loose-bottomed quiche/flan tin (pan). Prick the pastry (pie dough) with a fork and leave to chill for 30 minutes.

3 Line the pastry case (pie shell) with foil and baking beans and bake in a preheated oven, 190°C/375°F/ Gas Mark 5, for 15 minutes. Remove the foil and beans and cook for a further 15 minutes.

4 To make the filling, whisk the cream, sugar, eggs, lemon rind and juice together. Place the pastry case (pie shell), still in its tin (pan), on a baking tray (cookie sheet) and pour in the filling.

5 Bake in the oven for about 20 minutes or until just set. Leave to cool, then lightly dust with icing (confectioners') sugar before serving.

Orange Tart

Serves 6–8

INGREDIENTS

PASTRY (PIE DOUGH):
- 150 g/5 oz/1¼ cups plain (all-purpose) flour
- 25 g/1 oz/5 tsp caster (superfine) sugar
- 125 g /4½ oz/½ cup butter, cut into small pieces
- 1 tbsp water

FILLING:
- grated rind of 2 oranges
- 9 tbsp orange juice
- 50 g/1¾ oz/⅞ cups fresh white breadcrumbs
- 2 tbsp lemon juice
- 150 ml/¼ pint/⅔ cup single (light) cream
- 50 g/1¾ oz/¼ cup butter
- 50 g/1¾ oz/¼ cup caster (superfine) sugar
- 2 eggs, separated
- pinch of salt

1 To make the pastry (pie dough), place the flour and sugar in a bowl and rub in the butter. Add the cold water and work the mixture together until a soft pastry (pie dough) has formed. Wrap and leave to chill for 30 minutes.

2 Roll out the dough and line a 24 cm/9½ inch loose-bottomed quiche/flan tin (pan). Prick the pastry (pie dough) with a fork and chill for 30 minutes.

3 Line the pastry case (pie shell) with foil and baking beans and bake in a preheated oven, 190°C/ 375°F/ Gas Mark 5, for 15 minutes. Remove the foil and beans and cook for 15 minutes.

4 To make the filling, mix the orange rind, orange juice and breadcrumbs in a bowl. Stir in the lemon juice and cream. Melt the butter and sugar over a low heat. Remove the pan from the heat, add the 2 egg yolks, salt and breadcrumb mixture and stir.

5 Whisk the egg whites with the salt until they form soft peaks. Fold them into the egg yolk mixture.

6 Pour the filling into the pastry case (pie shell). Bake in a preheated oven, 170°C/325°F/Gas 3, for about 45 minutes or until just set. Leave to cool slightly and serve warm.

Coconut Cream Tart

Serves 6–8

INGREDIENTS

PASTRY (PIE DOUGH):

150 g/5½ oz/1¼ cups plain (all-purpose) flour

25 g/1 oz/5 tsp caster (superfine) sugar

125 g/4½ oz/½ cup butter, cut into small pieces

1 tbsp water

FILLING:

425 ml/¾ pint/2 cups milk

125 g /4½ oz creamed coconut

3 egg yolks

125 g/4½ oz/½ cup caster (superfine) sugar

50 g/1¾ oz/½ cup plain (all-purpose) flour, sieved

25 g/1 oz/⅓ cup desiccated (shredded) coconut

25 g/1 oz glacé (candied) pineapple, chopped

2 tbsp rum or pineapple juice

300 ml/½ pint/1⅓ cups whipping cream, whipped

1 Place the flour and sugar in a bowl and rub in the butter. Add the water and work the mixture together until a soft pastry (pie dough) has formed. Wrap and leave to chill for 30 minutes.

2 Roll out the dough and line a 24 cm/ 9½ inch loose-bottomed quiche/flan tin (pan). Prick the pastry with a fork and leave to chill for 30 minutes. Line the pastry case (pie shell) with foil and baking beans and bake in a preheated oven, 190°C/375°F/Gas 5, for 15 minutes. Remove the foil and beans and cook for a further 15 minutes. Leave to cool.

3 To make the filling, bring the milk and creamed coconut to just below boiling point, stirring to melt the coconut.

4 Whisk the egg yolks with the sugar until fluffy. Whisk in the flour. Add the hot milk, stirring. Return the mixture to the pan and gently heat for 8 minutes until thick, stirring. Leave to cool.

5 Stir in the coconut, pineapple and rum and spread the filling in the pastry case (pie shell). Cover with the whipped cream and leave to chill.

1

3

4

Pine Kernel Tart

Serves 8

INGREDIENTS

PASTRY (PIE DOUGH):
150 g /5 oz/1¼ cups plain (all-purpose) flour
25 g/1 oz/5 tsp caster (superfine) sugar
125 g/4½ oz/½ cup butter, cut into small pieces
1 tbsp water

FILLING:
350 g/12 oz curd cheese
4 tbsp double (heavy) cream
3 eggs
125 g/4½ oz/½ cup caster (superfine) sugar
grated rind of 1 orange
100 g/3½ oz pine kernels (nuts)

1 To make the pastry (pie dough), place the flour and sugar in a bowl and rub in the butter with your fingers. Add the water and work the mixture together until a soft pastry (pie dough) has formed. Wrap and leave to chill for 30 minutes.

2 On a lightly floured surface, roll out the dough and line a 24 cm/ 9½ inch loose-bottomed quiche/flan tin (pan). Prick the pastry (pie dough) with a fork and leave to chill for 30 minutes.

3 Line the pastry case (pie shell) with foil and baking beans and bake in a preheated oven, 190°C/ 375°F/ Gas Mark 5, for 15 minutes. Remove the foil and beans and cook the pastry case (pie shell) for a further 15 minutes.

4 To make the filling, beat together the curd cheese, cream, eggs, sugar, orange rind and half of the pine kernels (nuts). Pour the filling into the pastry case (pie shell) and sprinkle over the remaining pine kernels (nuts).

5 Bake in the oven at 170°C/325°F/Gas Mark 3 for 35 minutes or until just set. Leave to cool before serving.

1

2

4

Mixed Peel & Nut Tart

Serves 8

INGREDIENTS

PASTRY (PIE DOUGH):
- 150 g/5½ oz/1¼ cups plain (all-purpose) flour
- 25 g/1 oz/5 tsp caster (superfine) sugar
- 125 g/4½ oz/½ cup butter, cut into small pieces
- 1 tbsp water

FILLING:
- 75 g/2¾ oz/⅓ cup butter
- 50 g /1¾ oz/ ¼ cup caster (superfine) sugar
- 75 g/2¾ oz set honey
- 200 ml/7 fl oz/1¾ cups double (heavy) cream
- 1 egg, beaten
- 200 g/7 oz mixed nuts
- 200 g/7 oz mixed (candied) peel

1 To make the pastry (pie dough), place the flour and sugar in a bowl and rub in the butter with your fingers. Add the water and work the mixture together until a soft pastry (pie dough) has formed. Wrap and leave to chill for 30 minutes.

2 On a lightly floured surface, roll out the dough and line a 24 cm/ 9½ inch loose-bottomed quiche/flan tin (pan). Prick the pastry (pie dough) with a fork and leave to chill for 30 minutes.

3 Line the pastry case (pie shell) with foil and baking beans and bake in a preheated oven, 190°C/ 375°F/Gas Mark 5, for 15 minutes. Remove the foil and baking beans and cook for a further 15 minutes.

4 To make the filling, melt the butter, sugar and honey in a small saucepan. Stir in the cream and beaten egg, then add the nuts and mixed (candied) peel. Cook over a low heat for 2 minutes until the mixture is a pale golden colour, stirring constantly.

5 Pour the filling into the pastry case (pie shell) and bake for 15-20 minutes or until just set. Leave to cool, then serve in slices.

1

2

4

Apricot & Cranberry Frangipane Tart

Serves 8-10

INGREDIENTS

PASTRY (PIE DOUGH):
150 g/5½ oz/1¼ cups plain (all-purpose) flour
125 g/4½ oz/½ cup caster (superfine) sugar
125 g/4½ oz/½ cup butter, cut into small pieces
1 tbsp water

FILLING:
200 g/7 oz/1 cup unsalted butter
200g/7 oz/1 cup caster (superfine) sugar
1 egg
2 egg yolks
40 g/1½ oz/6 tbsp plain (all-purpose) flour, sieved (strained)
175 g/6 oz/1⅔ cups ground almonds
4 tbsp double (heavy) cream
411 g/14½ oz can apricot halves, drained
125 g/4½ oz fresh cranberries

1 Place the flour and sugar in a bowl and rub in the butter. Add the water and work the mixture together until a soft pastry (pie dough) has formed. Wrap and leave to chill for 30 minutes.

2 On a lightly floured surface, roll out the dough and line a 24 cm/9½ inch loose-bottomed quiche/flan tin (pan). Prick the pastry (pie dough) with a fork and chill 30 minutes.

3 Line the pastry case (pie shell) with foil and baking beans and bake in a preheated oven, 190°C/375°F/ Gas Mark 5, for 15 minutes. Remove the foil and beans and cook for a further 10 minutes.

4 Cream together the butter and sugar until fluffy. Beat in the egg and egg yolks, and stir in the flour, almonds and cream.

5 Place the apricots and cranberries in the pastry case (pie shell) and spoon the filling on top.

6 Bake in the oven for about 1 hour, or until the topping is just set. Leave to cool slightly, then serve warm or cold.

White Chocolate & Almond Tart

Serves 8

INGREDIENTS

PASTRY (PIE DOUGH):
- 150 g/5 oz/1¼ cups plain (all-purpose) flour
- 25 g/1 oz/5 tsp caster (superfine) sugar
- 125 g/4½ oz/½ cup butter, cut into small pieces
- 1 tbsp water

FILLING:
- 150 g/5½ oz/½ cup golden (light corn) syrup
- 50 g/1¾ oz/10 tsp butter
- 75 g/2¾ oz/⅓ cup soft brown sugar
- 3 eggs, lightly beaten
- 100 g/3½ oz/½ cup whole blanched almonds, roughly chopped
- 100 g/3½ oz white chocolate, chopped roughly
- cream, to serve (optional)

1 To make the pastry (pie shell), place the flour and sugar in a mixing bowl and rub in the butter with your fingers. Add the water and work the mixture together until a soft pastry (pie dough) has formed. Wrap and leave to chill for 30 minutes.

2 On a lightly floured surface, roll out the dough and line a 24 cm/9½ inch loose-bottomed quiche/flan tin (pan). Prick the pastry (pie dough) with a fork and leave to chill for 30 minutes. Line the pastry case (pie shell) with foil and baking beans and bake in a preheated oven, 190°C/375°F/ Gas Mark 5, for 15 minutes. Remove the foil and baking beans and cook for a further 15 minutes.

3 To make the filling, gently melt the syrup, butter and sugar together in a saucepan. Remove from the heat and leave to cool slightly. Stir in the beaten eggs, almonds and chocolate.

4 Pour the chocolate and nut filling into the prepared pastry case (pie shell) and cook in the oven for 30-35 minutes or until just set. Leave to cool before removing the tart from the tin (pan). Serve with cream, if wished.

Mincemeat & Grape Jalousie

Serves 4

INGREDIENTS

500 g/1lb 2 oz fresh ready-made puff pastry (pie dough)
411 g/14½ oz jar mincemeat
100 g/3½ oz grapes, seeded and halved
1 egg, for glazing
demerara (brown crystal) sugar, for sprinkling

1 Lightly grease a baking tray (cookie sheet).

2 On a lightly floured surface, roll out the pastry (pie dough) and cut it into 2 oblongs.

3 Place one pastry (pie dough) oblong on to the prepared baking tray (cookie sheet) and brush the edges with water.

4 Combine the mincemeat and grapes in a bowl. Spread the mixture over the pastry (pie dough) on the baking tray (cookie sheet), leaving a 2.5 cm/1 inch border.

5 Fold the second pastry (pie dough) oblong in half lengthways, and carefully cut a series of parallel lines across the folded edge, leaving a 2.5 cm/1 inch border.

6 Open out the pastry (pie dough) oblong and lay it over the mincemeat. Seal down the edges of the pastry (pie dough) and press together well.

7 Flute and crimp the edges of the pastry (pie dough). Lightly brush with the beaten egg and sprinkle with demerara (brown crystal) sugar.

8 Bake in a preheated oven, 220°C/425°F/Gas 7, for 15 minutes. Lower the heat to 180°C/350°F/Gas Mark 4 and cook for a further 30 minutes until the jalousie is well risen and golden brown. Leave to cool on a wire rack before serving.

COOK'S TIP

For an enhanced festive flavour, stir 2 tbsp sherry into the mincemeat.

4

5

6

Pear Tarts

Makes 6

INGREDIENTS

250 g/9 oz fresh ready-made puff pastry
25 g/1 oz/8 tsp soft brown sugar
25 g/1 oz/6 tsp butter (plus extra for brushing)
1 tbsp stem (candied) ginger, finely chopped
3 pears, peeled, halved and cored
cream, to serve

1 On a lightly floured surface, roll out the pastry (pie dough). Cut out six 10 cm/4 inch rounds.

2 Place the circles on to a large baking tray (cookie sheet) and leave to chill for 30 minutes.

3 Cream together the brown sugar and butter in a small bowl, then stir in the chopped stem (candied) ginger.

4 Prick the pastry circles with a fork and spread a little of the ginger mixture on to each one.

5 Slice the pears halves lengthways, keeping the pears intact at the tip. Fan out the slices slightly.

6 Place a fanned-out pear half on top of each pastry (pie dough) circle. Make small flutes around the edge of the pastry (pie dough) circles and brush each pear half with melted butter.

7 Bake in a preheated oven, 200°C/400°F/Gas Mark 6, for 15-20 minutes until the pastry is well risen and golden. Serve warm with a little cream.

COOK'S TIP

If you prefer, serve these tarts with vanilla ice cream for a delicious dessert.

Crème Brûlée Tarts

Makes 6

INGREDIENTS

PASTRY (PIE DOUGH):
150 g/5 oz/$1\frac{1}{4}$ cups plain (all-purpose) flour
25 g/1 oz/5 tsp caster (superfine) sugar
125 g/$4\frac{1}{2}$ oz/$\frac{1}{2}$ cup butter, cut into small pieces.
1 tbsp water

FILLING:
4 egg yolks
50 g/ $1\frac{3}{4}$ oz/9 tsp caster (superfine) sugar
400 ml 14 fl oz/$1\frac{3}{4}$ cups double (heavy) cream
1 tsp vanilla flavouring (extract)
demerara (brown crystal) sugar, for sprinkling

1 Place the flour and sugar in a bowl and rub in the butter. Add the water and work the mixture together until a soft pastry (pie dough) forms. Wrap and chill for 30 minutes.

2 Roll out the dough to line six 10 cm/4 inch tart tins (pans). Prick the bottom of the pastry (pie dough) with a fork and leave to chill for 20 minutes

3 Line the pastry cases (pie shells) with foil and baking beans and bake in a preheated oven, 190°C/375°F/Gas Mark 5, for 15 minutes. Remove the foil and beans and cook for 10 minutes until crisp and golden. Leave to cool.

4 Beat the egg yolks and sugar until pale. Heat the cream and vanilla until just below boiling point, then add to the egg mixture, whisking constantly.

5 Place the mixture in a pan and bring to just below the boil, stirring until thick. Do not allow to boil or it will curdle.

6 Leave the mixture to cool slightly, then pour it into the tart tins (pans). Leave to cool and then leave to chill overnight.

7 Sprinkle the tarts with the sugar. Place under a preheated hot grill (broiler) for a few minutes. Leave to cool, then chill for 2 hours before serving.

2

4

7

Mini Frangipane Tartlets with Lime

Makes 12

INGREDIENTS

125 g/4½ oz/1 cup plain (all-purpose) flour
100 g/3½ oz/⅓ cup butter, softened
1 tsp grated lime rind
1 tbsp lime juice
50 g/1¾ oz/9 tsp caster (superfine) sugar
1 egg
25 g/1 oz/¼ cup ground almonds
50 g/1¾ oz/⅓ cup icing (confectioners') sugar, sieved (strained)
½ tbsp water

1 Reserve 5 teaspoons of the flour and 3 teaspoons of the butter and set aside until required.

2 Rub the remaining butter into the remaining flour, until the mixture resembles fine breadcrumbs. Stir in the lime rind, then the lime juice and bring together to form a soft dough.

3 On a lightly floured surface, roll out the dough thinly. Stamp out twelve 7.5 cm/3 inch rounds and line a bun tin (pan).

4 In a bowl, cream together the reserved butter with the caster (superfine) sugar.

5 Mix in the egg, then the ground almonds and the reserved flour.

6 Divide the mixture between the pastry cases (pie shells).

7 Bake in a preheated oven, 200°C/400°F/Gas Mark 6, for 15 minutes until set and lightly golden. Remove the tartlets from the tin (pan) and leave to cool.

8 Mix the icing (confectioners') sugar with the water. Drizzle a little of the icing over each tartlet and serve.

Baked Tofu Cheesecake

Serves 6

INGREDIENTS

125 g/4½ oz digestive biscuits (graham crackers), crushed
50 g/1¾ oz/10 tsp vegan margarine, melted
50 g/1¾ oz stoned dates, chopped
4 tbsp lemon juice
rind of 1 lemon
3 tbsp water
350 g/12 oz or 2 x 285 g packets firm tofu (bean curd)
150 ml/¼ pint/⅔ cup apple juice
1 banana, mashed
1 tsp vanilla flavouring (extract)
1 mango, peeled and chopped

1 Lightly grease an 18 cm/7 inch round loose-bottomed cake tin (pan).

2 Mix together the digestive biscuit (graham cracker) crumbs and melted margarine in a bowl. Press the mixture into the base of the prepared tin (pan).

3 Put the chopped dates, lemon juice, rind and water into a saucepan and bring to the boil. Simmer for 5 minutes until the dates are soft, then mash them roughly with a fork.

4 Place the mixture in a blender or food processor with the tofu (bean curd), apple juice, mashed banana and vanilla flavouring (extract) and process until the mixture is a thick, smooth purée.

5 Pour the tofu (bean curd) purée into the prepared biscuit (cracker) crumb base.

6 Bake in a preheated oven, 180°C/350°F/ Gas Mark 4, for 30-40 minutes until lightly golden. Leave to cool in the tin (pan), then chill thoroughly before serving.

7 Place the chopped mango in a blender and process until smooth. Serve it as a sauce with the chilled cheesecake.

2

3

4

Pineapple Upside-Down Cake

Serves 6

INGREDIENTS

432 g/15 oz can unsweetened pineapple pieces, drained and juice reserved
4 tsp cornflour (cornstarch)
50 g/1¾ oz/3 tbsp soft brown sugar
50 g/1¾ oz/10 tsp vegan margarine, cut into small pieces
125 ml/4 fl oz/½ cup water
rind of 1 lemon

SPONGE:
50 ml/2 fl oz/¼ cup sunflower oil
75 g/2¾ oz/⅓ cup soft brown sugar
150 ml/¼ pint/⅔ cup water
150 g/5½ oz/1¼ cups plain (all-purpose) flour
2 tsp baking powder
1 tsp ground cinnamon

1 Grease a deep 18 cm/7 inch cake tin (pan). Mix the reserved juice from the pineapple with the cornflour (cornstarch) until it forms a smooth paste. Put the paste in a saucepan with the sugar, margarine and water and stir over a low heat until the sugar has dissolved. Bring to the boil and simmer for 2-3 minutes until thickened. Leave to cool slightly.

2 To make the sponge, place the oil, sugar and water in a saucepan. Heat gently until the sugar has dissolved; do not allow it to boil. Set aside to cool. Sieve the flour, baking powder and cinnamon into a mixing bowl. Pour over the cooled sugar syrup and beat well to form a batter.

3 Place the pineapple pieces and lemon rind on the bottom of the tin (pan) and pour over 4 tablespoons of the pineapple syrup. Spoon the sponge batter on top.

4 Bake in a preheated oven, 180°C/350°F/Gas Mark 4, for 35-40 minutes until set and a fine metal skewer inserted into the centre comes out clean. Invert on to a plate, leave to stand for 5 minutes, then remove the tin (pan). Serve with the remaining syrup.

2

3

3

Date & Apricot Tart

Serves 6-8

INGREDIENTS

225 g/8 oz/$1\frac{3}{4}$ cups plain wholemeal (whole wheat) flour
50 g/$1\frac{3}{4}$ oz mixed nuts, ground
100 g/$3\frac{1}{2}$ oz/$\frac{1}{3}$ cup vegan margarine, cut into small pieces
4 tbsp water
225 g/8 oz dried apricots, chopped
225 g/8 oz stoned dates, chopped
425 ml /$\frac{3}{4}$ pint/2 cups apple juice
1 tsp ground cinnamon
grated rind of 1 lemon
soya custard, to serve (optional)

1 Place the flour and ground nuts in a bowl and rub in the margarine until the mixture resembles breadcrumbs. Stir in the water and bring together to form a dough. Wrap the dough and leave to chill for 30 minutes.

2 Meanwhile, place the apricots and dates in a saucepan with the apple juice, cinnamon and lemon rind. Bring to the boil, cover and simmer for 15 minutes until the fruit softens and can be mashed to a purée.

3 Reserve a small ball of pastry (pie dough) for making lattice strips. On a lightly floured surface, roll out the rest of the dough to form a round and use to line a 23 cm/9 inch loose-bottomed quiche tin (pan).

4 Spread the fruit filling over the base of the pastry (pie dough). Roll out the reserved pastry (pie dough) and cut into strips 1 cm/$\frac{1}{2}$ inch wide. Cut the strips to fit the tart and twist them across the top of the fruit to form a lattice pattern. Moisten the edges of the strips with water and seal them around the rim.

5 Bake in a preheated oven, 200°/400°F/Gas Mark 6, for 25-30 minutes until golden brown. Cut into slices and serve with soya custard, if using.

Fruit Crumble

Serves 6

INGREDIENTS

6 dessert pears, peeled, cored, quartered and sliced
1 tbsp stem (candied) ginger, chopped
1 tbsp molasses (dark muscovado sugar)
2 tbsp orange juice

TOPPING:
175 g/6 oz/1½ cups plain (all-purpose) flour
75 g/2¾ oz/⅓ cup vegan margarine, cut into small pieces
25 g/1 oz almonds, flaked (slivered)
25 g/1 oz/⅓ cup porridge oats
50 g/1¾ oz molasses (dark muscovado sugar)
soya custard, to serve

1 Lightly grease a 1 litre/2 pint/4½ cup ovenproof dish.

2 In a bowl, mix together the pears, ginger, molasses (dark muscovado sugar) and orange juice. Spoon the mixture into the prepared dish.

3 To make the crumble topping, sieve (strain) the flour into a mixing bowl and rub in the margarine with your fingers until the mixture resembles fine breadcrumbs. Stir in the flaked (slivered) almonds, porridge oats and molasses (dark muscovado sugar). Mix until well combined.

4 Sprinkle the crumble topping evenly over the pear and ginger mixture in the dish.

5 Bake in a preheated oven, 190°C/375°F/Gas Mark 5, for 30 minutes until the topping is golden and the fruit tender. Serve with soya custard, if using.

VARIATION

Stir 1 tsp ground mixed spice (allspice) into the crumble mixture in step 3 for added flavour, if you prefer.

Lemon Mascarpone Cheesecake

Serves 8

INGREDIENTS

50 g/1¾ oz/1½ tbsp unsalted butter
150 g/5½ oz ginger biscuits (cookies), crushed
25 g/1 oz stem ginger (candied), chopped
500 g/1 lb 2 oz mascarpone cheese
finely grated rind and juice of 2 lemons
100 g/3½ oz caster (superfine) sugar
2 large eggs, separated
fruit coulis (see Cook's Tip), to serve

1 Grease and line the base of a 25 cm/10 inch spring-form cake tin (pan) or loose-bottomed tin (pan).

2 Melt the butter in a pan and stir in the crushed biscuits (cookies) and chopped ginger. Use the mixture to line the tin (pan), pressing the mixture about 6 mm/¼ inch up the sides.

3 Beat together the cheese, lemon rind and juice, sugar and egg yolks until smooth.

4 Whisk the egg whites until they are stiff and fold into the cheese and lemon mixture.

5 Pour the mixture into the tin (pan) and bake in a preheated oven, at180°C/ 350°F/Gas Mark 4, for 35–45 minutes until just set. Don't worry if it cracks or sinks – this is quite normal.

6 Leave the cheesecake in the tin (pan) to cool. Serve with fruit coulis (see Cook's Tip).

COOK'S TIP

Fruit coulis can be made by cooking 400 g/14 oz fruit, such as blueberries, for 5 minutes with 2 tablespoons of water. Sieve the mixture, then stir in 1 tablespoon (or more to taste) of sifted icing (confectioners') sugar. Leave to cool before serving.

VARIATION

Ricotta cheese can be used instead of the mascarpone to make an equally delicious cheesecake. However, it should be sieved before use to remove any lumps.

Breads & Savouries

Freshly baked bread has never been easier to make, especially with the easy-blend yeasts available nowadays. In this chapter 6 g/$^1/_5$ oz sachets of easy-blend dried yeast have been used as it is easy to obtain, simple to use and gives good results. If you want to use fresh yeast, replace one sachet of easy blend yeast with 25 g/1 oz of fresh yeast. Blend the fresh yeast into the warm liquid and add 1 teaspoon of sugar. Add to the flour and continue as usual.

Always choose a strong white or brown flour for the bread recipes using yeast, it contains a high proportion of gluten, the protein which gives the dough its elasticity. Always knead the dough thoroughly – this can be done in an electric mixer with the dough hook attachment for about 5-8 minutes, but kneading by hand is most enjoyable and allows the cook the pleasure of relieving their aggression and stress upon the dough!

This chapter also includes a selection of savouries, including a tasty selection of pies, pastries and flans to create a whole medley of delicious dishes that can be used as part of a main meal.

Teacakes

Serves 12

INGREDIENTS

450 g/1 lb/4 cups strong white bread flour
1 sachet easy blend dried yeast
50 g/1¾ oz/9 tsp caster sugar
1 tsp salt
25 g/1oz/6 tsp butter, cut into small pieces
300 ml/½ pint/1¼ cups tepid milk
75 g/2¾ oz luxury dried fruit mix
honey, for brushing

1 Grease several baking trays (cookie sheets).

2 Sieve (strain) the flour into a large mixing bowl. Stir in the dried yeast, sugar and salt. Rub in the butter with your fingers until the mixture resembles fine breadcrumbs. Add the milk and mix all of the ingredients together to form a soft dough.

3 Place the dough on a lightly floured surface and knead for about 5 minutes (alternatively, you can knead the dough with an electric mixer with a dough hook).

4 Place the dough in a greased bowl, cover and leave to rise in a warm place for about 1-1½ hours until it has doubled in size.

5 Knead the dough again for a few minutes and knead in the fruit. Divide the dough into 12 rounds and place on the baking trays (cookie sheets). Cover and leave for a further 1 hour or until springy to the touch.

6 Bake in a preheated oven, 200°C/400°F/Gas Mark 6, for 20 minutes. Brush the teacakes with honey while still warm.

7 Leave the teacakes to cool on a wire rack before serving them split in half. Spread with butter and serve.

3

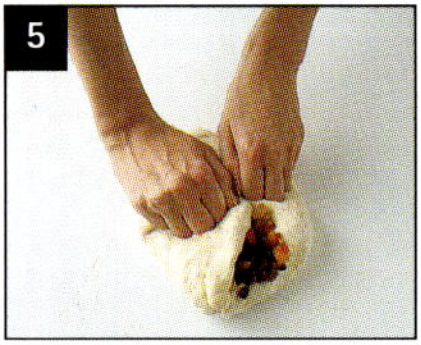
5

5

Cinnamon Swirls

Makes 12

INGREDIENTS

225 g/8 oz/2 cups strong white bread flour
$^{1}/_{2}$ tsp salt
1 sachet easy blend dried yeast
25 g/1 oz/6 tsp butter, cut into small pieces
1 egg, beaten
125 ml/4 fl oz/$^{1}/_{2}$ cup warm milk
2 tbsp maple syrup

FILLING:
50 g/1$^{3}/_{4}$ oz/10 tsp butter, softened
2 tsp ground cinnamon
50 g/1$^{3}/_{4}$ oz/3 tbsp soft brown sugar
50 g/1$^{3}/_{4}$ oz/$^{1}/_{3}$ cup currants

1 Grease a 23 cm/9 inch square baking tin (pan).

2 Sieve (strain) the flour and salt into a mixing bowl. Stir in the dried yeast. Rub in the butter with your fingers until the mixture resembles breadcrumbs. Add the egg and milk and mix everything together to form a dough.

3 Place the dough in a greased bowl, cover and leave in a warm place for about 40 minutes or until doubled in size.

4 Knead the dough for 1 minute to knock it back (punch down), then roll out to a rectangle 30 × 23 cm/12 × 9 inches.

5 To make the filling, cream together the butter, cinnamon and brown sugar until light and fluffy. Spread the filling over the dough, leaving a 2.5 cm/ 1 inch border. Sprinkle over the currants.

6 Roll up the dough like a swiss roll, starting at a long edge, and press down to seal. Cut the roll into 12 slices. Place them in the tin, cover and leave for 30 minutes.

7 Bake in a preheated oven, 190°C/375°F/ Gas Mark 5, for 20-30 minutes or until well risen. Brush with the syrup and leave to cool slightly before serving.

Cinnamon & Currant Loaf

Makes a 900 g/2 lb loaf

INGREDIENTS

350 g/12 oz/3 cups plain (all-purpose) flour
pinch of salt
1 tbsp baking powder
1 tbsp ground cinnamon
150 g/5½ oz/⅔ cup butter, cut into small pieces
125 g/4½ oz/¾ cup soft brown sugar
175 g/6 oz/¾ cup currants
finely grated rind of 1 orange
5-6 tbsp orange juice
6 tbsp milk
2 eggs, beaten lightly

1 Grease a 900 g/2 lb loaf tin and line the base with baking parchment.

2 Sieve (strain) the flour, salt, baking powder and ground cinnamon into a bowl. Rub in the butter pieces with your fingers until the mixture resembles coarse breadcrumbs.

3 Stir in the sugar, currants and orange rind. Beat the orange juice, milk and eggs together and add to the dry ingredients. Mix well together.

4 Spoon the mixture into the prepared tin. Make a slight dip in the middle of the mixture to help it rise evenly.

5 Bake in a preheated oven, 180°C/350°F/Gas Mark 4, for about 1-1 hour 10 minutes, or until a fine metal skewer inserted into the centre of the loaf comes out clean.

6 Leave the loaf to cool before turning out of the tin. Transfer to a wire rack and leave to cool completely before slicing.

COOK'S TIP

Once you have added the liquid to the dry ingredients, work as quickly as possible because the baking powder is activated by the liquid.

Orange, Banana & Cranberry Loaf

Serves 8-10

INGREDIENTS

175 g/6 oz/1½ cups self-raising flour
½ tsp baking powder
150 g/5½ oz/1 cup soft brown sugar
2 bananas, mashed
50 g/1¾ oz chopped mixed peel
25 g/1 oz chopped mixed nuts
50 g/1¾ oz dried cranberries
5-6 tbsp orange juice
2 eggs, beaten
150 ml/¼ pint/⅔ cup sunflower oil
75 g/2¾ oz icing (confectioners') sugar, sieved (strained)
grated rind of 1 orange

1 Grease a 900 g/2 lb loaf tin (pan) and line the base with baking parchment.

2 Sieve (strain) the flour and baking powder into a mixing bowl. Stir in the sugar, bananas, chopped mixed peel, nuts and cranberries.

3 Stir the orange juice, eggs and oil together until well combined. Add the mixture to the dry ingredients and mix until well blended. Pour the mixture into the prepared tin (pan).

4 Bake in a preheated oven, 180°C/350°F/Gas Mark 4, for about 1 hour until firm to the touch or until a fine skewer inserted into the centre of the loaf comes out clean.

5 Turn out the loaf and leave it to cool on a wire rack.

6 Mix the icing (confectioners') sugar with a little water and drizzle the icing over the loaf. Sprinkle the orange rind over the top. Leave the icing to set before serving the loaf in slices.

COOK'S TIP

This tea bread will keep for a couple of days. Wrap it carefully and store in a cool, dry place.

Banana & Date Loaf

Serves 6–8

INGREDIENTS

225 g/8 oz/2 cups self-raising flour
100 g/3½ oz/⅓ cup butter, cut into small pieces
75 g/2¾ oz/⅓ cup caster (superfine) sugar
125 g/4½ oz stoned dates, chopped
2 bananas, mashed roughly
2 eggs, beaten lightly
2 tbsp honey

1 Grease a 900 g/2 lb loaf tin (pan) and line the base with baking parchment.

2 Sieve (strain) the flour into a mixing bowl.

3 Rub the butter into the flour with your fingertips until the mixture resembles fine breadcrumbs.

4 Stir the sugar, chopped dates, bananas, beaten eggs and honey into the dry ingredients. Mix together to form a soft dropping consistency.

5 Spoon the mixture into the prepared loaf tin (pan) and level the surface with the back of a knife.

6 Bake in a preheated oven, 160°C/325°F/Gas Mark 3, for about 1 hour or until golden and a fine metal skewer inserted into the centre comes out clean.

7 Leave the loaf to cool in the tin (pan), then transfer to a wire rack.

8 Serve the loaf warm or cold, cut into thick slices.

COOK'S TIP

This tea bread will keep for several days if stored in an airtight container and kept in a cool, dry place.

Crown Loaf

Makes one loaf

INGREDIENTS

225 g/8 oz/2 cups strong white bread flour
½ tsp salt
1 sachet easy blend dried yeast
25 g/1 oz/6 tsp butter, cut into small pieces
125 ml/4 fl oz/½ cup tepid milk
1 egg, beaten

FILLING:
50 g/1¾ oz/10 tsp butter, softened
50 g/1¾ oz/3 tbsp soft brown sugar
25 g/1 oz chopped hazelnuts
25 g/1 oz stem (candied) ginger, chopped
50 g/1¾ oz mixed (candied) peel
1 tbsp rum or brandy
100 g/3½ oz/⅔ cup icing (confectioners') sugar
2 tbsp lemon juice

1 Grease a baking sheet (cookie sheet). Sieve (strain) the flour and salt into a bowl and stir in the yeast. Rub in the butter. Add the milk and egg and mix together to form a dough.

2 Place the dough in a greased bowl, cover and put in a warm place for 40 minutes until doubled in size. Knead for 1 minute then roll out to a rectangle 30 × 23 cm/12 × 9 inches.

3 Cream together the butter and sugar until light and fluffy. Stir in the hazelnuts, ginger, mixed (candied) peel and rum or brandy. Spread the filling over the dough, leaving a 2.5 cm/1 inch border.

4 Roll up the dough from the long edge to form a sausage shape. Cut into 5 cm/2 inch slices and place on the baking tray (cookie sheet) with the slices just touching. Cover and leave to rise in a warm place for 30 minutes.

5 Bake in a preheated oven, 190°C/325°F/ Gas Mark 5, for 20-30 minutes or until golden. Meanwhile, mix the icing sugar with enough lemon juice to form a thin icing.

6 Leave the loaf to cool slightly before drizzling with icing.

Date & Honey Loaf

Makes one loaf

INGREDIENTS

250 g/9 oz/1¼ cups strong white bread flour
75 g/2¾ oz/¼ cup strong brown bread flour
½ tsp salt
1 sachet easy blend dried yeast
200 ml/7 fl oz/¾ cup tepid water
3 tbsp sunflower oil
3 tbsp honey
75 g/2¾ oz dates, chopped
2 tbsp sesame seeds

1 Grease a 900 g/2 lb loaf tin (pan). Sieve (strain) the flours into a large mixing bowl, stir in the salt and dried yeast.

2 Pour in the tepid water, oil and honey. Mix everything together to form a dough.

3 Place the dough on a lightly floured surface and knead for about 5 minutes until smooth.

4 Place the dough in a greased bowl, cover and leave to rise in a warm place for about 1 hour or until doubled in size.

5 Knead in the dates and sesame seeds. Shape the dough and place in the tin (pan).

6 Cover and leave in a warm place for a further 30 minutes or until springy to the touch.

7 Bake in a preheated oven, 220°C/425°F/Gas Mark 7, for 30 minutes or until a hollow sound is heard when the base of the loaf is tapped.

8 Transfer the loaf to a wire rack and leave to cool. Serve cut into thick slices.

VARIATION

Replace the sesame seeds with sunflower seeds for a slightly different texture, if you prefer.

COOK'S TIP

If you cannot find a warm place, sit the bowl over a saucepan of warm water.

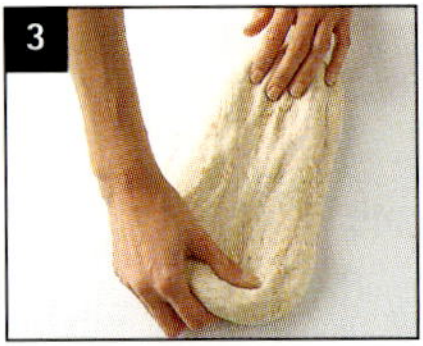

Pumpkin Loaf

Serves 6-8

INGREDIENTS

450 g/1 lb pumpkin flesh
125 g/ 4½ oz / ½ cup butter, softened
175 g /6 oz/¾ cup caster (superfine) sugar
2 eggs, beaten
225 g /8 oz/2 cups plain (all-purpose) flour, sifted
1½ tsp baking powder
½ tsp salt
1 tsp ground mixed spice (allspice)
25 g/1 oz pumpkin seeds

1 Grease a 900 g/2 lb loaf tin (pan) with oil.

2 Chop the pumpkin into large pieces and wrap in buttered foil. Cook in a preheated oven, 200°C/400°F/Gas Mark 6, for 30-40 minutes until they are tender.

3 Leave the pumpkin to cool completely before mashing well to make a thick purée.

4 In a bowl, cream the butter and sugar together until light and fluffy. Add the eggs a little at a time.

5 Stir in the pumpkin purée. Fold in the flour, baking powder, salt and mixed spice (allspice).

6 Fold the pumpkin seeds gently through the mixture, then spoon into the loaf tin (pan).

7 Bake in a preheated oven, 160°C/325°F/ Gas Mark 3, for 1¼-1½ hours or until a skewer inserted into the centre of the loaf comes out clean.

8 Leave the loaf to cool and serve buttered, if wished.

COOK'S TIP

To ensure that the pumpkin purée is dry, place it in a saucepan over a medium heat for a few minutes, stirring frequently, until it is thick.

Tropical Fruit Bread

Makes one loaf

INGREDIENTS

350 g/12 oz/3 cups strong white bread flour
50 g /1 3/4 oz/5 tbsp bran
1/2 tsp salt
1/2 tsp ground ginger
1 sachet easy blend dried yeast
25 g/1 oz/2 tbsp soft brown sugar
25 g/1 oz/6 tsp butter, cut into small pieces
250 ml/9 fl oz/generous 1 cup tepid water
75 g/2 3/4 oz glacé pineapple, chopped finely
25 g/1 oz dried mango, chopped finely
50 g/1 3/4 oz / 2/3 cup desiccated (shredded) coconut, toasted
1 egg, beaten
2 tbsp coconut shreds

1 Grease a baking sheet (cookie sheet). Sieve (strain) the flour into a large mixing bowl. Stir in the bran, salt, ginger, dried yeast and sugar. Rub in the butter with your fingers, then add the water and mix to form a dough.

2 On a lightly floured surface, knead the dough for about 5-8 minutes or until smooth (alternatively, use an electric mixer with a dough hook). Place the dough in a greased bowl, cover and leave to rise in a warm place until doubled in size.

3 Knead the pineapple, mango and desiccated (shredded) coconut into the dough. Shape into a round and place on the baking tray (cookie sheet). Score the top with the back of a knife. Cover and leave for a further 30 minutes in a warm place.

4 Brush the loaf with the egg and sprinkle with the 2 tbsp coconut. Bake in a preheated oven, 220°C/425°F/Gas Mark 7, for 30 minutes or until golden.

5 Leave the bread to cool on a wire rack before serving.

Citrus Bread

Makes one loaf

INGREDIENTS

- 450 g/1 lb/4 cups strong white bread flour
- ½ tsp salt
- 50 g/1¾ oz/9 tsp caster (superfine) sugar
- 1 sachet easy blend dried yeast
- 50 g/1¾ oz/10 tsp butter, cut into small pieces
- 5-6 tbsp orange juice
- 4 tbsp lemon juice
- 3-4 tbsp lime juice
- 150 ml/¼ pint/⅔ cup tepid water
- 1 orange
- 1 lemon
- 1 lime
- 2 tbsp runny honey

1 Lightly grease a baking tray (cookie sheet).

2 Sieve (strain) the flour and salt into a mixing bowl. Stir in the sugar and dried yeast.

3 Rub the butter into the mixture using your fingers. Add all of the fruit juices and the water and mix to form a dough.

4 Place the dough on a lightly floured working surface and knead for 5 minutes. Place the dough in a greased bowl, cover and leave to rise in a warm place for 1 hour.

5 Meanwhile, grate the rind of the orange, lemon and lime. Knead the fruit rinds into the dough.

6 Divide the dough into 2 balls, making one slightly bigger than the other.

7 Place the larger ball on the baking tray (cookie sheet) and set the smaller one on top.

8 Push a floured finger through the centre of the dough. Cover and leave to rise for about 40 minutes or until springy to the touch.

9 Bake in a preheated oven, 220°C/425°F/Gas Mark 7, for 35 minutes. Remove from the oven and glaze with the honey.

5

6

8

Mango Twist Bread

Makes one loaf

INGREDIENTS

450 g/1 lb/4 cups strong white bread flour
1 tsp salt
1 sachet easy blend dried yeast
1 tsp ground ginger
50 g/1¾ oz/3 tbsp soft brown sugar
40 g/1½ oz/9 tsp butter, cut into small pieces
1 small mango, peeled, cored and puréed
250 ml/9 fl oz/generous 1 cup tepid water
2 tbsp runny honey
125 g/4½ oz/⅔ cup sultanas (golden raisins)
1 egg, beaten
icing (confectioners') sugar, for dusting

1 Grease a baking tray (cookie sheet). Sieve (strain) the flour and salt into a large mixing bowl, stir in the dried yeast, ground ginger and brown sugar. Rub in the butter with your fingers.

2 Stir in the mango purée, water and honey and mix together to form a dough.

3 Place the dough on a lightly floured surface and knead for about 5 minutes until smooth (alternatively, use an electric mixer with a dough hook). Place the dough in a greased bowl, cover and leave to rise in a warm place for about 1 hour until it has doubled in size.

4 Knead in the sultanas (golden raisins) and shape the dough into 2 sausage shapes, each 25 cm/10 inches long. Carefully twist the 2 pieces together and pinch the ends to seal. Place the dough on the baking tray (cookie sheet), cover and leave in a warm place for a further 40 minutes.

5 Brush the loaf with the egg and bake in a preheated oven, 220°C/ 425°F/Gas Mark 7, for 30 minutes or until golden brown. Leave to cool on a wire rack. Dust with icing (confectioners') sugar before serving.

1

1

2

Chocolate Bread

Makes one loaf

INGREDIENTS

450 g/1 lb/4 cups strong white bread flour
25 g/1 oz/¼ cup cocoa powder
1 tsp salt
1 sachet easy blend dried yeast
25 g/1 oz/6 tsp soft brown sugar
1 tbsp oil
300 ml/½ pint/1⅓ cups tepid water

1 Lightly grease a 900 g/2 lb loaf tin (pan).

2 Sieve (strain) the flour and cocoa powder into a large mixing bowl.

3 Stir in the salt, dried yeast and brown sugar.

4 Pour in the oil together with the tepid water and mix the ingredients together to make a dough.

5 Place the dough on a lightly floured surface and knead for 5 minutes.

6 Place the dough in a greased bowl, cover and leave to rise in a warm place for about 1 hour or until the dough has doubled in size.

7 Knock back (punch down) the dough and shape it into a loaf. Place the dough in the prepared tin (pan), cover and leave to rise in a warm place for a further 30 minutes.

8 Bake in a preheated oven, 200°C/400°F/Gas Mark 6, for 25-30 minutes, or until a hollow sound is heard when the base of the bread is tapped.

9 Transfer the bread to a wire rack and leave to cool. Cut into slices to serve.

COOK'S TIP

This bread can be sliced and spread with butter or it can be lightly toasted.

Soda Bread

Makes one loaf

INGREDIENTS

300 g/10½ oz/2½ cups wholemeal (whole wheat) flour
300 g/10½ oz/2½ cups plain (all-purpose) flour
2 tsp baking powder
1 tsp bicarbonate of soda (baking soda)
2 tbsp caster (superfine) sugar
1 tsp salt
1 egg, beaten
425 ml/15 fl oz/1¾ cups natural yogurt

1 Grease and flour a baking tray (cookie sheet).

2 Sieve (strain) the flours, baking powder, bicarbonate of soda (baking soda), sugar and salt into a large bowl.

3 Beat together the egg and yogurt and pour the mixture into the dry ingredients. Combine well to make a soft and sticky dough.

4 On a lightly floured surface, knead the dough for a few minutes until it is smooth, then shape it into a round about 5 cm/2 inches deep.

5 Transfer the dough to the baking tray (cookie sheet). Using a sharp knife, mark a cross shape on the top of the dough.

6 Bake in a preheated oven, 190°C/375°F/Gas Mark 5, for about 40 minutes or until the bread is golden brown.

7 Transfer the loaf to a wire rack and leave to cool. Cut into slices to serve.

VARIATION

For a fruity version of this soda bread, add 125 g/4½ oz/¾ cup of raisins to the dry ingredients in step 2.

Spicy Bread

Makes one loaf

INGREDIENTS

225 g/8 oz/2 cups self-raising flour
100 g/3½ oz/¾ cup plain (all-purpose) flour
1 tsp baking powder
¼ tsp salt
¼ tsp cayenne pepper
2 tsp curry powder
2 tsp poppy seeds
25 g/1 oz/6 tsp butter, cut into small pieces
150 ml/¼ pint/⅔ cup milk
1 egg, beaten

1 Lightly grease a baking tray (cookie sheet) with butter.

2 Sieve (strain) the self-raising flour and the plain (all-purpose) flour into a mixing bowl along with the baking powder, salt, cayenne pepper, curry powder and poppy seeds.

3 Rub in the butter until everything is well mixed together.

4 Add the milk and the beaten egg and mix to a soft dough.

5 Turn the dough out on to a lightly floured surface, then knead lightly for a few minutes.

6 Shape the dough into a round and mark it with a cross shape in the centre of the top of the dough.

7 Bake in a preheated oven, 190°C/375°F/Gas Mark 5, for 45 minutes.

8 Transfer the bread to a wire rack and leave to cool. Serve in chunks or slices.

COOK'S TIP

If the bread looks as though it is browning too much, cover it with a piece of foil for the remainder of the cooking time.

3

4

6

Chilli Corn Bread

Makes 12 bars

INGREDIENTS

25 g/4½ oz/1 cup plain (all-purpose) flour
125 g/4½ oz polenta
1 tbsp baking powder
½ tsp salt
1 green chilli, deseeded and chopped finely
5 spring onions (scallions), chopped finely
2 eggs
142 ml/4 ½ fl oz/generous ½ cup soured cream
125 ml/4 fl oz/½ cup sunflower oil

1 Grease a 20 cm/8 inch square cake tin (pan) and line the base with baking parchment.

2 In a large bowl, mix together the flour, polenta, baking powder and salt.

3 Add the finely chopped green chilli and the spring onions (scallions) to the dry ingredients and mix well.

4 In a mixing jug (pitcher), beat the eggs with the soured cream and sunflower oil. Pour the mixture into the bowl of dry ingredients. Mix everything together quickly and thoroughly.

5 Pour the mixture into the prepared cake tin (pan).

6 Bake in a preheated oven, 200°C/ 400°F/ Gas Mark 6, for about 20-25 minutes or until the loaf has risen and is lightly browned.

7 Leave the bread to cool slightly before turning out of the tin (pan). Cut into bars or squares to serve.

VARIATION

Add 125 g/4½ oz of sweetcorn kernels to the .mixture in step 3, if you prefer.

Cheese & Potato Bread

Serves 4

INGREDIENTS

225 g/8 oz/2 cups plain (all-purpose) flour
1 tsp salt
½ tsp mustard powder
2 tsp baking powder
125 g/4½ oz Red Leicester cheese, grated
175 g/6 oz potatoes, cooked and mashed
200 ml/7 fl oz/¾ cup water
1 tbsp oil

1 Lightly grease a baking tray (cookie sheet).

2 Sieve (strain) the flour, salt, mustard powder and baking powder into a mixing bowl.

3 Reserve 2 tbsp of the grated cheese and stir the rest into the bowl with the cooked and mashed potatoes.

4 Pour in the water and the oil, and stir all the ingredients together (the mixture will be wet at this stage). Mix them all to make a soft dough.

5 Turn out the dough on to a floured surface and shape it into a 20 cm/8 inch round.

6 Place the round on the baking tray (cookie sheet) and mark it into 4 portions with a knife, without cutting through. Sprinkle with the reserved cheese.

7 Bake in a preheated oven, 220°C/425°F/Gas Mark 7, for about 25-30 minutes.

8 Transfer the bread to a wire rack and leave to cool. Serve the bread as fresh as possible.

COOK'S TIP

You can use instant potato mix for this bread, if wished.

VARIATION

Add 50 g/1¾ oz chopped ham to the mixture in step 3, if you prefer.

3

4

6

Cheese & Ham Loaf

Serves 6

INGREDIENTS

225 g/8 oz/2 cups self-raising flour
1 tsp salt
2 tsp baking powder
1 tsp paprika
75 g/2¾ oz/⅓ cup butter, cut into small pieces
125 g/4½ oz mature (sharp) cheese, grated
75 g/ 2¾ oz smoked ham, chopped
2 eggs, beaten
150 ml/¼ pint/⅔ cup milk

1 Grease a 450 g/1 lb loaf tin (pan) and line the base with baking parchment.

2 Sieve (strain) the flour, salt, baking powder and paprika into a bowl.

3 Rub in the butter with your fingers until the mixture resembles fine breadcrumbs. Stir in the cheese and ham.

4 Add the beaten eggs and milk to the dry ingredients and mix well.

5 Spoon the cheese and ham mixture into the prepared loaf tin (pan).

6 Bake in a preheated oven, 180°C/350°F/Gas Mark 4, for about 1 hour or until the loaf is well risen.

7 Leave the bread to cool in the tin (pan), then turn out and transfer to a wire rack to cool slightly.

8 Serve the bread cut into thick slices.

COOK'S TIP

This tasty bread is best eaten on the day it is made as it does not keep well for very long.

VARIATION

Any grated hard cheese can be used for this bread; use a milder one, if preferred.

Cheese & Chive Bread

Serves 8

INGREDIENTS

225 g/8 oz/2 cups self-raising flour
1 tsp salt
1 tsp mustard powder
100 g/3½ oz mature (sharp) cheese, grated
2 tbsp chopped fresh chives
1 egg, beaten
25 g/1 oz/6 tsp butter, melted
150 ml/¼ pint/⅔ cup milk

1 Grease a 23 cm/9 inch square cake tin (pan) and line the base with baking parchment.

2 Sieve (strain) the flour, salt and mustard powder into a large mixing bowl.

3 Reserve 3 tbsp of the grated mature (sharp) cheese for sprinkling over the top of the loaf before baking in the oven.

4 Stir the remaining cheese into the bowl along with the chopped fresh chives. Mix well.

5 Add the beaten egg, melted butter and milk and stir the mixture thoroughly.

6 Pour the mixture into the prepared tin (pan) and spread with a knife. Sprinkle over the reserved grated cheese.

7 Bake in a preheated oven, 190°C/375°F/Gas Mark 5, for 30 minutes.

8 Leave the bread to cool slightly in the tin (pan). Turn out on to a wire rack to cool further. Cut into triangles to serve.

COOK'S TIP

You can use any hard mature (sharp) cheese of your choice for this recipe.

Garlic Bread Rolls

Makes 8

INGREDIENTS

12 cloves garlic, peeled
350 ml/12 floz/1½ cups milk
450 g/1 lb/4 cups strong white bread flour
1 tsp salt
1 sachet easy blend dried yeast
1 tbsp dried mixed herbs
2 tbsp sunflower oil
1 egg, beaten
milk, for brushing
rock salt, for sprinkling

1 Grease a baking tray (cookie sheet). Place the garlic cloves and milk in a saucepan, bring to the boil and simmer gently for 15 minutes. Leave to cool slightly, then process in a blender or food processor to purée the garlic.

2 Sieve (strain) the flour and salt into a large mixing bowl and stir in the dried yeast and mixed herbs.

3 Add the garlic-flavoured milk, sunflower oil and beaten egg to the dry ingredients and mix everything to a dough.

4 Place the dough on a lightly floured work surface and knead lightly for a few minutes until smooth and soft.

5 Place the dough in a greased bowl, cover and leave to rise in a warm place for about 1 hour or until doubled in size.

6 Knock back (punch down) the dough by kneading it for 2 minutes. Shape into 8 rolls and place on the baking tray (cookie sheet). Score the top of each roll with a knife, cover and leave for 15 minutes.

7 Brush the rolls with milk and sprinkle rock salt over the top.

8 Bake in a preheated oven, 220°C/425°F/Gas Mark 7, for 15-20 minutes.

9 Transfer the rolls to a wire rack and leave to cool before serving.

1

3

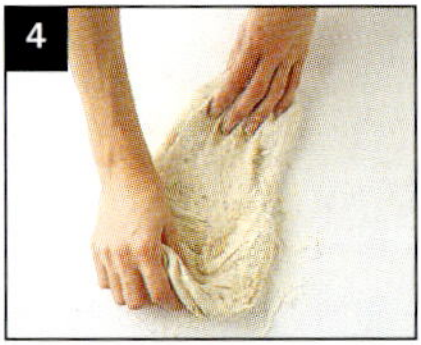
4

Mini Focaccia

Makes 4

INGREDIENTS

350 g/12 oz/3 cups strong white flour
½ tsp salt
1 sachet easy blend dried yeast
2 tbsp olive oil
250 ml/9 fl oz tepid water
100 g/3½ oz green or black olives, halved

TOPPING:
2 red onions, sliced
2 tbsp olive oil
1 tsp sea salt
1 tbsp thyme leaves

1 Lightly oil several baking trays (cookie sheets). Sieve (strain) the flour and salt into a large mixing bowl, then stir in the yeast. Pour in the olive oil and tepid water and mix everything together to form a dough.

2 Turn the dough out on to a lightly floured surface and knead it for about 5 minutes (alternatively, use an electric mixer with a dough hook and knead for 7-8 minutes).

3 Place the dough in a greased bowl, cover and leave in a warm place for about 1-1½ hours until it has doubled in size. Knock back (punch down) the dough by kneading it again for 1-2 minutes.

4 Knead half of the olives into the dough. Divide the dough into quarters and then shape the quarters into rounds. Place them on the baking trays (cookie sheets) and push your fingers into the dough to achieve a dimpled effect.

5 Sprinkle the red onions and remaining olives over the rounds. Drizzle the olive oil over the top and sprinkle each round with the sea salt and thyme leaves. Cover and leave the dough to rise again for 30 minutes.

6 Bake in a preheated oven, 190°C/375°F/ Gas Mark 5, for 20-25 minutes or until the focaccia are well cooked and golden. Transfer to a wire rack and leave to cool before serving.

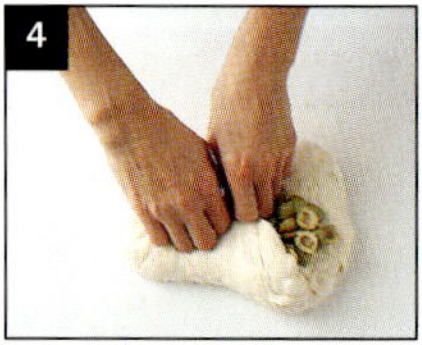

Sun-Dried Tomato Rolls

Makes 8

INGREDIENTS

225 g/8 oz/2 cups strong white bread flour
½ tsp salt
1 sachet easy blend dried yeast
100 g/3½ oz/⅓ cup butter, melted and cooled slightly
3 tbsp milk, warmed
2 eggs, beaten
50 g/1¾ oz sun-dried tomatoes, well drained and chopped finely
milk, for brushing

1 Lightly grease a baking tray (cookie sheet).

2 Sieve (strain) the flour and salt into a large mixing bowl. Stir in the yeast, then pour in the butter, milk and eggs. Mix together to form a dough.

3 Turn the dough on to a lightly floured surface and knead for about 5 minutes (alternatively, use an electric mixer with a dough hook).

4 Place the dough in a greased bowl, cover and leave to rise in a warm place for 1-1½ hours until the dough has doubled in size. Knock back (punch down) the dough by kneading it for a few minutes.

5 Knead the sun-dried tomatoes into the dough, sprinkling the work surface (counter) with extra flour as the tomatoes are quite oily.

6 Divide the dough into 8 balls and place them on to the baking tray (cookie sheet). Cover and leave to rise for about 30 minutes until the rolls have doubled in size.

7 Brush the rolls with milk and bake in a preheated oven, 230°C/450°F/Gas Mark 8, for 10-15 minutes until the rolls are golden brown.

8 Transfer the rolls to a wire rack and leave to cool slightly before serving.

3

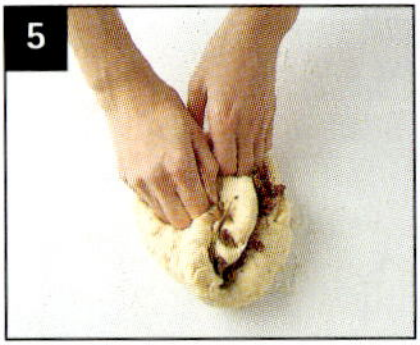
5

6

Thyme Crescents

Makes 8

INGREDIENTS

250 g/9 oz fresh ready-made puff pastry (pie dough)
100 g/3½ oz/⅓ cup butter, softened
1 garlic clove, crushed
1 tsp lemon juice
1 tsp dried thyme
salt and pepper

1 Lightly grease a baking tray (cookie sheet).

2 On a lightly floured surface, roll out the pastry (pie dough) to form a 25 cm/10 inch round and cut into 8 wedges.

3 In a small bowl, mix the softened butter, garlic clove, lemon juice and dried thyme together until soft. Season with salt and pepper to taste.

4 Spread a little of the butter and thyme mixture on to each of the pastry (pie dough) wedges.

5 Carefully roll up each wedge, starting from the wide end.

6 Arrange the crescents on the prepared baking tray (cookie sheet) and chill for 30 minutes.

7 Dampen the baking tray (cookie sheet) with cold water. This will create a steamy atmosphere in the oven while the crescents are baking and help the pastries to rise.

8 Bake in a preheated oven, 200°C/400°F/ Gas Mark 6, for 10-15 minutes until the crescents are well risen and golden.

COOK'S TIP

Dried herbs have a stronger flavour than fresh ones, which makes them perfect for these pastries. The crescents can be made with other dried herbs of your choice, such as rosemary and sage, or mixed herbs.

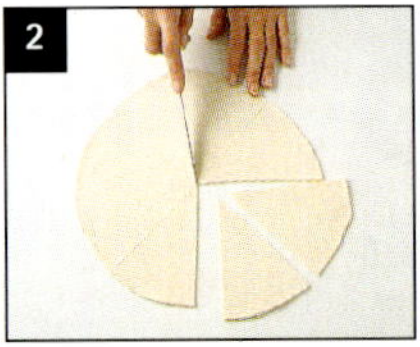

Cheese & Mustard Scones

Makes 8

INGREDIENTS

225 g/8 oz/2 cups self-raising flour
1 tsp baking powder
pinch of salt
50 g/1¾ oz/10 tsp butter, cut into small pieces
125 g/4½ oz mature (sharp) cheese, grated
1 tsp mustard powder
150 ml/¼ pint/⅔ cup milk
pepper

1 Lightly grease a baking tray (cookie sheet).

2 Sieve (strain) the flour, baking powder and salt into a mixing bowl. Rub in the butter with your fingers until the mixture resembles breadcrumbs.

3 Stir in the grated cheese, mustard and enough milk to form a soft dough.

4 On a lightly floured surface, knead the dough very lightly, then flatten it out with the palm of your hand to a depth of about 2.5 cm/1 inch.

5 Cut the dough into 8 wedges with a knife. Brush each one with a little milk and sprinkle with pepper to taste.

6 Bake in a preheated oven, 220°C/425°F/ Gas Mark 7, for 10-15 minutes until the scones are golden brown.

7 Transfer the scones to a wire rack and leave to cool slightly before serving.

COOK'S TIP

Scones should be eaten on the day they are made as they quickly go stale. Serve them split in half and spread with butter.

Cheese Sables

Makes about 35

INGREDIENTS

150 g/5½ oz/1¼ cups plain (all-purpose) flour
150 g/5½ oz mature (sharp) cheese, grated
150 g/5½ oz/⅔ cup butter, cut into small pieces
1 egg yolk
sesame seeds, for sprinkling

1 Lightly grease several baking trays (cookie sheets).

2 Mix the flour and cheese together in a bowl.

3 Add the butter and mix with your fingers until combined.

4 Stir in the egg yolk and mix to form a dough. Wrap the dough and leave to chill in the refrigerator for about 30 minutes.

5 On a lightly floured surface, roll out the cheese dough thinly. Cut out 6 cm/2½ inch rounds, re-rolling the trimmings to make about 35 rounds.

6 Place the rounds on to the prepared baking trays (cookie sheets) and sprinkle the sesame seeds over the top of them.

7 Bake in a preheated oven, 200°C/400°F/ Gas Mark 6, for 20 minutes until the sables are lightly golden.

8 Transfer to a wire rack and leave to cool slightly before serving.

COOK'S TIP

Cut out any shape you like for your savoury biscuits. Children will enjoy them cut into animal or other fun shapes.

2

5

6

Savoury Curried Biscuits

Makes 40

INGREDIENTS

100 g/3½ oz/¾ cup plain (all-purpose) flour
1 tsp salt
2 tsp curry powder
100 g/3½ oz Cheshire cheese (mellow hard cheese), grated
100 g/3½ oz Parmesan cheese, grated
100 g/3½ oz/⅓ cup butter, softened

1 Lightly grease about 4 baking trays (cookie sheets).

2 Sieve (strain) the plain (all-purpose) flour and salt into a mixing bowl.

3 Stir in the curry powder and the grated Cheshire and Parmesan cheeses. Rub in the softened butter with your fingers until the mixture comes together to form a soft dough.

4 On a lightly floured surface, roll out the dough thinly to form a rectangle.

5 Using a 5 cm/2 inch biscuit cutter, cut out 40 round biscuits (cookies).

6 Arrange the biscuits neatly on the baking trays (cookie sheets).

7 Bake in a preheated oven, 180°C/350°F/Gas Mark 4, for 10-15 minutes.

8 Leave the biscuits to cool slightly on the baking trays (cookie sheets). Transfer the biscuits to a wire rack until completely cold and crisp, then serve.

COOK'S TIP

These biscuits can be stored for several days in an airtight tin or plastic container.

3

4

5

Cheese Pudding

Serves 4

INGREDIENTS

150 g/5$\frac{1}{2}$ oz/2$\frac{1}{2}$ cups fresh white breadcrumbs
100 g/3$\frac{1}{2}$ oz Gruyère cheese, grated
150 ml/$\frac{1}{4}$ pint/$\frac{2}{3}$ cup tepid milk
125 g/4$\frac{1}{2}$ oz/$\frac{1}{2}$ cup butter, melted
2 eggs, separated
salt and pepper
2 tbsp chopped fresh parsley

1 Grease a 1 litre/2 pint/ 4 cup ovenproof dish.

2 Place the breadcrumbs and cheese in a bowl and mix.

3 Pour the milk over the cheese and breadcrumb mixture and stir to mix. Add the melted butter, egg yolks, salt and pepper to taste and parsley. Mix well.

4 Whisk the egg whites until firm. Fold the cheese mixture into the egg whites.

5 Transfer the mixture to the prepared ovenproof dish.

6 Bake the pudding in a preheated oven, 190°C/375°F/Gas Mark 5, for about 45 minutes or until golden and slightly risen, and a fine skewer inserted into the middle of the pudding comes out clean.

7 Serve the cheese pudding hot, with a green salad.

VARIATION

Any strongly flavoured cheese of your choice can be used instead of the Gruyère to make this tasty savoury pudding.

COOK'S TIP

For a slightly healthier alternative, make the cheese pudding with fresh wholemeal (whole wheat) breadcrumbs instead of white ones.

2

4

4

Cheese & Onion Pies

Makes 4

INGREDIENTS

3 tbsp vegetable oil
4 onions, peeled and sliced finely
4 garlic cloves, crushed
4 tbsp finely chopped fresh parsley
75 g/2¾ oz mature (sharp) cheese, grated
salt and pepper

PASTRY (PIE DOUGH):
175 g/6 oz/1½ cups plain (all-purpose) flour
½ tsp salt
100 g/3½ oz/⅓ cup butter, cut into small pieces
3-4 tbsp water

1 Heat the oil in a frying pan (skillet). Add the onions and garlic and fry for 10-15 minutes or until the onions are soft. Remove the pan from the heat and stir in the parsley and cheese and season.

2 To make the pastry (pie dough), sieve (strain) the flour and salt into a mixing bowl and rub in the butter until the mixture resembles breadcrumbs. Stir in the water and mix to a dough.

3 On a lightly floured surface, roll out the dough and divide it into 8 portions.

4 Roll out each portion to a 10 cm/4 inch round and use half of the rounds to line 4 individual tart tins (pans).

5 Fill each round with a quarter of the onion mixture. Cover with the remaining 4 pastry (pie dough) rounds. Make a slit in the top of each tart with the point of a knife and seal the edges with the back of a teaspoon.

6 Bake in a preheated oven, 220°C/425°F/Gas Mark 7, for 20 minutes. Serve hot or cold.

COOK'S TIP

You can prepare the onion filling in advance and store it in the refrigerator.

1

1

5

Red Onion Tart

Serves 4

INGREDIENTS

50 g/1¾ oz/10 tsp butter
25 g/1oz/6 tsp sugar
500 g/1 lb 2 oz red onions, peeled and quartered
3 tbsp red wine vinegar
2 tbsp fresh thyme leaves
250 g/8 oz fresh ready-made puff pastry (pie dough)
salt and pepper

1 Place the butter and sugar in a 23 cm/9 inch ovenproof frying pan (skillet) and cook over a medium heat until melted.

2 Add the red onion quarters and sweat them over a low heat for 10-15 minutes until golden, stirring occasionally.

3 Add the red wine vinegar and thyme leaves to the pan. Season with salt and pepper to taste, then simmer over a medium heat until the liquid has reduced and the red onion pieces are coated in the buttery sauce.

4 On a lightly floured surface, roll out the pastry (pie dough) to a circle slightly larger than the frying pan (skillet).

5 Place the pastry (pie dough) over the onion mixture and press down, tucking in the edges to seal the pastry (pie dough).

6 Bake in a preheated oven, 180°C/350°F/Gas Mark 4, for 20-25 minutes. Leave the tart to stand for 10 minutes.

7 To turn out, place a serving plate over the frying pan (skillet) and carefully invert them both so that the pastry (pie dough) becomes the base of the tart. Serve warm.

VARIATION

Replace the red onions with shallots, leaving them whole, if you prefer.

Puff Potato Pie

Serves 6

INGREDIENTS

750 g/1 lb 9 oz potatoes, peeled and sliced thinly
2 spring onions (scallions), chopped finely
1 red onion, chopped finely
150 ml/$^1/_4$ pint/$^2/_3$ cup double (heavy) cream
500 g/1 lb 2 oz fresh ready-made puff pastry (pie dough)
2 eggs, beaten
salt and pepper

1 Lightly grease a baking tray (cookie sheet). Bring a saucepan of water to the boil, add the sliced potatoes, bring back to the boil and then simmer for a few minutes. Drain the potato slices and leave to cool. Dry off any excess moisture with paper towels.

2 In a bowl, mix together the spring onions (scallions), red onion and the cooled potato slices. Stir in 2 tbsp of the cream and plenty of seasoning.

3 Divide the pastry (pie dough) in half and roll out one piece to a 23 cm/9 inch round. Roll the remaining pastry (pie dough) to a 25 cm/ 10 inch round.

4 Place the smaller circle on to the baking tray (cookie sheet) and top with the potato mixture, leaving a 2.5 cm/1 inch border. Brush this border with a little of the beaten egg.

5 Top with the larger circle of pastry (pie dough), seal well and crimp the edges of the pastry (pie dough). Cut a steam vent in the middle of the pastry (pie dough) and, using the back of a knife, mark with a pattern. Brush with the beaten egg and bake in a preheated oven, 200°C/ 400°F/Gas Mark 6, for 30 minutes.

6 Mix the remaining beaten egg with the rest of the cream and pour into the pie through the steam vent. Return to the oven for 15 minutes, then leave to cool for 30 minutes. Serve warm or cold.

Fresh Tomato Tarts

Serves 6

INGREDIENTS

250 g/9 oz fresh ready-made puff pastry (pie dough)
1 egg, beaten
2 tbsp pesto
6 plum tomatoes, sliced
salt and pepper
fresh thyme leaves, to garnish (optional)

1 On a lightly floured surface, roll out the pastry (pie dough) to a rectangle measuring 30 × 25 cm/12 × 10 inches.

2 Cut the rectangle in half and divide each half into 3 pieces to make 6 even-sized rectangles. Leave to chill for 20 minutes.

3 Lightly score the edges of the pastry (pie dough) rectangles and brush with the beaten egg.

4 Spread the pesto over the rectangles, dividing it equally between them, leaving a 2½ cm/1 inch border on each one.

5 Arrange the tomato slices along the centre of each rectangle on top of the pesto.

6 Season well with salt and pepper to taste and lightly sprinkle with fresh thyme leaves, if using.

7 Bake the tarts in a preheated oven, 200°C/400°F/Gas Mark 6, for about 15-20 minutes until well risen and golden brown.

8 Transfer the tomato tarts to warm serving plates straight from the oven and serve while they are still piping hot.

VARIATION

Instead of individual tarts, roll the pastry (pie dough) out to form 1 large rectangle. Spoon over the pesto and arrange the tomatoes over the top.

Provençal Tart

Serves 6–8

INGREDIENTS

250 g/9 oz ready-made fresh puff pastry (pie dough)
3 tbsp olive oil
2 red (bell) peppers, seeded and diced
2 green (bell) peppers, seeded and diced
150 ml/¼ pint/⅔ cup double (heavy) cream
1 egg
2 courgettes (zucchini), sliced
salt and pepper

1 Roll out the pastry (pie dough) on a lightly floured surface and line a 20 cm/8 inch loose-bottomed quiche/flan tin (pan). Leave to chill in the refrigerator for 20 minutes.

2 Meanwhile, heat 2 tbsp of the olive oil in a pan and fry the (bell) peppers for about 8 minutes until softened, stirring frequently.

3 Whisk the double (heavy) cream and egg together in a bowl and season to taste with salt and pepper. Stir in the cooked (bell) peppers.

4 Heat the remaining oil in a pan and fry the courgette (zucchini) slices for 4-5 minutes until lightly browned.

5 Pour the egg and (bell) pepper mixture into the pastry case (pie shell).

6 Arrange the courgette (zucchini) slices around the edge of the tart.

7 Bake in a preheated oven, 180°C/350°F/Gas Mark 4, for 35-40 minutes or until just set and golden brown.

COOK'S TIP

This recipe could be used to make 6 individual tarts – use 15 × 10 cm/6 × 4 inch tins (pans) and bake them for 20 minutes.

Celery & Onion Pies

Makes 12

INGREDIENTS

PASTRY (PIE DOUGH):
- 125 g/4½ oz/1 cup plain (all-purpose) flour
- ½ tsp salt
- 25 g/1 oz/6 tsp butter, cut into small pieces
- 25 g/1 oz mature (sharp) cheese, grated
- 3-4 tbsp water

FILLING:
- 50 g/1¾ oz/10 tsp butter
- 125 g/4½ oz celery, chopped finely
- 2 garlic cloves, crushed
- 1 small onion, chopped finely
- 1 tbsp plain (all-purpose) flour
- 50 ml/2 fl oz/¼ cup milk
- salt
- pinch of cayenne pepper

1 To make the filling, melt the butter, add the celery, garlic and onion and fry for 5 minutes or until softened.

2 Remove from the heat and stir in the flour, then the milk. Heat gently until the mixture is thick, stirring freqently. Season with salt and cayenne pepper. Leave to cool.

3 To make the pastry, sieve (strain) the flour and salt into a mixing bowl and rub in the butter with your fingers. Stir the cheese into the mixture together with the cold water and mix to form a dough.

4 Roll out three quarters of the dough and using a 6 cm/2½ inch biscuit (cookie) cutter, cut out 12 rounds. Line a patty tin (pan) with the rounds.

5 Divide the filling between the rounds. Roll out the remaining dough and, using a 5 cm/2 inch cutter, cut out 12 circles. Place the circles on top of the pies and seal. Make a slit in each pie and chill them for 30 minutes.

6 Bake in a preheated oven, 220°C/425°F/ Gas Mark 7, for about 15-20 minutes. Leave to cool in the tin (pan) for about 10 minutes before turning out. Serve warm.

Asparagus & Goat's Cheese Tart

Serves 6

INGREDIENTS

250 g/9 oz fresh ready-made shortcrust pastry (pie dough)
250 g/9 oz asparagus
1 tbsp vegetable oil
1 red onion, chopped finely
200 g/7 oz goat's cheese
25 g/1 oz hazelnuts, chopped
2 eggs, beaten
4 tbsp single (light) cream
salt and pepper

1 On a lightly floured surface, roll out the pastry (pie dough) and line a 24 cm/9½ inch loose-bottomed quiche/flan tin (pan). Prick the base of the pastry (pie dough) with a fork and leave to chill for 30 minutes.

2 Line the pastry case (pie shell) with foil and baking beans and bake in a preheated oven, 190°C/375°F/Gas Mark 7, for about 15 minutes.

3 Remove the foil and baking beans and return the pastry case (pie shell) to the oven for a further 15 minutes.

4 Cook the asparagus in boiling water for 2-3 minutes, drain and cut into bite-size pieces.

5 Heat the oil in a small frying pan (skillet) and fry the onion until soft. Spoon the asparagus, onion and hazelnuts into the prepared pastry case (pie shell).

6 Process the cheese, eggs and cream in a blender until smooth, or beat by hand. Season well, then pour the mixture over the asparagus, onion and hazelnuts.

7 Bake in the oven for 15-20 minutes or until the cheese filling is just set. Serve warm or cold.

VARIATION

Omit the hazelnuts and sprinkle Parmesan cheese over the top of the tart just before cooking in the oven, if you prefer.

2

4

6

Onion Tart

Serves 6

INGREDIENTS

250 g/9 oz fresh ready-made shortcrust pastry (pie dough)
40 g/1½ oz/8 tsp butter
75 g/2¾ oz bacon, chopped
700 g/1lb 9 oz onions, peeled and sliced thinly
2 eggs, beaten
50 g/1¾ oz Parmesan cheese, grated
1 tsp dried sage
salt and pepper

1 Roll out the pastry (pie dough) on a lightly floured work surface (counter) and line a 24 cm/9½ inch loose-bottomed quiche/flantin (pan).

2 Prick the base of the pastry (pie dough) with a fork and leave to chill for 30 minutes.

3 Heat the butter in a saucepan, add the chopped bacon and sliced onions and sweat them over a low heat for about 25 minutes until tender. If the onion slices start to brown, add 1 tbsp water to the saucepan.

4 Add the beaten eggs to the onion mixture and stir in the cheese, sage and salt and pepper to taste. Mix well to combine all the ingredients.

5 Spoon the onion mixture into the prepared pastry case (pie shell).

6 Bake in a preheated oven, 180°C/350°F/Gas Mark 4, for about 20-30 minutes or until the tart has just set.

7 Leave to cool slightly in the tin (pan). Serve the tart warm or cold.

VARIATION

For a vegetarian version of this tart, replace the bacon with the same amount of chopped mushrooms.

2

3

5

Pissaladière

Serves 8

INGREDIENTS

4 tbsp olive oil
700 g/1 lb 9 oz red onions, sliced thinly
2 garlic cloves, crushed
2 tsp caster (superfine) sugar
2 tbsp red wine vinegar
350 g/12 oz fresh ready-made puff pastry (pie dough)
salt and pepper

TOPPING:
2 x 50 g/1¾ oz cans anchovy fillets
12 green stoned (pitted) olives
1 tsp dried marjoram

1 Lightly grease a swiss roll tin (pan). Heat the olive oil in a large saucepan. Add the onions and garlic and cook over a low heat for about 30 minutes, stirring occasionally.

2 Add the sugar and red wine vinegar to the pan and season with plenty of salt and pepper.

3 On a lightly floured surface, roll out the pastry (pie dough) to a rectangle 33 × 23 cm/ 13 × 9 inches. Place the pastry (pie dough) rectangle on to the prepared tin (pan), pushing the pastry (pie dough) well into the corners of the tin (pan).

4 Spread the onion mixture over the pastry (pie dough).

5 Arrange the anchovy fillets and green olives on top, then sprinkle with the marjoram.

6 Bake in a preheated oven, 220°C/425°F/ Gas Mark 7, for about 20-25 minutes until the pissaladière is lightly golden. Serve piping hot, straight from the oven.

VARIATION

Cut the pissaladière into squares or triangles for easy finger food at a party or barbecue (grill).

Mini Cheese & Onion Tarts

Serves 12

INGREDIENTS

PASTRY (PIE DOUGH):
100 g/4½ oz/1 cup plain (all-purpose) flour
¼ tsp salt
75 g/2¾ oz/⅓ cup butter, cut into small pieces
1-2 tbsp water

FILLING:
1 egg, beaten
100 ml/3½ fl oz/generous ⅓ cup single (light) cream
50 g/1¾ oz Red Leicester cheese, grated
3 spring onions (scallions), chopped finely
salt
cayenne pepper

1 To make the pastry (pie dough), sieve (strain) the flour and salt into a mixing bowl. Rub in the butter with your fingers until the mixture resembles breadcrumbs. Stir in the water and mix to form a dough.

2 Roll out the pastry (pie dough) on to a lightly floured surface. Using a 7.5 cm/3 inch biscuit cutter, stamp out 12 rounds from the pastry (pie dough) and line a patty tin (pan).

3 To make the filling, whisk together the beaten egg, single (light) cream, grated cheese and chopped spring onions (scallions) in a mixing jug (pitcher). Season to taste with salt and cayenne pepper.

4 Pour the filling mixture into the pastry cases (pie shells) and bake in a preheated oven, 180°C/350°F/Gas Mark 4, for about 20-25 minutes or until the filling is just set.

Serve the mini tarts warm or cold.

VARIATION

Top each mini tartlet with slices of fresh tomato before baking, if you prefer.

COOK'S TIP

If you use 175 g/6 oz of ready-made shortcrust pastry (pie dough), these tarts can be made in minutes.

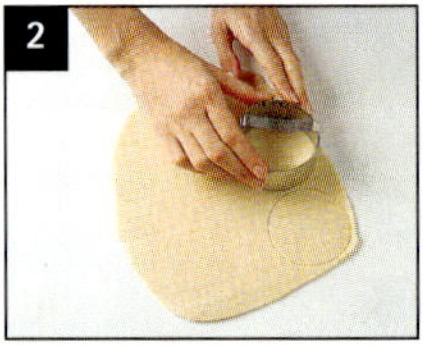

2

3

4

Ham & Cheese Lattice Pies

Makes 6

INGREDIENTS

250 g/9 oz fresh ready-made puff pastry (pie dough)
50 g/1¾ oz ham, finely chopped
125 g/4½ oz full fat soft cheese
2 tbsp chopped fresh chives
1 egg, beaten
2 tbsp freshly grated Parmesan cheese
pepper

1 Roll out the pastry (pie dough) thinly on to a lightly floured work surface (counter). Cut out 12 rectangles measuring 15 × 5 cm/6 × 2 inches.

2 Place the rectangles on to greased baking trays (cookie sheets) and leave to chill for 30 minutes.

3 Combine the ham, cheese and chives in a small bowl. Season with pepper to taste.

4 Spread the ham and cheese mixture along the centre of 6 of the rectangles, leaving a 2.5 cm/1 inch border around each one. Brush the border with the beaten egg.

5 To make the lattice pattern, fold the remaining rectangles lengthways. Leaving a 2.5 cm/1 inch border, cut vertical lines across one edge of the rectangles.

6 Unfold the rectangles and place them over the rectangles topped with the ham and cheese mixture set on the baking trays (cookie sheets). Seal the pastry (pie dough) edges well and lightly sprinkle with the Parmesan cheese.

7 Bake in a preheated oven, 180°C/350°F/Gas Mark 4, for 15-20 minutes. Serve hot or cold.

COOK'S TIP

These pies can be made in advance, frozen uncooked and baked fresh when required.

3

4

5

Curry Pasties

Serves 4

INGREDIENTS

225 g/8 oz/1¾ cups plain wholemeal (whole wheat) flour
100 g/3½ oz/⅓ cup vegan margarine, cut into small pieces
4 tbsp water
2 tbsp oil
225 g/8 oz diced root vegetables (potatoes, carrots and parsnips)
1 small onion, chopped
2 garlic cloves, chopped finely
½ tsp curry powder
½ tsp ground turmeric
½ tsp ground cumin
½ tsp wholegrain mustard
5 tbsp vegetable stock
soya milk, to glaze

1 Place the flour in a mixing bowl and rub in the vegan margarine with your fingertips until the mixture resembles breadcrumbs. Stir in the water and bring together to form a soft dough. Wrap and leave to chill in the refrigerator for 30 minutes.

2 To make the filling, heat the oil in a large saucepan. Add the diced root vegetables, chopped onion and garlic. Fry for 2 minutes, then stir in all of the spices, turning the vegetables to coat them with the spices. Fry the vegetables for a further 1 minute.

3 Add the stock to the pan and bring to the boil. Cover and simmer for about 20 minutes, stirring occasionally, until the vegetables are tender and the liquid has been absorbed. Leave to cool.

4 Divide the pastry (pie dough) into 4 portions. Roll each portion into a 15 cm/6 inch round. Place the filling on one half of each round.

5 Brush the edges of each round with soya milk, then fold over and press the edges together to seal. Place on a baking sheet (cookie sheet). Bake in a preheated oven, 200°C/ 400°F/Gas Mark 6, for 25-30 minutes until the pastry is golden brown.

1

2

5

Brazil Nut & Mushroom Pie

Serves 4-6

INGREDIENTS

PASTRY:
225 g/8 oz/1¾ cups plain wholemeal (whole wheat) flour
100 g/3½ oz/⅓ cup vegan margarine, cut into small pieces
4 tbsp water
soya milk, to glaze

FILLING:
25 g/1oz/6 tsp vegan margarine
1 onion, chopped
1 garlic clove, chopped finely
125 g/4½ oz button mushrooms, sliced
1 tbsp plain (all-purpose) flour
150 ml/¼ pint/⅔ cup vegetable stock
1 tbsp tomato purée (paste)
175 g/6 oz brazil nuts, chopped
75 g/2¾ oz fresh wholemeal (whole wheat) breadcrumbs
2 tbsp chopped fresh parsley
½ tsp pepper

1 To make the pastry, rub the margarine into the flour until it resembles fine breadcrumbs. Stir in the water and bring together to form a dough. Wrap and chill for 30 minutes.

2 Melt the margarine for the filling in a pan, add the onion, garlic and mushrooms and fry for 5 minutes until softened. Add the flour and cook for 1 minute, stirring. Slowly add the stock, stirring until the sauce is smooth and beginning to thicken. Stir in the tomato purée (paste), nuts, breadcrumbs, parsley and pepper. Cool slightly.

3 Roll out two thirds of the pastry (pie dough) and use to line a 20 cm/8 inch loose-bottomed quiche/flan tin (pan). Spread the filling in the pastry case (pie shell). Brush the edges of the pastry (pie dough) with soya milk. Roll out the remaining pastry (pie dough) to fit the top of the pie. Seal the edges, make a slit in the top of the pastry (pie dough) and brush with soya milk.

4 Bake in a preheated oven, 200°C/400°F/Gas Mark 6, for 30-40 minutes until golden brown.

Lentil & Red Pepper Flan

Serves 6-8

INGREDIENTS

PASTRY:
225 g/8 oz/1¾ cups plain wholemeal (whole wheat) flour
100 g/3½ oz/⅓ cup vegan margarine, cut into small pieces
4 tbsp water

FILLING:
175 g/6 oz red lentils, rinsed
300 ml/½ pint/1¼ cups vegetable stock
15 g/½ oz/3 tsp vegan margarine
1 onion, chopped
2 red (bell) peppers, cored, seeded and diced
1 tsp yeast extract
1 tbsp tomato purée (paste)
3 tbsp chopped fresh parsley
pepper

1 To make the pastry (pie dough), place the flour in a mixing bowl and rub in the vegan margarine with your fingertips until the mixture resembles fine breadcrumbs. Stir in the water and bring together to form a dough. Wrap and chill for 30 minutes.

2 To make the filling, put the lentils in a pan with the stock, bring to the boil and simmer for 10 minutes until the lentils are tender and can be mashed to a purée.

3 Melt the margarine in a small pan and fry the onion and red (bell) peppers and fry until soft.

4 Add the lentil purée, yeast extract, tomato purée (paste) and parsley. Season with pepper. Mix until well combined.

5 On a lightly floured surface, roll out the dough and line a 24 cm/9½ inch loose-bottomed quiche tin (pan). Prick the base of the pastry (pie dough) with a fork and spoon the lentil mixture into the pastry case (pie shell).

6 Bake in a preheated oven, 200°C/400°F/Gas Mark 6, for 30 minutes until the filling is firm.

1

2

4

Garlic & Sage Bread

Serves 4-6

INGREDIENTS

250 g/9 oz/2¼ cups strong brown bread flour
1 sachet easy blend dried yeast
3 tbsp chopped fresh sage
2 tsp sea salt
3 garlic cloves, chopped finely
1 tsp honey
150 ml /¼ pint/⅔ cup tepid water

1 Grease a baking tray (cookie sheet). Sieve (strain) the flour into a large mixing bowl and stir in the husks remaining in the sieve.

2 Stir in the dried yeast, sage and half of the sea salt. Reserve 1 teaspoon of the chopped garlic for sprinkling and stir the rest into the bowl. Add the honey with the tepid water and mix together to form a dough.

3 Turn the dough out on to a lightly floured surface and knead it for 5 minutes (alternatively, use an electric mixer with a dough hook).

4 Place the dough in a greased bowl, cover and leave to rise in a warm place until doubled in size.

5 Knead the dough again for a few minutes, shape it into a circle and place on the baking tray (cookie sheet).

6 Cover and leave to rise for a further 30 minutes or until springy to the touch. Sprinkle with the rest of the sea salt and garlic.

7 Bake in a preheated oven, 200°C/400°F/ Gas Mark 6, for 25-30 minutes. Leave to cool on a wire rack before serving.

3

5

6

Sweets & Drinks

There is nothing quite as nice as home-made chocolates and sweets – they leave the average bought box of chocolates in the shade!

You'll find recipes in this chapter to suit everybody's taste. Wonderful, rich, melt-in-the-mouth chocolate truffles, crispy florentines, nutty chocolate creams and rich chocolate liqueurs – they're all here. There is even some simple-to-make chocolate fudge, so there is no need to fiddle about with sugar thermometers.

Looking for something to wash it all down? We have included two delightfully cool summer chocolate drinks and for warmth and comfort on winter nights two hot drinks that will simply put instant hot chocolate to shame. Enjoy!

Rocky Road Bites

Makes 18

INGREDIENTS

125 g/4½ oz milk chocolate
50 g/2½ oz mini multi-coloured marshmallows
25 g/1 oz/¼ cup chopped walnuts
25 g/1 oz no-soak apricots, chopped

1 Line a baking tray (cookie sheet) with baking parchment and set aside.

2 Break the milk chocolate into small pieces and place in a large mixing bowl. Set the bowl over a pan of simmering water and stir until the chocolate has melted.

3 Stir in the marshmallows, walnuts and apricots and toss in the melted chocolate until well covered.

4 Place heaped teaspoons of the mixture on to the prepared baking tray (cookie sheet).

5 Leave the sweets (candies) to chill in the refrigerator until set.

6 Once set, carefully remove the sweets from the baking parchment.

COOK'S TIP

These sweets (candies) can be stored in a cool, dry place for up to 2 weeks.

VARIATION

Light, fluffy marshmallows are available in white or pastel colours. If you cannot find mini marshmallows, use large ones and snip them into smaller pieces with kitchen scissors before mixing them into the melted chocolate in step 3.

Easy Chocolate Fudge

Makes 25–30 pieces

INGREDIENTS

500 g/1 lb 2 oz dark chocolate
75 g/2¾ oz/⅓ cup unsalted butter
400 g/14 oz can sweetened condensed milk
½ tsp vanilla flavouring (extract)

1 Lightly grease a 20 cm/ 8 inch square cake tin (pan).

2 Break the chocolate into pieces and place in a large saucepan with the butter and condensed milk.

3 Heat gently, stirring until the chocolate and butter melts and the mixture is smooth. Do not allow to boil.

4 Remove from the heat. Beat in the vanilla flavouring (extract), then beat the mixture for a few minutes until thickened. Pour it into the prepared tin (pan) and level the top.

5 Chill the mixture in the refrigerator until firm.

6 Tip the fudge out on to a chopping board and cut into squares to serve.

VARIATION

For chocolate peanut fudge, replace 50 g/1½ oz/4 tbsp of the butter with crunchy peanut butter.

COOK'S TIP

Store the fudge in an airtight container in a cool, dry place for up to 1 month. Do not freeze.

COOK'S TIP

Don't use milk chocolate as the results will be too sticky.

No-Cook Fruit & Nut Chocolate Fudge

Makes about 25 pieces

INGREDIENTS

250 g/9 oz dark chocolate
25 g/1 oz/2 tbsp butter
4 tbsp evaporated milk
450 g/1 lb/3 cups icing (confectioners') sugar, sieved (strained)
50 g/$1^3/4$ oz/$^1/2$ cup roughly chopped hazelnuts
50 g/$1^3/4$ oz/$^1/3$ cup sultanas (golden raisins)

1 Lightly grease a 20 cm/8 inch square cake tin (pan).

2 Break the chocolate into pieces and place it in a bowl with the butter and evaporated milk. Set the bowl over a pan of gently simmering water and stir until the chocolate and butter have melted and the ingredients are well combined.

3 Remove the bowl from the heat and gradually beat in the icing (confectioners') sugar. Stir the hazelnuts and sultanas (golden raisins) into the mixture. Press the fudge into the prepared tin (pan) and level the top. Chill until firm.

4 Tip the fudge out on to a chopping board and cut into squares. Place in paper sweet (candy) cases. Chill until required.

VARIATION

Vary the nuts used in this recipe; try making the fudge with almonds, brazil nuts, walnuts or pecans.

COOK'S TIP

The fudge can be stored in an airtight container for up to 2 weeks.

3

3

3

Nutty Chocolate Clusters

Makes about 30

INGREDIENTS

175 g/6 oz white chocolate
100 g/3½ oz digestive biscuits (graham crackers)
100 g/3½ oz macadamia nuts or brazil nuts, chopped
25 g/1 oz stem ginger, chopped (optional)
175 g/6 oz dark chocolate

1 Line a baking tray (cookie sheet) with a sheet of baking parchment. Break the white chocolate into small pieces and place in a large mixing bowl set over a pan of gently simmering water; stir until melted.

2 Break the digestive biscuits (graham crackers) into small pieces. Stir the biscuits (graham crackers) into the melted chocolate with the chopped nuts and stem ginger, if using.

3 Place heaped teaspoons of the mixture on to the prepared baking tray (cookie sheet).

4 Chill the mixture until set, then carefully remove from the baking parchment.

5 Melt the dark chocolate and leave it to cool slightly. Dip the clusters into the melted chocolate, allowing the excess to drip back into the bowl. Return the clusters to the baking tray (cookie sheet) and chill in the refrigerator until set.

COOK'S TIP

The clusters can be stored for up to 1 week in a cool, dry place.

COOK'S TIP

Macadamia and brazil nuts are both rich and high in fat, which makes them particularly popular for confectionery, but other nuts can be used, if preferred.

2

3

5

Chocolate Cherries

Makes 24

INGREDIENTS

12 glacé (candied) cherries
2 tbsp rum or brandy
250 g/9 oz marzipan
125 g/5½ oz dark chocolate
extra milk, dark or white chocolate, to decorate (optional)

1 Line a baking tray (cookie sheet) with a sheet of baking parchment.

2 Cut the cherries in half and place in a small bowl. Add the rum or brandy and stir to coat. Leave the cherries to soak for at least 1 hour, stirring occasionally.

3 Divide the marzipan into 24 pieces and roll each piece into a ball. Press half a cherry into the top of each marzipan ball.

4 Break the chocolate into pieces, place in a bowl and set over a pan of hot water. Stir until the chocolate has melted.

5 Dip each sweet (candy) into the melted chocolate, allowing the excess to drip back into the bowl. Place the coated cherries on the baking parchment and chill until set.

6 If liked, melt a little extra chocolate and drizzle it over the top of the coated cherries. Leave to set.

VARIATION

Flatten the marzipan and use it to mould (mold) around the cherries to cover them, then dip in the chocolate as above.

VARIATION

Use a whole almond in place of the halved glacé (candied) cherries and omit the rum or brandy.

Chocolate Marzipans

Makes about 30

INGREDIENTS

450 g/1 lb marzipan
25 g/1 oz/1/3 cup glacé (candied) cherries, chopped very finely
25 g/1 oz stem ginger, chopped very finely
50 g/1 3/4 oz no-soak dried apricots, chopped very finely
350 g/12 oz dark chocolate
25 g/1 oz white chocolate
icing (confectioners') sugar, to dust

1 Line a baking tray (cookie sheet) with a sheet of baking parchment. Divide the marzipan into 3 balls and knead each ball to soften it.

2 Work the glacé (candied) cherries into one portion of the marzipan by kneading on a surface lightly dusted with icing (confectioners') sugar.

3 Do the same with the stem ginger and another portion of marzipan and then the apricots and the third portion of marzipan.

4 Form each flavoured portion of marzipan into small balls, keeping the different flavours separate.

5 Melt the dark chocolate. Dip one of each flavoured ball of marzipan into the chocolate by spiking each one with a cocktail stick (toothpick) or small skewer, allowing the excess chocolate to drip back into the bowl.

6 Carefully place the balls in clusters of the three flavours on the prepared baking tray (cookie sheet). Repeat with the remaining marzipan balls. Chill until set.

7 Melt the white chocolate and drizzle a little over the tops of each cluster of marzipan balls. Chill until hardened, then remove from the baking parchment and dust with sugar to serve.

VARIATION

Coat the marzipan balls in white or milk chocolate and drizzle with dark chocolate, if you prefer.

2

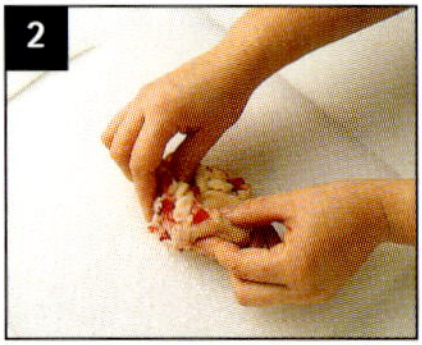

5

6

Chocolate Liqueurs

Makes 20

INGREDIENTS

100 g/3½ oz dark chocolate
about 5 glacé (candied) cherries, halved
about 10 hazelnuts or macadamia nuts
150 ml/¼ pint/⅔ cup double (heavy) cream
25 g/1 oz/2 tbsp icing (confectioners') sugar
4 tbsps liqueur

TO FINISH:
50 g/1¾ oz dark chocolate, melted
a little white chocolate, melted or white chocolate curls or extra nuts and cherries

1 Line a baking tray (cookie sheet) with a sheet of baking parchment. Melt the chocolate and spoon it into 20 paper sweet (candy) cases, spreading up the sides with a small spoon or pastry brush. Place upside down on the prepared baking tray (cookie sheet) and leave to set.

2 Carefully peel away the paper cases. Place a cherry or nut in the base of each cup.

3 To make the filling, place the double (heavy) cream in a mixing bowl and sieve (strain) the icing (confectioners') sugar on top. Whisk the cream until it is just holding its shape, then whisk in the liqueur.

4 Place the cream in a piping bag fitted with a 1 cm/½ inch plain nozzle (tip) and pipe a little into each chocolate case. Leave to chill for 20 minutes.

5 To finish, spoon the melted dark chocolate over the cream to cover it and pipe the melted white chocolate on top, swirling it into the dark chocolate with a cocktail stick (toothpick). Leave to harden. Alternatively, cover the cream with the melted dark chocolate and decorate with white chocolate curls before setting. Or, place a small piece of nut or cherry on top of the cream and then cover with dark chocolate.

COOK'S TIP

Sweet (candy) cases can vary in size. Use the smallest you can find for this recipe.

Chocolate Cups with Mascarpone Filling

Makes 20

INGREDIENTS

- 100 g/3½ oz dark chocolate

FILLING:

- 100 g/3½ oz milk or dark chocolate
- ¼ tsp vanilla flavouring (extract)
- 200 g/7 oz mascarpone cheese
- cocoa powder, to dust

1 Line a baking tray (cookie sheet) with a sheet of baking parchment. Melt the chocolate and spoon it into 20 paper sweet (candy) cases, spreading up the sides with a small spoon or pastry brush. Place upside down on the prepared baking tray (cookie sheet) and leave to set.

2 When set, carefully peel away the paper cases.

3 To make the filling, melt the dark or milk chocolate. Place the mascarpone cheese in a bowl and beat in the vanilla flavouring (extract) and melted chocolate and beat until well combined. Leave the mixture to chill, beating occasionally until firm enough to pipe.

4 Place the mascarpone filling in a piping bag fitted with a star nozzle (tip) and pipe the mixture into the cups. Decorate with a dusting of cocoa powder.

COOK'S TIP

Mascarpone is a rich Italian soft cheese made from fresh cream, so it has a high fat content. Its delicate flavour blends well with chocolate.

VARIATION

You can use lightly whipped double (heavy) cream instead of the mascarpone cheese, if preferred.

1

3

4

Mini Chocolate Cones

Makes 10

INGREDIENTS

75 g/2¾ oz dark chocolate
100 ml/3½ fl oz/⅓ cup double (heavy) cream
15 g/½ oz/1 tbsp icing (confectioners') sugar
1 tbsp crème de menthe
chocolate coffee beans, to decorate (optional)

1 Cut ten 7.5 cm/3 inch circles of baking parchment. Shape each circle into a cone shape and secure with sticky tape.

2 Melt the chocolate. Using a small pastry brush or clean artists' brush, brush the inside of each cone with melted chocolate.

3 Brush a second layer of chocolate on the inside of the cones and leave to chill until set. Carefully peel away the paper.

4 Place the double (heavy) cream, icing (confectioners') sugar and crème de menthe in a mixing bowl and whip until just holding its shape. Place in a piping bag fitted with a star nozzle (tip) and pipe the mixture into the chocolate cones.

5 Decorate the cones with chocolate coffee beans (if using) and chill until required.

COOK'S TIP

The chocolate cones can be made in advance and kept in the refrigerator for up to 1 week. Do not fill them more than 2 hours before you are going to serve them.

VARIATION

Use a different flavoured liqueur to flavour the cream: a coffee-flavoured liqueur is perfect. If you want a mint flavour without using a liqueur, use a few drops of peppermint flavouring (extract) to flavour the cream according to taste.

Collettes

Makes 20

INGREDIENTS

100 g/3½ oz white chocolate

FILLING:

150 g/5½ oz orange-flavoured dark chocolate

150 ml/¼ pint/⅔ cup double (heavy) cream

25 g/1 oz/2 tbsp icing (confectioners') sugar

1 Line a baking tray (cookie sheet) with a sheet of baking parchment. Melt the chocolate and spoon it into 20 paper sweet (candy) cases, spreading up the sides with a small spoon or pastry brush. Place upside down on the prepared baking tray (cookie sheet) and leave to set.

2 When set, carefully peel away the paper cases.

3 To make the filling, melt the orange-flavoured chocolate and place in a mixing bowl with the double (heavy) cream and the icing (confectioners') sugar. Beat until smooth. Chill until the mixture becomes firm enough to pipe, stirring occasionally.

4 Place the filling in a piping bag fitted with a star nozzle (tip) and pipe a little into each case. Leave to chill until required.

VARIATION

Add 1 tbsp orange-flavoured liqueur to the filling, if preferred.

COOK'S TIP

If they do not hold their shape well, use 2 cases to make a double thickness mould (mold). Foil cases are firmer so use these if you can find them.

Use the smallest sweet (candy) cases you can find for these cups.

2

3

4

Mini Florentines

Makes about 40

INGREDIENTS

75 g/2$\frac{3}{4}$ oz/$\frac{1}{3}$ cup butter
75 g/2$\frac{3}{4}$ oz/$\frac{1}{3}$ cup caster (superfine) sugar
25 g/1 oz/2 tbsp sultanas (golden raisins) or raisins
25 g/1 oz/2 tbsp glacé (candied) cherries, chopped
25 g/1 oz/2 tbsp crystallised ginger, chopped
25 g/1 oz sunflower seeds
100 g/3$\frac{1}{2}$ oz/$\frac{3}{4}$ cup flaked (slivered) almonds
2 tbsp double (heavy) cream
175 g/6 oz dark or milk chocolate

1 Lightly grease and flour 2 baking trays (cookie sheets) or line with baking parchment. Place the butter in a small pan and heat gently until melted. Add the sugar, stir until dissolved, then bring the mixture to the boil. Remove from the heat and stir in the sultanas (golden raisins) or raisins, cherries, ginger, sunflower seeds and almonds. Mix well, then beat in the cream.

2 Place small teaspoons of the fruit and nut mixture on to the prepared baking tray (cookie sheet), allowing plenty of space for the mixture to spread. Bake in a preheated oven, 180°C/350°F/Gas Mark 4, for 10–12 minutes until light golden in colour.

3 Remove from the oven and, whilst still hot, use a circular biscuit (cookie) cutter to pull in the edges to form a perfect circle. Leave to cool and crispen before removing from the baking tray (cookie sheet).

4 Melt most of the chocolate and spread it on a sheet of baking parchment. When the chocolate is on the point of setting, place the biscuits (cookies) flat-side down on the chocolate and leave to harden completely.

5 Cut around the florentines and remove from the paper. Spread a little more chocolate on the already coated side of the florentines and use a fork to mark waves in the chocolate. Leave to set. Arrange the florentines on a plate (or in a presentation box for a gift) with alternate sides facing upwards. Keep them cool.

2

3

4

Mini Chocolate Tartlets

Makes about 18

INGREDIENTS

175 g/6 oz/1½ cups plain (all-purpose) flour
75 g 2¾ oz/⅓ cup butter
15 g/½ oz/1 tbsp caster (superfine) sugar
about 1 tbsp water

FILLING:
100 g/3½ oz full-fat soft cheese
25 g/1 oz/5 tsp caster (superfine) sugar
1 small egg, lightly beaten
50 g/1¾ oz dark chocolate

TO DECORATE:
100 ml/3½ fl oz/⅓ cup double (heavy) cream
dark chocolate curls
cocoa powder, to dust

1 Sieve (strain) the flour into a mixing bowl. Cut the butter into small pieces and rub in with your fingertips until the mixture resembles fine breadcrumbs. Stir in the sugar. Add enough water to mix to a soft dough, then cover and chill for 15 minutes.

2 Roll out the pastry (pie dough) on a lightly floured surface and use to line 18 mini tartlet tins (pans) or mini muffin tins (pans). Prick the bases with a cocktail stick (toothpick).

3 Beat together the full-fat soft cheese and the sugar. Beat in the egg. Melt the chocolate and beat it into the mixture. Spoon into the pastry cases (pie shells) and bake in a preheated oven, 190°C/375°F/Gas Mark 5, for 15 minutes until the pastry (pie dough) is crisp and the filling set. Place the tins (pans) on a wire rack to cool completely.

4 Chill the tartlets. Whip the cream until it is just holding its shape. Place in a piping bag fitted with a star nozzle (tip). Pipe rosettes of cream on top of the tartlets. Decorate with chocolate curls and dust with cocoa powder.

COOK'S TIP

The tartlets can be made up to 3 days ahead. Decorate on the day of serving, preferably no more than 4 hours in advance.

Rum Truffles

Makes about 20

INGREDIENTS

125 g/5½ oz dark chocolate
small knob of butter
2 tbsp rum
50 g/1¾oz desiccated (shredded) coconut
100 g/3½ oz cake crumbs
75 g/2¾ oz/6 tbsp icing (confectioners') sugar
2 tbsp cocoa powder

1 Break the chocolate into pieces and place in a bowl with the butter. Set the bowl over a pan of gently simmering water, stir until melted and combined.

2 Remove from the heat and beat in the rum. Stir in the desiccated (shredded) coconut, cake crumbs and 50 g/1¾ oz of the icing (confectioners') sugar. Beat until combined. Add a little extra rum if the mixture is stiff.

3 Roll the mixture into small balls and place them on a sheet of baking parchment. Leave to chill until firm.

4 Sieve (strain) the remaining icing (confectioners') sugar on to a large plate. Sieve (strain) the cocoa powder on to another plate. Roll half of the truffles in the icing (confectioners') sugar until coated and roll the remaining truffles in the cocoa powder.

5 Place the truffles in paper sweet (candy) cases and leave to chill until required.

VARIATION

Make the truffles with white chocolate and replace the rum with coconut liqueur or milk, if you prefer. Roll them in cocoa powder or dip in melted milk chocolate.

COOK'S TIP

These truffles will keep for about 2 weeks in a cool place.

2

3

4

White Chocolate Truffles

Makes about 20

INGREDIENTS

25 g/1 oz/2 tbsp unsalted butter
75 ml/3 fl oz/5 tbsp double (heavy) cream
225 g/8 oz good quality Swiss white chocolate
1 tbsp orange-flavoured liqueur (optional)

TO FINISH:
100 g/3½ oz white chocolate

1 Line a Swiss roll tin (pan) with baking parchment.

2 Place the butter and cream in a small saucepan and bring slowly to the boil, stirring constantly. Boil for 1 minute, then remove from the heat.

3 Break the chocolate into pieces and add to the cream. Stir until melted, then beat in the liqueur, if using.

4 Pour into the prepared tin (pan) and chill for about 2 hours until firm.

5 Break off pieces of mixture and roll them into balls. Chill for a further 30 minutes before finishing the truffles.

6 To finish, melt the white chocolate. Dip the balls in the chocolate, allowing the excess to drip back into the bowl. Place on non-stick baking parchment and swirl the chocolate with the prongs of a fork. Leave to harden.

7 Drizzle a little melted dark chocolate over the truffles if you wish and leave to set. Place the truffles in paper cases to serve.

COOK'S TIP

The truffle mixture needs to be firm but not too hard to roll. If the mixture is too hard, allow it to stand at room temperature for a few minutes to soften slightly. During rolling the mixture will become sticky but will reharden in the refrigerator before coating.

COOK'S TIP

The chocolates can be kept in the refrigerator for up to 2 weeks.

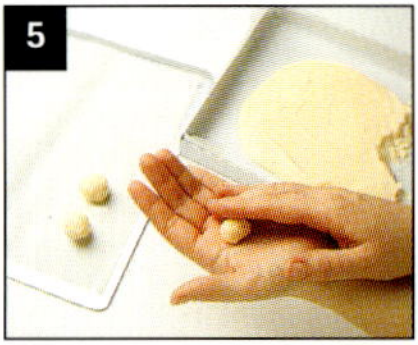

Italian Chocolate Truffles

Makes about 24

INGREDIENTS

175 g/6 oz dark chocolate
2 tbsp almond-flavoured liqueur (amaretto) or orange-flavoured liqueur
40 g/1½ oz/3 tbsp unsalted butter
50 g/1¾ oz icing (confectioners') sugar
50 g/1¾ oz/½ cup ground almonds
50 g/1¾ oz grated chocolate

1 Melt the dark chocolate with the liqueur in a bowl set over a saucepan of hot water, stirring until well combined.

2 Add the butter and stir until it has melted. Stir in the icing (confectioners') sugar and the ground almonds.

3 Leave the mixture in a cool place until firm enough to roll into about 24 balls.

4 Place the grated chocolate on a plate and roll the truffles in the chocolate to coat them.

5 Place the truffles in paper sweet (candy) cases and chill.

COOK'S TIP

These truffles will keep for about 2 weeks in a cool place.

VARIATION

The almond-flavoured liqueur gives these truffles an authentic Italian flavour. The original almond liqueur, Amaretto di Saronno, comes from Saronno in Italy.

VARIATION

For a sweeter truffle, use milk chocolate instead of dark. Dip the truffles in melted chocolate to finish, if desired.

2

2

4

Hot Chocolate Drinks

Serves 2

INGREDIENTS

SPICY HOT CHOCOLATE:
600 ml/1 pint/2½ cups milk
1 tsp ground mixed spice (allspice)
100 g/3½ oz dark chocolate
4 cinnamon sticks
100 ml/3½ fl oz/⅓ cup double (heavy) cream, lightly whipped

HOT CHOCOLATE & ORANGE TODDY:
75 g/2½ oz orange-flavoured dark chocolate
600 ml/1 pint/2½ cups milk
3 tbsp rum
2 tbsp double (heavy) cream
grated nutmeg

1 To make Spicy Hot Chocolate, pour the milk into a small pan. Sprinkle in the mixed spice (allspice).

2 Break the dark chocolate into squares and add to the milk. Heat the mixture over a low heat until the milk is just boiling, stirring all the time to prevent the milk burning on the bottom of the pan.

3 Place 2 cinnamon sticks in 2 cups and pour in the spicy hot chocolate. Top with the whipped double (heavy) cream and serve.

4 To make Hot Chocolate & Orange Toddy, break the orange-flavoured dark chocolate into squares and place in a small saucepan with the milk. Heat over a low heat until just boiling, stirring constantly.

5 Remove the pan from the heat and stir in the rum. Pour into cups.

6 Pour the cream over the back of a spoon or swirl on to the top so that it sits on top of the hot chocolate. Sprinkle with grated nutmeg and serve at once.

COOK'S TIP

Using a cinnamon stick as a stirrer will give any hot chocolate drink a sweet, pungent flavour of cinnamon without overpowering the flavour of the chocolate.

2

3

5

Cold Chocolate Drinks

Serves 2

INGREDIENTS

CHOCOLATE MILK SHAKE:
- 450 ml/16 fl oz/2 cups ice cold milk
- 3 tbsp drinking chocolate powder
- 3 scoops chocolate ice cream
- cocoa powder, to dust (optional)

CHOCOLATE ICE CREAM SODA:
- 5 tbsp chocolate dessert sauce
- soda water
- 2 scoops of chocolate ice cream
- double (heavy) cream, whipped
- dark or milk chocolate, grated

1 To make Chocolate Milk Shake, place half of the ice-cold milk in a blender.

2 Add the drinking chocolate powder to the blender and 1 scoop of the chocolate ice cream. Blend until the mixture is frothy and well mixed. Stir in the remaining milk.

3 Place the remaining 2 scoops of chocolate ice cream in 2 serving glasses and carefully pour the chocolate milk over the ice cream.

4 Sprinkle a little cocoa powder (if using) over the top of each drink and serve at once.

5 To make Chocolate Ice Cream Soda, divide the chocolate dessert sauce between 2 glasses.

6 Add a little soda water to each glass and stir to combine the sauce and soda water. Place a scoop of ice cream in each glass and top up with more soda water.

7 Place a dollop of whipped heavy (double) cream on the top, if liked, and sprinkle with a little grated dark or milk chocolate.

COOK'S TIP

Served in a tall glass, a milk shake or an ice cream soda makes a scrumptious snack in a drink. Serve with straws, if wished.

3

5

6

Index